PRAISE FOR *Your Are Woman, You Are Divine*

You Are Woman, You Are Divine is inspired. You can't read it without feeling the presence of The Divine Feminine, the ancient goddess energy, moving in your bones. It is so beautifully written and woven together; I'm enthralled and I can't stop reading it even though I should be packing for a trip. My suitcase sits empty as I turn the pages . . . filling my soul with much needed food. Women, we are being called home to our true essential natures. By nurturing the timeless presence of Her, we realize She is already within us. Open this book and unlock the door to important myths, mysteries, goddesses and rituals that were lovingly chosen by Renée Starr. Her deep connection with The Divine Feminine leaps off the pages and enters the psyche in rich and meaningful ways. This extraordinary work brings us close to The Beloved, to Freedom and ultimately to honor our own Sacred–Self. I will give this book to my friends.

~TERRY LASZLO-GOPADZE
Editor of *The Spirit of a Woman: Stories to Empower and Inspire*

We live in a modern world where women are expected to achieve greatness, look perfect and made to feel like they are never enough. *You Are Woman You Are Divine* is a great handbook that gracefully leads women into "beingness" and less into "doingness" and ultimately into their divine feminine self. Through her writing, Renée Starr strives to guide women to restore their inner feminine light, create an energetic shift to claim peace, harmony and well-being. Through transforming ourselves, we can transform the world.

~MARY ANN HALPIN
Photographer and Author of *Fearless Women: Visions of a New World*

Divine Femininity is a mystery, and the experience of it is always mystical. We can only speak about it in metaphor—it cannot be directly defined, but instead must be evoked from within. Renée Starr in her amazing book *You Are Woman You Are Divine* uses myth, storytelling, concrete examples, and ceremonial instruction to give the reader a roadmap for what she calls the "journey back to The Goddess." Every woman would benefit from reading it, no matter how old. In my opinion, it should be required reading for every female high school senior so that she will enter her journey into mature womanhood fully aware of her own power, facing her destiny well-informed and metaphorically girded!

~CONNIE KAPLAN
Author of *The Woman's Book of Dreams, Dreams are Letters from the Soul*
and *The Invisible Garment*

Renée Starr has provided us with divine reading material. Her renditions of the ancient Goddesses are creative, diverse, and inspirational. *You Are Woman, You Are Divine* is a wonderful and flowing addition to the literature of the Divine Feminine, and a much needed resource for young women.

~RABBI LEAH NOVICK
Author of *On the Wings of Shekhinah: Re-Discovering Judaism's Divine Feminine*

Beautifully designed, thorough and inspirational, Renée Starr's *You Are Woman, You Are Divine* captures the essence of the Sacred Feminine reawakened within its pages. It is a creative and splendidly researched vehicle for those walking down the Goddess path for the first time, as well as a delightful refresher for those already enjoying a sacred relationship with Goddess. Appealing to both left and right brain, Renée Starr's new book combines Goddess mythology and its relevance today, along with how to work with different facets of the Feminine essence. Readers find their understanding of Goddess mythology morphing into self-help and self-knowledge, encouraging women in particular to heal, come into wholeness and find their Sacred Roar!

~REV. DR. KAREN TATE
Author of *Goddess Calling* and Host of "Voices of the Sacred Feminine Radio"

The return of the Divine Feminine is essential to the maturation of human spirituality both as individuals and as a species. In the Bible's Book of Proverbs, we learn that Wisdom, the Divine Feminine, sends out her disciples, all of whom are women, to call humanity to Her feast of enlightenment. Renée Starr's *You Are Woman, You Are Divine* not only introduces you to the Divine Feminine, but trains you to share Her invitation to wisdom. Read this book, and more importantly, practice what she teaches.

~RABBI RAMI SHAPIRO
Author of *The Divine Feminine* and *Embracing the Divine Feminine*

Weaving the history and stories of Goddesses throughout time, *You Are Woman, You Are Divine* invites you on a sacred journey to reclaim your feminine wisdom. With Renée's practical activities and rituals, you will reconnect with your true essence and the beauty that is you.

~SHERI GAYNOR
Author of *Creative Awakenings: Envisioning the Life of Your Dreams Through Art*

May
the Goddess
bless you
in every way!

Renee
Starr

YOU ARE WOMAN
YOU ARE DIVINE

The Modern Woman's Journey Back to The Goddess

RENÉE STARR

OVER AND ABOVE
PRESS

Editorial Direction: Rick Benzel

Editing: Rick Benzel and Susan Shankin

Art Direction and Design: Susan Shankin & Associates

Cover Photograph: Robert E Thune II

Cover and Interior Illustrations: Susan Shankin & Renée Starr

Author Photograph: Deja Cross Photography

Published by Over And Above Press

Over And Above Creative Group

Los Angeles, CA

www.overandabovecreative.com

First edition

10 9 8 7 6 5 4 3 2 1

Library of Congress Control Number: 2015902361

ISBN 978-0-9907924-7-5

Visit our website and blog: www.BackToTheGoddess.com

Printed at Bang Printing in the United States of America

Distributed by SCB Distributors

CONTENTS

PART TWO—RESTORE

PART THREE—REMEMBER

I can think of nothing more spectacular than a woman
who is returning to her goddess-self.

THIS BOOK IS DEDICATED TO YOU.

ACKNOWLEDGMENTS

NO ONE WRITES A BOOK ALONE.
I did not know this when I first started out writing *You Are Woman, You Are Divine*. I had imagined long, joyous hours of solitude typing away on my laptop, with more long hours of thoughtful, private reverie waiting for inspiration to strike. I imagined waking up at all hours to capture subconscious inspirations, wading through piles of post-its, pages of notes and several notebooks for ideas until just the right word, phrase, or concept emerged. I saw myself uninterested in doing anything but writing, crazed with creative passion and dedication. I fantasized that after only few short months, I would emerge from my creative confinement to present the most perfect first draft and declare myself finished. I would smile, certain that there would be no need for a rewrite, and I would then wait patiently for publication.

Yes, that was what I imagined—but that is not at all what happened. Oh, I did spend many joyous hours writing and daydreaming this book into the world and I did wake up at all hours to capture flashes of inspiration, and I was crazed and dedicated, and I did write a wonderful first draft. But what I did not foresee were the many more drafts and the two years it would take me to complete this book, nor the profound personal challenges and deep healing that would come from writing it, nor the many people who would stand by me, support me, coach me, encourage me and help me to birth this book into being. No one writes a book alone.

This book demanded that I face deeply buried fears, overcome lingering doubts and heal many deep-rooted issues from my past that needed to be released from my heart and soul in order to offer up these words on paper. I learned so much about myself as a writer, a reader and a woman during each and every chapter. I experienced this book just as I hope that you will . . . fully, completely and with The Goddess by your side.

I am blessed to have had so many friends—in person and online, as well as the many clients and students who have all cheered me on and offered me their kindness, strength, and wisdom while I wrote. This book is filled with your presence and I deeply, deeply thank you all.

To my publisher and editor-in-chief, Rick Benzel, your literary expertise and uncanny ability to challenge me in ways that I needed most has taught me to be true to myself. Your vision of me as a writer, and of this book has encouraged me to know myself more deeply, to venture into the uncharted territories of my psyche, and to write from this deep, mysterious place. From you, I have learned excellence.

To my publisher, co-editor and book designer, Susan Shankin, your design expertise and vision has brought each of the goddesses stunningly and enchantingly to life. Your unfaltering patience, understanding, and support of my creative process have taught me how to find serenity and be kinder to myself. Your loving friendship and invaluable, spot-on insights have encouraged me to let this book—and my life unfold in its own time, to set my voice free and to light my words on fire. From you, I have learned to trust both myself, and life.

To Shell Ariel and Cori Bardo, whose precious friendship I treasure every day; you are my touchstones, my guiding lights and the sacred witnesses to every one of my life's struggles and triumphs—you hold such safe space and give such wise counsel. You never lost faith in me or in this book. You know me in ways that only soul sisters can. From you, I have learned to see myself as you do.

With Her infinite wisdom and Her endless love, The Divine Feminine has taken me on a journey to find myself—my goddess-self. It is to Her that I am most grateful. I am in such awe of the words that She has inspired me to write. Without Her, this book and this path would not exist.

FOREWORD

AS A DESIGNER OF CLOTHING FOR THE MODERN WOMAN, my intention is to create a tool that inspires a woman to feel her greatness. To be confident and creative, feminine and empowered, comfortable with herself and sincerely sexy—because, ultimately that is how I want to feel. Nothing is more satisfying to me than hearing feedback from women that echoes my intention.

And nothing was more powerful than learning how to feel this way for myself while working with Renée Starr. I first began working with Renée in 2011, for personal and professional coaching. At that time in my life, I needed guidance. My life looked successful and wonderful on the outside, but on the inside, it was a mess. I was experiencing many personal challenges, and feeling out of touch with myself.

Just six years into building my namesake fashion label, *Raquel Allegra,* my professional success was becoming a reality. I was gaining major international accounts and fans, and I had a coveted celebrity, stylist, and editor following. But even with this success, I was struggling. I longed to develop my leadership skills, to speak with a voice that would direct and inspire my teams—and remain connected to my creative spirit. I had no idea then of the magnitude of healing I would experience, nor the depth of positive change that Renée would bring to my life.

Renée is truly a modern goddess. I'll be honest and say that I used to have a difficult time with the concept of 'goddess' in my life. But over the years, as I worked with

Renée, she inspired me to develop and hone my *inner* goddess—which to my surprise meant becoming more confident, stronger, and courageous, but in the most feminine of ways. Her recounting of stories from her own life as well as from goddess lore has helped me see myself more clearly. She has skillfully empowered me to understand what this concept could mean for me—how I could be a strong female leader in my professional life and a deeply connected and spiritual woman in my personal life. I learned that I needed stillness and meditation to recharge, that I could speak up and express my needs without feeling ashamed, and that being a woman was a very special, very sacred thing.

Renée's way of relating to the archetypes, and her tools towards self-care taught me ways to conjure and inspire the Goddess essence inside me. Through this I have found a deeper internal connection, a personal voice, and the strength to communicate and be a more effective and joyful human. My work with her has been wildly transformational, and I am truly grateful. Her kindness and unconditional love, her wisdom, and her support have all been my saving grace.

In *You Are Woman, You Are Divine*, Renée reminds us that every culture in history has honored women through story. These ancient mythologies recognized the woman as goddess-like, and they are expressions of The Divine Feminine and of our own divine femininity. They are essential models for us today, teaching us in their own way that every woman is sacred and divine. As women living in a complex and hectic society, we can still reclaim our feminine essences of power, stillness, passion, creativity, vision, wisdom, and awakening—and within these pages you will learn how.

I highly encourage any woman who is called to this book to dive in fully and freely! And I am excited for her inevitable transformation.

RAQUEL ALLEGRA

PROLOGUE

I have found God in myself and I love Her fiercely.

~Ntotzake Shange

THE AGE OF WOMAN IS HERE.

The time has come, right now, for you to know that being a woman is special, sacred, and divine. You are more than you think you are. So much more. You are a spectacular creature and you are beautifully built. You have been specifically designed to be a creatress, the bearer of our species, and to be powerful in the most feminine of ways. You carry within the space of your womb the Light of the world, which you birth anew every morning when you open your eyes. Your very existence makes the world lovelier.

You are woman; your body is sacred, and your essence is Divine.
You are the embodiment of The Divine Feminine.

After many thousands of years, the time has come for the predominant presence of masculine energy in the world to be rebalanced by the presence of feminine energy. The age of Woman is upon us; a relationship with The Divine Feminine is on its way back to the world and to you.

Every woman deserves to know The Divine Feminine in a personal, intimate way and she deserves to know herself as a woman filled with the qualities of The Divine Feminine. All women should be free to feel the magnificence of their Feminine Power.

Once this Feminine Essence is made more present in your life, it will fill and nourish you with the highest wisdom, intuition, creativity, and love. As a woman, you are designed to be a sacred vessel, and to embody these Divine Feminine qualities. It is through you, as this sacred vessel, that the Feminine Essence is poured out into the world.

When the daily presence of The Divine Feminine fills you, and the joy and power of seeing yourself as a goddess is fully restored to your spirit, you will know how to:

❖ live a better, happier, more fulfilled life as a woman
❖ feel more confident and free to express your feminine wisdom
❖ be more creative and feel more alive with inspiration and energy
❖ love more authentically
❖ have more harmonious relationships

The acknowledgment and integration of the Feminine Presence within you will bring about much needed relief from the society in which we find ourselves living today. It will bring back harmony and healing not only for us as women, but also for the entire world.

WHO IS THE DIVINE FEMININE?

The Divine Feminine is an immaterial, abstract and co-creational principle that, along with The Divine Masculine, fashions our world into being. They are the active and receptive essences that flow through all life on the planet. Together, they are The One. Many of us today understand this as a singular God, but long ago, the ancients used dual terms to describe the fundamental principles of The Divine as both 'God' and 'Goddess.'

We cannot entirely know The Divine Feminine and Masculine because they are pure, infinite essences. We can, however, understand and experience them through their appearances as goddesses and gods, which are the archetypal and mythological representations of Divine qualities. The Goddess is The Divine Feminine personified and you are made to be like Her, to embody Her qualities. The Divine Feminine looks out from behind your eyes, touches with your hands, and loves through your heart. Life, healing, grace, and peace are all attributed to you, as a woman and a goddess on earth.

Here on this earth, The Divine Feminine, the holiest of holy presences, is beyond logical understanding. She is an immeasurable and limitless Essence that cannot be known only with the mind. To write a book about the most indescribably indescribable and infinitely infinite of energies would be like attempting to put all the light of the universe into one small box. It simply cannot be done. The Divine Feminine is too awesome and all-encompassing an essence to describe just with words and to know just through thoughts. She must primarily be felt with our heart and recognized by our soul.

No one can truly say just what The Divine Feminine actually is. Attempts to convey Her splendor in plain language will fail; for only the cadent language of poetry and the dreamy language of love will do. To describe Her radiance with ordinary, everyday language, is to explain the wind only as a scientific event. The rational words of science cannot possibly convey how delicious a soft wind feels as it passes over your skin on a warm summer day, nor can it capture its glorious power as it blows across the ocean, raising waves in a storm.

So it is with The Divine Feminine who is Woman, most High. As it is with all women, The Divine Feminine must be experienced, not defined. She is the Feminine Beingness of all beings, and my desire to write this book comes from my desire to share with you all of my experiences of Her being in my life.

The return of The Divine Feminine to the world may not be immediately clear to women today. Where did She go, why did She go, and how is She returning are questions I often hear when I discuss this movement with women. I answer that The Divine Feminine did not literally ever leave the world in the first place, as She is one of its two principle essences. Rather Her presence in the world was methodically concealed, Her guidance was slowly removed from our lives, and as a result, women (and men) eventually stopped experiencing Her.

There are many historical reasons for this disappearance, such as: the predominance of patriarchal rule, the fear of woman as witches, and many religious beliefs blaming women for the woes of the world based on the creation story of Adam and Eve and other anti-women depictions among the main religions of humanity. The return of The Divine Feminine is really more about the return of women to Her, by inviting today's woman to accept Her, express Her, and recognize that we can no longer live without Her. This is how our relationship with Her will find its way back to us, and we must prepare ourselves and make room in our lives for Her homecoming. This book is designed to help you do just that.

MY JOURNEY TO THE DIVINE FEMININE

I did not receive knowledge of The Divine Feminine from my mother. She did not receive it from her mother. Being a female was not special in the home of my childhood and I did not think of myself as sacred.

I remember how, as a young girl, I loved reading the stories of women who were special in some way. Without yet realizing that I was searching for The Divine Feminine, I read goddess mythology, biblical stories and even faery tales that depicted women as magical and intuitive, as having special powers of prophecy, healing, and knowing. I daydreamed that I, too, was special at my core—that as a woman, I am a special being. I have been in search of confirming this feeling my entire life.

As I grew into adulthood, my longing for a deeper sense of Self led me to explore many different paths, hoping to move myself closer to the Truth, the Absolute, to God—especially to the Feminine aspect of God. My journey in search of spirituality has taken me through many traditions, introducing me to many rituals and ways of connecting with Spirit, feeling at one with the Universe, and especially experiencing The Divine Feminine essence.

I practiced Buddhism where I read about the hand of Siddhartha reaching for Mother Earth to witness him, to show him the truth beyond illusion while the demon Mara tempted him with fear and desire. I browsed through the ancient texts of Gnostic Christianity and found The Sophia, the abstract concept of absolute truth and wisdom. Deeply attracted to ancient Egypt's pantheon of goddesses, I found myself seeking answers at the feet of Isis and Hathor, eventually visiting their temples in Egypt, completely in awe. The royal path of Yoga inspired me to call upon Kali, Lakshmi and Shakti, chanting their names over and over in devotion to Ma, the Divine Mother. In Hawai'i I called upon Pele; in Greece, Aphrodite, and in the south of France, the Magdalene. My search meandered into the realms of Wicca where the earth, the moon, and all of nature is The Goddess, and women are intrinsically connected to Her. Within Wicca, I reconnected to the natural rhythms of the seasons of nature, reinforcing my relationship with the moon and the lunar cycles that affect my female body, my emotions, and my life.

My search eventually led me back to my Jewish roots and to the Kabbalah—the mystic teachings of Judaism. Here, among the ancient rituals of my ancestors, I was inspired to begin the practice of lighting the Sabbath candles. For years on Fridays before sundown, I would clean my apartment from top to bottom, prepare an elaborate meal, bathe with scented soaps, and anoint myself with special oils as I called into my home the Shekhinah, who is the Queen of Heaven, the Bride of The Divine Masculine and also the Feminine aspect of God.

As I lit candles for Her at the precise moment of sunset, I helped light Her way in the darkness towards Her Beloved. I prayed to Her for understanding, for peace, and for my own true beloved to find me. I prayed for Her to light my way in this life as a woman.

I treasured those Fridays and kept them for my own. While the Jewish Shabbat is traditionally a time for family, friends, and company, for me it was a reverent, private space to be alone with The Shekhinah. Often during my prayers, tears would stream from my eyes, and my heart would break open as I expressed all of my worries, fears, and hopes to Her with the light of the candles flickering behind my closed eyes. Eventually a sense of profound gratitude for having been built in Her image, for having been made a woman, came into my life. And always, my prayers brought forth a weighty longing to know and experience Her and to become more and more like Her.

I eventually had a deeply transformational, personal experience with The Divine Feminine several years ago. On a crisp, California winter night, in a meditation class with many other seekers, She came to me, touched my core—and I was forever changed. Her visit was so intimate, Her energy touched me so profoundly that it immediately moved me to tears. Shaking with excitement and awe, I shared my experience with the others in the class.

The Divine Feminine came to me first as a profound stillness, so quiet that Her presence caused an unusually calm motionlessness to pass over me as if time had stopped, as if my heart and breath had stopped, too.

As She made Her way into and through me, I felt a soulful yearning for Her, a keen desire that was saturated with a love unlike any I have ever known. She sent waves of insight and knowing coursing through me. It was as if I suddenly grasped the meaning of and understood the sacredness of my womanhood and the purpose of my being a woman here on earth. All sensation of the physical world around me slipped away except for one thing—the delicious and intoxicating taste of honey in my mouth. And then She left.

It is said in Kabbalah that the Feminine aspect of God, The Shekhinah, will taste like honey in your mouth when She appears. I now know this to be true.

The essence of The Divine Feminine presented Herself to me on that day. She gave me the momentary experience of pure feminine energy that has left me entranced by the mystery of Her ever since. In my many meditations that have followed, I have learned that there is no end to this mystery. She is, much like life itself, unknowable, enigmatic and will never fully reveal Herself to me.

EXPERIENCING THE DIVINE FEMININE FOR YOURSELF

How can you experience The Divine Feminine? How do you bring Her essence into your life? The mystical poet Rumi said once: *There are hundreds of ways to kneel and kiss the ground.* This quote reminds me that there are literally hundreds of ways to seek Her, and hundreds of ways to experience Her.

In this book, I have chosen my favorite ways to guide you towards your own relationship with The Divine Feminine as you bring Her into your life. In these chapters, I offer myths, rituals, invocations, meditations and more. Each of these methods serves as an invitation for you to move closer to Her, sensing Her with you as you step over the threshold from the ordinary into the extraordinary. This book will guide you through the portal that leads you to experience Her as I did—with the taste of honey in your mouth.

Opening yourself up to experiencing The Divine Feminine and to knowing yourself as a goddess may feel strange at first. For some women, it may seem too religious or too spiritual, perhaps repelling, intimidating or awkward. It may conflict with your personal beliefs—or it may challenge them.

It is not intended to do any of these. Allowing The Divine Feminine into your life is purely an invitation to empower yourself as a woman—to own your feminine essence, to be the goddess that you were created to be. Reading the myths and performing the rituals in this book can be as spiritual or religious as you want them to be. It is up to you to embrace them in the ways in which you are most comfortable.

I invite you to open your heart to learn more about Her, to allow yourself to become curious enough, interested enough to continue on and experience how She can reveal your true self to you and bring divine sweetness into your life. Once you have experienced this, even if it is for the briefest of moments or in the smallest of ways, you will be forever changed. For once you know of your own sacredness, your own divine purpose and design—you can never undo this knowing. You will look upon yourself in new ways, forever aware of who you truly are as a woman . . . and as a goddess.

Today, my journey with The Divine Feminine is not over, but my search to find Her is. I have discovered that She is everywhere that I go and everything that I am. I am naturally designed to know Her, be Her, and express Her. You are, too.

HOW TO ENJOY
THIS BOOK

This book was created with you, today's woman, in mind. Everything presented within these pages has been lovingly crafted to lead The Divine Feminine and The Goddess back into your life, and, from there, to your becoming a goddess on earth.

The book is the result of my years of research and personal experiences with The Divine Feminine, all of which I am excited to share with you. My research has its roots in many spiritual practices, religions, rituals and the goddess stories of many cultures but is not affiliated with any one particular religion or spiritual practice. It is universal and inclusive, which is a principle feminine quality. This book is about showing you how to connect to your own unique essence as a woman from whatever your spiritual and religious callings are.

I have crafted a guide that will help you reclaim all of the beauty, grace, and spe-cialness that being female is. This book is a treasury filled with the Divine wisdom of The Feminine and the magical ways of The Goddess—helping you to become whole and to fill yourself with Feminine Essence, which is your divine birthright.

The book is divided into three parts—Return, Restore, and Remember, plus another section entitled Reflections, which can be found separately as a companion journal. Each part offers you insight, instruction, and inspiration on your journey back to The Goddess. Each part will bring you closer to having a more personal relationship with The Divine Feminine and discovering your own divine femininity.

Part 1, Return

This is the beginning of our journey with The Divine Feminine, where we find our own history as women in the world and learn that the female was once honored and considered sacred in most ancient human cultures. From the dawn of pre-history, women have been perceived as the holy, sacred, and divine incarnations of the universal Great Mother, or Great Goddess. The earliest of our human ancestors adored the voluptuous shape of a woman. Her wide hips, full breasts, and sexy curves were carved into fertility statuettes and figurines that have been found in archaeo-logical digs throughout the world. Many anthropologists believe our ancestors wor-shipped these carvings because they embodied the mystery of creation.

The Return shows us that within many of the world's first religions, there was a rev-erence for The Divine Feminine first as an abstraction, and later as The Goddess, who is

The Divine Feminine personified. Within every culture of the world, The Goddess has played a key role among their pantheons of deities. She was often a powerful figure, full of strength, wisdom, leadership, and feminine essence. Over the many centuries of religious and patriarchal rule, however, our relationship with Her and Her presence in our lives has become increasingly lost to us . . . and to the world.

Part 2, Restore

In this part, we will explore seven of the many qualities of The Divine Feminine as seen through the mythology of The Goddess. The sacred stories of the past that come to us from Egypt, Africa, Greece, India, Tibet, the Lakota, and the creation myths of the Judeo-Christian Bible—all reflect ancient archetypes of The Goddess that were passed down from generation to generation.

While writing this section, it became clear to me that you will not be restoring these seven qualities—power, creativity, stillness, passion, voice, wisdom, and awakening—literally into yourself, as they are already and innately within you. Rather you will be restoring your relationship to them—reclaiming them as truly feminine qualities you can reconnect with as you journey back to The Divine Feminine.

I chose to present just seven of the many qualities of The Divine Feminine because seven is a spiritually potent and sacred number. It is a number often seen in nature, recognized by many religions and used in many spiritual and magical rituals. In numerology, seven represents the Divine Mystery, intuition, the soul, the mystic, intellect, research (usually of ancient wisdom), and expertise. It stands for universal truth, introspection, revelation, and spiritual realization. Furthermore, the primarily masculine nature of seven is to investigate, study and evaluate. This brings structural balance and grounding to this book, which is otherwise heavily saturated with the ethereal, mystical, and intuitive nature of The Feminine. There is another association with the number seven I had in mind while writing this book, one that is very powerful. It is found in the myth of Ishtar, an ancient Assyrian/Babylonian goddess.

In her myth, Ishtar travels to visit her sister who resides in the underworld, which is guarded by seven gates, representing seven spiritual rites of passage. When Ishtar passes through each of the gates, she must shed a piece of clothing, representing her earthly attachments. When she finally passes the seventh gate, she is naked, representing complete detachment from earthly things. She is then imprisoned by her sister but later rescued and must then pass back through the seven gates up to the middle world. Ishtar is given one piece of her clothing back at each gate, and is once again fully clothed as she passes through the last gate. This story is often thought to be the origin for the biblical story of Salome, who performed 'The Dance of The Seven Veils' for King Herod. One by one, she removed a veil until she stood unclothed and completely revealed before him. In this way, Salome personifies The Goddess, unveiled and revealed to the human soul.

Each one of the seven myths that I chose for you is like one of the seven gates, or rites of passage, that will take you deeper and deeper into the realm of The Goddess, revealing Her to you and within you. As you read them, it is my hope that you will shed your own false attachments and misperceptions, one by one, about who you really are, and then re-clothe yourself in seven new ways to discover that you are truly a goddess on earth.

The Divine Feminine is a creative, imaginative energy that often expresses Herself through innovation and invention—and my experience in writing this section was no exception. As I studied the traditional telling of these myths, I found myself inspired to write fresh, new versions of them. Her stories came to me in new ways, as Her words and Her messages were revealed for women today. These adaptations of the myths are invitations to Her teachings; strengthening your relationship to Her qualities as you reclaim and restore them to your life.

At the end of each myth in *Restore*, I provide ways for you to work with each goddess and get to know her. I offer rituals tailored to each goddess, such as her colors, crystals, herbs, essential oils, associated totems, and more. These rituals are ways for you to activate The Divine Feminine and The Goddess within you.

As you take part in these exercises, know that these are *your* sacred rituals, invocations, and prayers to The Divine Goddess. Perform them with reverence and care to honor Her and yourself. For example, when I take a ritual bath, I transform my bathroom into sacred space so that my experience takes on an air of holiness and devotion—both to The Divine and to my own divinity. I light candles, take deep breaths, and make all of my movements slow and deliberate. I use frankincense and herbal smoke, such as sage, to purify the room and my body. I treat myself as if I am beautiful and precious . . . because I am. So are you. You are a goddess in Her name.

These are some of the rituals you will find:

CRYSTALS OF THE GODDESS. Crystals are used for their special metaphysical properties in healing, divination, and magic. Everything in our world is vibrating, so working with the crystals associated with each goddess is a way to capture, infuse, and imprint their vibrations into your energy by working with them. If you have never worked with crystals before, I invite you to open to their special nature and the energy they can bring to you. Working with crystals can be the same as enjoying the beauty of the gemstones in a special piece of jewelry that you may have—and noticing how they can help you to feel beautiful, serene, and confident.

TOTEMS OF THE GODDESS. Totems are sacred symbols, representing something special and divine. They can be plants, animals, or objects that are deeply connected with a spirit being and have special wisdom, powers, or gifts that can be shared with us. In the native and shamanic traditions, animals that appear to us while we are out in nature or in a meditative state are considered powerful messengers for our spirit. Many cultures connect certain flowers, trees, plants or even ritual objects to gods and goddesses. Learning about these helpful and wise totem teachers will enrich your experience with each goddess profoundly.

THE MOONS OF THE GODDESS. The moon is an essential part of working with The Divine Feminine and The Goddess, given that lunar rhythm is so inherent to women. Each of the goddesses in the myths I have chosen has a corresponding lunar phase. Celebrating Her moon helps you gather the power of each goddess and amplify your experience of Her. Some phases of the moon are associated with more than one goddess, in which case, I have presented a different feature of that lunar phase. At the end of this book, in Resources, I have provided you with a link to an online lunar calendar.

THE ANOINTED GODDESS. Anointing is the blessing of your body and the attuning of your essence towards the sacred, aligning it with the Divine. Essential oils, once called esoteric oils, are highly aromatic, deriving their scents from the botanicals they are made from. I have created a recipe in each chapter for an aromatic treasure you can easily make on your own and use to anoint your body—and you can also use any oil of choice for this, as well. The key is to use it with the intention that you are blessing yourself. Essential oils are considered the spirit or essence of the plant; whether derived from its flowers, leaves, roots or bark. Some essential oils have been clinically proven to vibrate at rates higher than the human energy field—causing our own vibrations to elevate.

THE ALTAR OF THE GODDESS. Before or soon after you begin this book, I invite you to dedicate an area of your home to create an altar that honors The Goddess and reflects your experiences with Her. Your altar space can be as simple as a small silver tray atop your dresser or shelf, or as elaborate as an entire table set up in a room, or it can be in addition to or combined with an existing altar. Your altar can even travel with you as a carved wooden box.

I want to encourage and support your journey to The Divine Feminine in every way I can, so on my website I have designed a beautiful altar card for each Goddess, along with affirmations, invocations, and prayers that you can download—free of charge—to print and place upon your altar. By the end of this book, your altar will be overflowing with essence of The Divine Feminine and images of the goddesses, reminding you of your journey with Her each time you see it.

SACRED WATERS OF THE GODDESS. The bathing rituals I offer are designed for you to spend quiet, private time connecting directly with each goddess. Blessing the water of your bath—making it sacred water—will cleanse and purify you, releasing any negative energy that may be attached to your energetic field. In each chapter of this section, I also include a special intention for your bath, along with bath salt formulas you can make yourself.

Part 3, Remember

To remember something is to *re-member* it—to put it back together, to collect all the parts and make it whole once again. In the third part of this book, *Remember,* you will do the same, by learning how to integrate the teachings of The Goddesses into your everyday life.

As you re-member yourself into wholeness, you will also reawaken to the sacredness of your goddess body and learn to see it as a temple and a vessel—beautiful in every way. I'll share with you the cyclical seasons of a woman's life and also reacquaint you with the Great Mother Moon who guides your lunar nature and your moontime blood.

Many women are drawn to do this work in groups—they are often called Goddess Circles. If this interests you, I highly recommend it, as being part of a circle is an enjoyable and inclusive way to create community and sisterhood. In this part, I offer suggestions and instructions for how this book can be used within your own Goddess Circle.

Part 4, Reflections

This part is an optional companion Journal, existing separately from this book. Just like a mirror showing you your truest, most authentic self, it is designed to unveil yourself to *yourself*—revealing your innermost thoughts, feelings and musings about your own goddessness and your own divine specialness. The Journal is filled with further wisdom, teachings, exploration, inspiration, rituals, and blank space for writing, sketching, collaging—or anything else that delights you. Used alongside this book, it is a treasury of your *own* wisdom, which is the perfect compliment to the wisdom of The Goddess found within these pages.

CHOOSE HOW YOU READ

I have designed the book to be read sequentially. However, if you are feeling a little unsure on your life's journey and you need immediate inspiration or guidance, The Goddess is here to help. Flip through the book randomly without looking, and when it feels right, stop and see which page you have landed on—Her message is there . . . even if it takes some time to make sense. If you have landed on a page with a ritual, The Goddess is indicating that you need to do this activity at this time.

Once you have finished your journey with this book, I encourage you to revisit it from time to time, as you may find that what did not speak to you at first may be calling to you now.

A WORD ABOUT
TERMINOLOGY

The Divine Feminine and *Feminine* are words used to convey the highest, holiest, most sacred—and intangibly abstract essence of feminine power that there is. While we will be working only with The Divine Feminine, it is important to note that *The Divine Masculine* and *Masculine* are terms used to convey the highest, holiest, and most sacred energy of the masculine power.

The term *The Goddess* can be used interchangeably with *The Divine Feminine*, referring to the Feminine Essence that flows through the entire natural world as well as the Feminine nature of all things in this world. I use the word *goddess* (with a lower-case 'g') to describe the individual personifications of The Divine Feminine in Her tangible appearances, i.e., the mythic archetypes of The Goddess. Through these goddesses, we are able to have a more intimate and personal relationship with The Divine Feminine.

Please know that your sexual orientation, gender identity and your own individual expressions of love are embraced within these pages. For me, all love is sacred. The terms 'man' and 'woman' are used only to simplify what would be a very lengthy and complex discussion on the dynamic nature of the Masculine and the Feminine in same sex relationships, for the transgender woman and the two spirited person. Know that the elegant and persevering dynamic of these two core essences will always surface—regardless of gender, identity and orientation. Even in same sex relationships, each partner will express their predominant divine essence of either masculine or feminine.

CELEBRATE THE GODDESS
WITHIN YOU!

It is my hope that this book will restore your inner feminine light and show you how to shine it into the world. You can create the energetic shift needed to heal the world today by returning to your true feminine self and restoring your wholeness.

Every human born here on earth comes through the female. This is a magnificent feat that women do. Through you, many magnificent things are possible.

Together we can transform our lives and the world.

I am ancient,
much older than God.

I am the celestial alchemy of the night sky,
the sacred fires of passion and the awakened soul.

I am the essence of power,
the voice of intuition and the wisdom of the earth.

I am the stillness of the mind,
the abundance of the ocean and all that
is re-membered with love.

You are these things too,
for that is how I made you.

PART ONE
RETURN

And yet the real wisdom remains, because it belongs to life itself.
In the cells and in the soul of every woman
this ancient knowing is waiting to be awakened.
~Llewellyn Vaughan-Lee

THE GODDESS
NUT

Her proper role is not to be worshipped,
but to be actualized in the material of our own lives.
~Rev. Cynthia Bourgeault, Ph.D.

LONG, LONG AGO, BEFORE THE LAND OF EGYPT ever was, and long before the river Nile ran through it, the great god Atum was alone in the universe. All around him, energy and matter swirled in disorder. With only the darkness for company, he longed for companionship. And so, when the time was just right, he swung his mighty arm and cut across the void.

All at once, and for the first time, there was a separation. There was an above and also a below. What rose up was the air, thick and smoky from the sparks of his handiwork. What formed beneath was the water, churning and chaotic, hissing with cold and wet.

Now that there were two things in the world, where just a moment ago there was only one, names were necessary. He looked up, and gazing upon the air he named it 'Shu.' As soon as he heard his name, Shu began to quiver and shake with movement. Atum watched as the air busily formed itself into various cloud forms, strong gusty winds, and gentle breezes.

Looking down beneath him, Atum gazed upon the water and named it 'Tefnut.'

Just as with her brother, the moment she heard her name, Tefnut began to transform. The water began to vibrate, collecting into small puddles at first, and then joining these puddles together into running streams, then rushing rivers, and lastly roaring oceans spilling out as far as the eye could see.

Drifting above Tefnut, Shu often caught sight of himself reflected back in the waters below. At first he could only see himself, and so he watched and studied himself in all his forms. But as he gazed day after day, he soon saw beyond his own refection and began to see his sister with all of her different moods and expressions. Shu noticed that she was dark, mysterious, still, serene, roiling with energy, reflective and ever changing.

Shu fell in love.

His early courtship consisted of gentle, light breezes blown across her watery surface and he watched with pleasure the little ripples she made, happy that he had caused them.

His passion for her grew. Now he blew gusty winds, hoping to access her inky depth with his power. She responded with huge salty waves arching to meet him above her. From their elemental union materialized the quiet mist of atmosphere; moisture clung to everything, rain fell softly down. They carried on like this for some time, each one reaching for the other endlessly, pressing up side to side.

There was joy and pleasure in the world, and Atum was pleased.

As it is with all living things, when two are joined, a third is born, and so it was for Shu and Tefnut. They gave life to lovely Nut, who was the night sky with her many stars and whirling galaxies floating high above her father's atmosphere. And they gave life to Nut's fine-looking brother, Geb, who was the solid land that appeared below his mother's waters. Tefnut and Shu were proud to see the green abundant land that was their son, and were made breathless by the beauty of their starry-eyed daughter Nut.

It was not long before Nut and Geb began to see each other as more than siblings. Geb took notice of Nut's long, slender legs and arms and her graceful hands. He began to wait for her, in awe of her beauty as she emerged each night when the sun disappeared into her immense body. Each dawn, he lamented her leaving as she labored the sun out into the world from deep inside of herself. He watched her with longing as she disappeared against the morning sky. He waited eagerly for nighttime when he could lay beneath her again, gazing upon her body above him and losing himself in her twinkling skin of diamond stars.

Showing off in courtship, Geb heaved large tectonic plates of land, thrusting the tops of mountains powerfully towards her. He grew tall trees whose branches reached upwards for her, and she responded by lowering her night sky down upon it all, receiving him into her sparkling blackness.

Nut and Geb were in love.

One late evening, just before the sun was to be born again, Nut and Geb were talking. Their eyes were closed and they were wrapped tightly in each other's arms.

Feeling the sun begin to stir within her, Nut slowly opened her eyes, still drowsy from their loving.

"It is time for me to go, Geb," she said softly.

She could feel him frown in the stillness of the dark.

"Where is it that you go, sister?" Geb complained like a child. "What in the world could be so important that you must leave me each morning?"

"Well," Nut said, turning her face from him to hide her smile, "I have things to do."

"What are these things?"

Turning back towards him, her lips lightly brushing his, she whispered with her face close to his, "While you are growing grass and trees, blooming flowers, and heaving land from the seas to the surface, I am creating new stars to shine down on you."

Geb pouted, unconvinced that this was more important than himself.

"I am spinning planets, moons and galaxies round and round, I am spinning you round and round as well, lover, day after day. It is with my arms that I encircle this world, holding it close and dear. It is within my embrace that all elements of the cosmos are born, and die."

Geb busied himself with a patch of grass that needed filling in, and so she continued.

"All day I am sweeping up the dust of nebulae and I am blowing the solar winds, tending to the black holes and cleaning up after dwarf stars. And, brother of mine," raising her voice a bit to get his attention, "who do you think births the blessed sun each morning to nourish all the life that grows upon you, and to warm your huge round body?"

Geb looked self-consciously down at his huge, round body.

She was suddenly irritated that Geb, who watched her all night long, did not see all she had to do, all that she was. Nut moved herself a bit further away from the quiet Geb, thus revealing a thin line of crimson dawn at the horizon. The sun was getting quite full in her belly; it was becoming uncomfortable. Very soon she would need to push it out.

"I must go now, Geb," she said softly as her anger cooled.

Hiding her discomfort and the great effort it took for her to bring forth the sun, Nut looked tenderly over to her brother, sorry that she had been cross with him. Her dark, violet eyes became lavender as the night turned unhurriedly into day. She looked longingly towards Geb and felt his deep love for her. She also felt his puzzlement of her anger.

The sun could not wait a moment more and in a sudden, silent burst of blinding orange pink light, another day was born as Nut released the sun from her womb. With her image fading against the morning sky, the sibling lovers reached for each other one last time and then, Nut was gone.

All that day, Geb was preoccupied, thinking of Nut. They had never quarreled before and he was confused by her irritation with him. Did she not know how much he adored her and loved to gaze upon her?

Geb could not yet really see Nut in all of her power and all of her glory. Her mystery was still unrevealed to him. Geb spent the day thinking back to all that Nut had said and all the nights he had spent looking up at her with desire.

Still perplexed, he went to seek the guidance of his father. Shu asked his son what he knew of Nut thus far. "Well," said Geb, "she is beautiful. And her skin sparkles . . . oh how I love looking at her!"

Shu said gently, and with great wisdom, "Geb my son. You know very little of the one that you love. You must look deeper than her physical form, past her twinkling skin and perfect beauty. Look deeper, look into the depth of her very essence, and witness her great work in this world. It is there that you will see your own essence reflected back to you. It is there that you will find your own true self and your true purpose with Nut."

Geb could not wait to see his sister that night, for he had much to say.

When Nut appeared as the evening sky that night, Geb was waiting for her. He had spent the entire day growing thousands of jasmine vines that he had woven high up on all the tallest branches of a grove of sycamore trees, hoping to praise her with their intoxicating perfume.

Nut smiled down at her brother while breathing in the jasmine. He looked deep into her eyes and with his heart overflowing he spoke to her these words:

My sister.

My lover.

O great goddess.

I see you now. I know you now.

You, who births the sun into the world each day

and becomes the moon and the stars each night

You, who has filled this world with your beauty,

and has given this world the light of the sun,

the light that gives life to all things.

I know that it is you who holds up the heavens.

You alone, are holding up the sky and I honor you.

The whole of my body lying beneath you knows all of this to be true.

I and everything else rests within your arms, is born and dies in your embrace.

Beloved, I shall join my whole self to you, in every way.

You are the light of the world, the light of my life.

Rest your beautiful hands on my hands, and your delicate feet upon my feet.

I ask that you receive my support and together we will be as one.

Nut's eyes filled with tears of joy that fell upon Geb like shooting stars tumbling from the sky.

Then she positioned herself gracefully above her brother, tenderly placing her hands on his hands, and her feet upon his feet, and she arched herself upwards as they became the above and the below of this world.

Immediately, Nut felt her whole being relax in the power of her beloved's strength. And in that moment she opened her heart to him, more so than ever before. Between them grass grew and flowers bloomed. Gentle breezes floated across rippled oceans. New stars were made and galaxies spiraled round and round.

There was joy and pleasure in the world, and Atum was pleased.

Nut was a creation goddess of ancient Egypt. Her name means 'sky,' which is in reference to both her elemental nature and her embodiment of the night sky.

Often depicted as an elongated, naked female body with legs and arms outstretched or bent over at the waist with her fingertips and toes upon the earth, each of her hands and feet were thought to be touching one the four cardinal directions of north, south, east, and west. Nut was the firmament that separated the earth and sky, chaos from order, and the living from the dead.

As a sky goddess, she governed all heavenly bodies, and was thought of as protectress of the dead as they traveled across her body into the afterlife. During the day, the sun, moon and other celestial bodies also made their way across her body, then at dusk she would swallow them all, only to give birth to them one by one again at dawn to create each new day.

CHAPTER ONE

RETURNING TO YOUR DIVINE FEMININE SELF

Return to yourself, to who you are...
you will discover yourself, like a lotus flower in full bloom,
even in a muddy pond, beautiful and strong.

~Masaru Emoto

THE WORLD IS OUT OF BALANCE TODAY. This is because women are out of balance—and women have a profound effect on the equilibrium of life.

The way of the world is such that it requires both the feminine and the masculine essence to be present in equivalent amounts, as counterparts of each other, in order for there to be harmony. Whenever a woman is out of balance, wherever she is and whatever she is doing is also out of balance. The goddess Nut (*pronounced with a long 'u' as in 'Noot'*) reminds us that the Feminine Essence is in balance whenever she is in harmony with the Masculine. This is true for both a woman's relationship with the man in her life, as well as her relationship with her own inner masculine essence.

Today's feminine imbalance is the result of generations of women living in a patriarchal society and striving to be treated and recognized in the same way as men. In their attempt to become equalized, many women have minimized their feminine essence and maximized their masculine.

Just like the effects of chronic stress upon a body, the stress of this feminine imbalance on our culture has been devastating. The word *devastating* means 'highly destructive or damaging, causing severe shock, distress, or grief,' according to the Merriam-Webster dictionary. Within the word itself is contained another word—*deva* which is Sanskrit for god or male deity and has its origins in the word *deiwos*, which means to shine. In other words, the stress of the feminine imbalance has caused damage; it has caused the light women give to the world to stop shining. And when women's light is dimmed, so too is men's. The whole world experiences a spiritual darkness when women do not shine their feminine essence into it. Like the sun eclipsing the moon, the light of The Goddess has been blocked from our lives.

While there can be many underlying reasons for the following harmful behaviors, for many women they are indications of this feminine imbalance:

- ❖ being excessively goal driven
- ❖ allowing work to take precedence over other activities
- ❖ having an aversion to being in stillness
- ❖ letting her body and her schedule always be in motion
- ❖ experiencing difficulty with intimacy and relationships with men
- ❖ feeling that the male is the enemy—confusing, confounding or irritating to her
- ❖ overthinking and analyzing everything
- ❖ having difficulty expressing her feelings and emotions
- ❖ experiencing a disconnection from her body (feeling her body image is distorted, or needing to use plastic surgery to alter her body)
- ❖ feeling that self-pleasure is taboo

The imbalance may also manifest in physical ways such as health issues on the right side of the body—as this is the energetically masculine side. Anything that is overused eventually wears out or wears down, and will display the wear and tear by not working properly. So it is with our bodies.

Forgiveness, compassion, and harmony are fundamental aspects of your feminine essence. As a woman, you carry within your cells and within your womb all of the collective experiences that all women on Earth have endured—both joyous and painful. This energetic ancestry anxiously awaits for *your* healing, your forgiveness, and your compassion.

As you heal your own feminine essence, all the spirits of all the women of the world who came before you will heal as well. Your own healing will cause a profound shift in you, one that will spark a deep, personal restoration that will spiral out into the world, reestablishing the balance we so desperately need. The way for you to become balanced is to open up to The Divine Feminine. A woman who is balanced is able to operate easily within both her feminine and her masculine essences, as she has both, but her primary essence, which is feminine, must lead.

I have come to understand that the injuries men have inflicted upon women throughout history are actually a symptom of The Goddess' absence in all of our lives—men's as much as women's. While The Divine Feminine is not a presence that humans can ever remove from the world, She is a presence that they can most certainly choose to ignore . . . and they have been doing so for too long now. Through my study and observation, I have learned that She is the life force of the world, and we cannot live without Her.

The qualities of The Divine Feminine are the very qualities that will heal our collective wounds and calm women's rage—conscious or unconscious—towards men. These qualities help create an understanding and closeness between the sexes that naturally leads to rebalancing the world. The Divine Feminine is not only wise, loving, and compassionate towards women. She is also here to share these qualities with men—but She does this *through* women. All women can and must teach these qualities to men; these are our divine gifts to share.

A woman was designed to shine her light into the world. She was created to offer beauty, healing, and love to all living things. Women are sacred beings capable of huge acts of healing for themselves, for others and for the planet. We have worshipped The Great Mother, The Goddess, and The Divine Feminine since early humans first understood that all of humankind comes from the female. Sufi teachings say that a woman is most certainly pure, because every newborn child is pure (from the pure comes the pure). In Judaism it is believed that women have been blessed with a higher degree of intuition and understanding than men. And this Taoist teaching deeply reflects the sacredness of The Feminine: *Know the masculine. Keep to the feminine.*

Today's woman is mostly unaware of her sacred essence, which comes from The Divine Feminine. With this awareness awakening within us, we must go in search of ways to reconnect to our sacred roots as women. By returning to the wisdom of our true essence, we restore our ability to be more loving towards others, and ourselves— enjoying our natural feminine state of being and sacrificing nothing in order to be powerful, successful, and happy. Our lives will be filled with the wisdom of the Divine and the ways of The Goddess when we make ourselves whole again. Once a woman restores her own divine feminine essence, she can then transform herself into her truest Self—a goddess on earth.

Your own return to The Divine Feminine and the renewal of Her principles to your life will bring about an enormous personal transformation for you, and this will result in a massive shift of healing that resonates through the entire planet. This long overdue return of the feminine into your life heralds the return of The Divine Feminine into the world.

Bless my tears as I cry to You,
O Goddess of the Sea;
tear of the first woman's tear;

Bless my body as it grows like You,
O Goddess of the Earth;
bone of the first woman's bone;

Bless my hands as I pray to You,
O Goddess of the Stars;
fire of first woman's fire;

Bless my heart as it longs for You,
O Goddess of the Air;
breath of first woman's breath;

Bless me into wholeness,
beloved Goddess,
first Mother of us all.

CHAPTER TWO

THE DIVINE FEMININE

She is with everyone and in everyone, and so beautiful is her secret
that no person can know the sweetness with which
she sustains people, and spares them in inscrutable mercy.
~Hildegard of Bingen

THE GODDESS IS THE FEMININE ESSENCE OF GOD. For many of you, this statement may challenge your spiritual and religious beliefs. For others, this information is surprising because you did not know that God had a feminine aspect. And for still others, you are aware of this idea but did not realize that its truth has everything to do with how you feel about yourself as a woman.

For all of us, the idea that The Divine is both Masculine *and* Feminine is monumental to our wholeness as human beings. And for women especially, this concept is the missing link in our journey back to our true Self.

Today is very different than when the world's most powerful religions were first forming, when women and their feminine essence were feared and suppressed. Today, in most cultures, a woman is not so externally feared nor as suppressed as she was in those ancient times. Many women, however, remain extraordinarily disconnected from their true Self and this has led us into a spiritual and energetic predicament.

For you to see yourself as divine, you must first begin to see The Divine as Feminine.

THE SUPREME ESSENCE
OF WOMAN

What is The Divine Feminine? It is impossible to define. How can something that is everything be described as only one thing?

The Divine Feminine is best defined as that which is the intangibility of life, the mystery of the mysterious universe. Conceptual by nature, She is the *beingness* of life, rather than the *doing* in life.

Penned elusively onto the scrolls of the first Torah, recited faintly in the first telling of The Bhagavad Gita and found hidden within the original parchments of the New Testament, The Divine Feminine is acknowledged, hinted at, but not stated specifically. This is not an injustice, nor an omission. She has not been kept a secret from us—She *is* the secret and all this mystery is simply Her way of being.

The Divine Feminine is a Presence hidden within the Presence of God. She is not obvious and not observable to the naked eye. Like veins of gold concealed within the earth, Her radiance lies unrevealed until mined from within. She is the Feminine Essence of God, an indwelling aspect of God as a Whole.

Her existence is much like a riddle—She is everywhere known and yet one can spend an entire lifetime continually searching for Her. Like a fish that is searching for water to swim in, what we are seeking is all around us; so obvious that we miss seeing it.

The key to finding The Divine Feminine is to stop looking for Her—and just be like Her. In being like Her, you will find more compassion, more understanding, more wisdom, more peace and more love—for both yourself and for others—than ever before. With the essence and qualities of The Divine Feminine held securely in your heart, and active in your life, you will begin to see Her everywhere and experience Her in all that you do. Both men and women can experience The Divine Feminine, but only a woman can embody Her . . . this is Her gift to you.

As the Supreme Mother, The Divine Feminine nourishes the universe with Her Light and Essence. She is both the source of creation *and* creation itself—a concept that can baffle the human mind. She is unknowable by our human minds. She is the Master Architect with the sacred design for all living things within Her.

When the catalytic, activating force of The Divine Masculine joins with Her, life is made. Without this joining, no life in our world may come forth; no thing can be made physical until their Union occurs.

The Divine Feminine resides in all things that bring us closer to experiencing our own divinity—e.g., Tantra, Kundalini, Yoga, meditation, prayer, dance and song. She is the natural, wild, and untamed nature of the anima part of our psyche, speaking to us from the hidden and shadowy depths of our unconscious. She is both a mystery, and She is The Mystery. Men desire Her, women seek to be like Her and we have all come from Her sacred womb to be born into this world. In the end, at the close of our lives, we shall all return to Her.

She, of 10,000 names, has been called The Cosmic Mother, The Great Mother, The Holy Mother, The Grace of God, The Bride of God, and The Queen of Heaven. Throughout the Old Testament and in other spiritual texts of the world, She is described as a light or radiance. Veiled within God's entirety, She is the *glory* in the phrase *the glory of God* that we find throughout the Bible and in poems, songs and spiritual literature. The American Heritage Dictionary defines *glory* as 'majestic beauty and splendor; resplendence; the splendor and bliss of heaven; perfect happiness.' The Divine Feminine is all of this . . . and you are made in Her image.

Once you, as a woman, embrace that you are the physical embodiment of the Glory of God, then the realm of The Divine Feminine and all of Her magnificence, splendor and grandeur will not only be revealed *to* you, you will discover them *within* you.

Restoring our relationship with The Divine Feminine is the only hope for our world to heal—and Her Divine Wisdom of how this will come about lies within you. She is the Divine Essence of mercy, truth, and love—all of which are encoded into your cells, your consciousness, and your heart. Activating this within yourself and in all that you do, not only feeds the part of you that is longing for Divine Feminine Essence but it also sends ripples, then waves of mercy, truth, and love out into the world, quenching the collective thirst and feeding the hunger of a peace-starved planet.

Throughout history, the magnificence of The Divine Feminine and Her gifts to women have been suppressed, denied and minimized by those who held earthly power and who feared Her Divine Power. And yet, She has prevailed. Her wisdom has seeped into every religion and Her goddess personifications have long endured through myth, art and song.

THE GODDESS
WALKS AMONG US

The Divine Feminine Essence is found within all cultures and all spiritualities. Throughout human history many goddesses have walked with us, and the underlying essence of each and every one is The Divine Feminine. Many of these various goddess personifications are revisions or versions of the same Supreme Essence that, having spread from culture to culture, were adopted into familiar, local religious traditions. However, in most cultures, Her pure Essence was usually diluted, rewritten or censored, leaving only that which the patriarchal religious leaders would allow.

The Feminine as an energy, elemental force, or essence can be found as early as ancient Egypt, whose goddess Ma'at represented the principles of cosmic order, balance, and justice. In Hindu India, The Divine Feminine is the Shakti—the highest, most supreme energy of the universe. For the Jewish people, She is The Shekhinah—the Queen, Bride, and Feminine aspect of God. She appears within later religions such as Gnostic and Esoteric Christianity as The Sophia, or God's Essence of Wisdom—a belief that may have been inspired by The Shekhinah and *Chochma,* which is the feminine essence of Wisdom found on the Kabbalistic Tree of Life, which itself perhaps even dates back to Ma'at.

Ma'at

Ma'at was a Goddess of measurement, standards and discernment for the ancient Egyptians. She stood for the abstract principles of cosmic and earthly order, balance, harmony and justice. Ma'at was not considered the single Divine Feminine principle nor an ultimate Supreme Being; however, her 42 laws of right living reigned supreme in the land of the Egypt. To follow them was to gain entry into the afterlife. To break even one of them meant risking your entrance into the paradisal land of *Aaru*. As the personification of right and wrong, Ma'at's laws were the standard for discerning between them. Her laws were the laws of nature; to live with Ma'at in your life was to live in harmony with the natural world.

Like the earliest Egyptian goddesses, Ma'at appeared first as an abstraction but eventually took the human form of a beautiful young woman. She was often painted into Egyptian hieroglyphs as just a feather, which is her chief symbol acknowledging her as an unseen force in the world. Later she was depicted as a goddess wearing her feather in a headdress. Scholarly research suggests that she was even more closely related to The Divine Feminine principle than Isis, who was the supreme mother-healer-magician goddess of Egypt. Ma'at's law of order prevented chaos in the world and governed all beings—humans, gods, and goddesses. Some experts believe that Isis and Ma'at were actually one goddess, appearing in two forms, both as personifications of The Divine Feminine principle.

Surviving records of Ma'at found on papyrus and within excavated tombs tell us her story. Ma'at spreads her glorious wings wide enough to hold the world within them and her feather of truth, light as air, was enough to tip the scales of balance in either one direction or another. She awaits each soul of men and women at the time of their death, so that she can hear their negative confession of her 42 laws. This ancient Egyptian confession differs from the Judeo-Christian one in that deceased beings declare acts that they did *not* commit rather than those which they did. Recited in the presence of this goddess along with a jury of ten, the confession was a report of right-doing for the deceased.

Intention meant everything for the Egyptians. While the soul was confessing, Ma'at weighed their heart for the intent of every action confessed against the feather of truth. If the heart weighed less than her feather throughout the confession, the soul was allowed to pass into the afterlife. But if the heart was heavy with ill intent, even if its actions were righteous, then the fierce crocodile-headed god Ammut immediately ate the soul.

Ma'at was both loved and respected; her laws kept peace and order among the people of Egypt while infusing their lives with spirituality, kindness, and respect.

The 42 Laws of Ma'at

While the following translation of Ma'at's Law, from Professor E. A. Wallis Budge in *The Book of the Dead* (1995) is debated among scholars as to its accuracy, it is still interesting to read. These laws changed from tomb to tomb, perhaps reflecting the right and wrongdoing of each individual buried there. When I first read them, my mind began to wonder what laws would be written to reflect my own life.

I have not committed sin.

I have not committed robbery with violence.

I have not stolen.

I have not slain men and women.

I have not stolen grain.

I have not purloined offerings.

I have not stolen the property of the god.

I have not uttered lies.

I have not carried away food.

I have not uttered curses.

I have not committed adultery; I have not lain with men.

I have made none to weep.

I have not eaten the heart [i.e., I have not grieved uselessly, or felt remorse].

I have not attacked any man.

I am not a man of deceit.

I have not stolen cultivated land.

I have not been an eavesdropper.

I have slandered [no man].

I have not been angry without just cause.

I have not debauched the wife of any man.

I have not polluted myself.

I have terrorized none.

I have not transgressed [the Law].

I have not been wroth (angry).

I have not shut my ears to the words of truth.

I have not blasphemed.

I am not a man of violence.

I am not a stirrer up of strife (or a disturber of the peace).

I have not acted (or judged) with undue haste.

I have not pried into matters.

I have not multiplied my words in speaking.

I have wronged none. I have done no evil.

I have not worked witchcraft against the King (or blasphemed against the King).

I have never stopped [the flow of] water.

I have never raised my voice (spoken arrogantly, or in anger).

I have not cursed (or blasphemed) God.

I have not acted with evil rage.

I have not stolen the bread of the gods.

I have not carried away the khenfu cakes from the Spirits of the dead.

I have not snatched away the bread of the child,

nor treated with contempt the god of my city.

I have not slain the cattle belonging to the god.

Shakti   ————————————

In the Hindu practice of Tantra, Shakti is the Divine Feminine whose power flows through all living beings as well as through the Gods and Goddesses. Shakti can take any form and manifest as any one of the Hindu goddesses. Her name means 'empowerment' or 'force,' and She is thought of as the highest, most sacred, supreme energy, also known as *Mahadevi* (Mother Goddess) of the universe. She is the sum of all *Devis* (Goddesses) and the complement and consort to the Supreme Masculine known as Deva, Brahman, or Shiva. The power of Shakti is so expansive, that all things—including Shiva—exist within Her and Hindu wisdom reveres the woman as life itself, believing her to be Goddess-like, because She embodies the essence and principle of Shakti.

The energy of Shakti is creative and balancing, but it can also be destructive. She is both restless and still. Her essence gives life to the universe, and supports all living things. Shakti creates life, preserves life and *is* the life-force that runs through us. She can also withdraw Her essence from us as well—which She does at the time of our death.

In the healing science of Ayurveda, Shakti is the vibrant radiance of our *prana shakti* (physical energy), *chitta shakti* (mental energy) and *alma shakti* (spiritual energy). Ayurveda treats the person as a whole, balancing all aspects of life. Every remedy and each practice of Ayurveda derives from this idea, and seeks to create a body, mind, and spirit through which Shakti can freely flow. When Shakti runs unobstructed through us, we are in perfect physical, mental, and spiritual balance and can enjoy the riches She brings into our life. Often, Shakti is called 'the wish-fulfilling gem,' and this jewel is available to all.

In Tantric Yoga, Shakti is the Supreme Divine Feminine, and is also called the Kundalini, when referring to the dormant Feminine energy that lies sleeping, coiled like a snake at the base of our spine along with the Supreme Divine Masculine energy, which is Her compliment. To awaken the Kundalini is to awaken one's very being to the divine within and to the Divine nature of the Universe. Through the practice of *pranayama* (breathing exercises), *asana* (yogic postures), a *sattvic* diet (a sentient, vegetarian diet eating foods such as honey, cheese, butter, cream, cereals, grains, legumes, nuts and fruit—*sattvic* means 'pure, simple') and devotional chanting of mantras (repetition of sacred sounds or words), one awakens the Kundalini and attains self-realization.

Repeating a mantra 108 times daily or more creates a vibrational sound current that calls forth the Kundalini, or Shakti energy that awakens Her. This promotes health, well-being, creativity, happiness and spiritual growth. The use of a *mala* (which means 'garland' in Sanskrit) assists with focus and attention as the user gently moves from one bead to the next while reciting the chant over and over. A mala is a necklace or bracelet usually made from precious and semi-precious stones, sacred rudraksha seeds, or beads made from precious woods such as sandalwood. A mala has either 108 beads for one revolution of chanting, or 54 beads for two revolutions.

Here is a powerful mantra for Lalita, a supreme Shakti goddess of Divine Femininity and bliss as presented by Thomas Ashley-Farrand in his book, *Shakti Mantras*. It is originally from the sacred Hindu texts of the Brahmanda Purana:

> *Om Bhakta Saubhagya Dayinyei Namaha*
> *(Om Bhahk-tah Sauw-bhag-giya Dah-yeen-yei Nahm-ah-hah)*
>
> *Om and salutations to She who compassionately gives*
> *qualities of herself to Her devotees, including illumination, glory,*
> *beauty and other attributes making their future bright.*

Shekhinah

The Shekhinah is the indwelling, feminine aspect of God for the Jewish people and for other religions whose roots grew from within Judaism. She is The Divine Feminine both of and for God.

Her name, which means 'dwelling' in Hebrew, is not written nor mentioned in the Old Testament (the Torah), save for a few obscure and similar words. Rather, She was referred to specifically in Talmudic discussion and in the *Targumim,* which are the oral traditions of the Jewish spiritual teachings.

The Judaic God (Yahweh or Adonai) is not referred to as either Feminine or Masculine, but contains both aspects within it. This presence of The Divine Feminine that dwells within God is known as the Light of God, sometimes referred to as His Glory in early Talmudic texts. It is through this light that the ordinary world of Earth is connected to the extraordinary world of The Divine.

First published in the 13th century with disputed authorship, a group of books called the *Zohar* (a Hebrew word meaning 'the radiance' or 'the splendor') represent the fundamental texts of Jewish mysticism. In them, they discuss that God manifests Itself into the world through and with this Light. Much like our prayers as we send them upwards towards heaven, the Zohar describes that God sends us Its Light, Its Feminine aspect, The Shekhinah, down towards us. It is through this infinite Feminine presence that we are able to make contact with God.

At one time, The Shekhinah's dwelling place was in the Temple of Israel. There She was unified with and within God in that She was joined with The Divine Masculine. Once the Temple was destroyed, She was severed from Her union with The Divine Masculine and Her dwelling place came to be out among the people of Israel, wandering with them in the world until the Temple could be rebuilt. It can be argued whether The Shekhinah Herself is in exile, or if She was sent to dwell with the exiled Jewish people to provide them with comfort and guidance.

On the eve of the Jewish Sabbath, called *Shabbat*, it is thought that we can temporarily wed or reunite The Shekhinah with The Divine Masculine by the lighting of Shabbat candles and the reciting of the Shabbat prayers. It is also said that when all of humankind fulfills all of the Divine commandments, it will cause the permanent reunification of The Shekhinah to God.

Jewish Mysticism teaches that when three or more individuals study the Torah together, or when ten or more people gather for prayer, The Shekhinah dwells among them. It is also taught that She sits at the head of every person who is ill or in need of Her. Many Kabbalistic healers do not stand near the head of those in need, leaving space for The Shekhinah to be present.

The Shekhinah is the Essence of the essence of woman. Her Essence comes into the world through you, as you. This is exquisitely expressed in this lovely version of Psalm 139:13-16, as presented by Rabbi Rami Shapiro in his book, *The Divine Feminine in Biblical Wisdom Literature.*

> *You created my inmost parts;*
> *weaving me together in my mother's womb.*
> *I thank You for that,*

for I am awesomely and wondrously made.
Your work is subtle and steeped in wonder;
I know it well.
My body was not hidden from You;
You gave me shape in secret recesses of the womb.
You knit me whole in the depths of the earth.
Your eyes saw my unformed limbs;
and You knew the deeds I could do
even before there was an I *to do them.*

RESTORING THE DIVINE FEMININE IN OUR MODERN WORLD

The return of our relationship with The Divine Feminine and welcoming Her back into our awareness and into our lives means that She is reappearing to rebalance our world. She is an inextinguishable fire, a presence that cannot ever be obliterated. She is *the* primal life force that is pulsing through every living thing. To annihilate Her is to annihilate all life, in all forms.

The age of Man, and The Masculine as the primary force in the world, has caused much disruption and destruction, because *when acting on its own,* that is the Masculine nature. As we reunite with the long absent Feminine, we assist Her to reunite with The Masculine so that order and balance can be restored.

This Divine reunion cannot happen solely on the energetic plane. It must be also be enacted here, on Earth, by women and men, feminine and masculine. This reunion is a healing both for earthly women and men as well as for the Divine Woman and Divine Man. We return ourselves to The Divine Feminine and bring Her forth into the world so that this may happen.

The Divine Feminine will not take the place of The Masculine in the world, for that would be yet another imbalance in the opposite direction. Rather, She will stand next to, and with The Masculine as His beloved Beloved . . . as it should be.

Unseen, unknown, and unrevealed;
She is the breath between the breath,
the thought behind the thought,
and the heart within the heart.

Visible, understood, and revealed;
She is the face of our face,
the body of our body,
and the essence of our essence.

See Her within you.
Know Her as you.
Reveal yourself to Her
and you will become
as a goddess upon the earth.

CHAPTER THREE

WE ARE THE GODDESS

God may be in the details, but the goddess is in the questions.
Once we begin to ask them, there's no turning back.

~Gloria Steinem

OUR EARLY SISTERS DEEPLY DESIRED TO KNOW the faceless and formless power of The Divine Feminine. They wanted a personal experience, interacting with Her directly. This longing to look upon the face of The Divine Feminine eventually took form—and along with the gods of the earliest religions, many goddesses were also born.

The goddesses of mythology are the tangible manifestations of the intangible Divine Feminine; they are the personifications of Her. The Goddess is, by nature, coexistent with The Divine Feminine—they are technically one and the same. However, through Goddess archetypal story, song and art, the Feminine abstraction can be seen, related to, and interacted with. This occurs through any of Her individual embodiments or as a single being who possesses all of the essence and power of The Divine Feminine.

In any of Her forms, The Goddess looks like us, loves like us, and feels like us. She is more powerful than we are, often having supernatural abilities. If she is inspired to do so, she can either give us one or more of Her Divine abilities—or take away the ones that we already have. Both actions are decisions based upon Her Divine Feminine wisdom. The Goddess is not punitive, nor is she retaliatory; She loves us dearly and wants our lives to be filled with joy and happiness. She offers us healing, comfort, protection, guidance, inspiration, support, balance, and abundance. While The Goddess is the face of The Divine Feminine, She is also the heart of every woman.

We have abundant evidence of Goddess worship in many cultures dating back for millennia. These are embedded in the ancient myths that have been passed down for generations, as well as in the many small, stylized and beautifully formed statues of women found at archaeological excavation sites.

The idea of woman/mother as goddess and female fertility was so captivating that in almost all prehistoric cultures we have found abundant representations of pregnant and voluptuous statuettes, called Venus figurines by archaeologists.

In the earliest known carving to date, the Acheulian Figurine, which was found in soil layers thought to be from 232,000 to 800,000 years old, we are reunited with The Great Mother Goddess. This small carving far predates another ancient statue, called the Venus of Willendorf, a figurine of similar design thought to be created only about 24,000 years ago. Both statuettes have pendulous breasts and wide hips along with disproportionately small heads and almost non-existent limbs. In each statue, the artist's focus was specifically on the female reproductive parts of the body. We can imagine why this emphasis had meaning and significance for early peoples. It has even been suggested that the artists who created these statuettes were female, so gracefully represented was the female body.

Made of bone, rock, or clay, Mother Goddess figures have been found in nearly every early culture that inhabited Africa, Europe, North and South America, Asia, and elsewhere. Often found near shrines and burial sites, these fertile, curvaceous representations of the female suggest that they reflected a woman's unique ability to give life.

Perhaps our foremothers believed these statues had the power to assist them with fertility or childbirth, or maybe they were used to assure the fertileness of the land to produce abundant crops and harvests. Or perhaps they were fashioned to honor the creative energies of the universe, reminding women of their own divine, reproductive femaleness whenever they looked upon it. Quite possibly, they were potent talismans, or magical charms believed to transfer the power of The Goddess to whoever held them. The fact that these womanly figurines have survived at all is wondrous enough, but the idea that early humankind recognized female extraordinariness is spectacular.

From these early representational figurines of archaic cultures, there later emerged more lifelike goddesses, as seen in Sumerian, Mesopotamian, African, Egyptian, Eastern, Greek, and Roman art. Taking on more human features, behaviors and attributes, these goddesses became less figurative and more realistic. We see examples of this in the art and mythology of the numerous pantheons of goddesses that many ancient civilizations have left for us to find, such as the Sumerian goddess Inanna, the ancient Egyptian goddess Isis, the Greek goddess Aphrodite and her appearance later as the Roman goddess Venus.

Throughout the world's various cultures, the many goddesses each expressed one or more of the Divine qualities embodied in the nature of women—the mother, the lover, the seductress, the healer, the midwife, the warrior, the creatress, or the destroyer of life. Some goddesses were personifications of the elements—air, earth, fire, and water, while others were the representations of land, water, and valleys. Individual goddesses were also portrayed as the personification of the moon, natural forces, all of nature, various animals, creative arts such as dance or music, or as abstract notions such as abundance.

THE FACE OF
THE GODDESS

In each culture in which The Goddess appeared, one or more of Her representations usually stood out as the principal expression of The Divine Feminine.

This Goddess was usually the primary Creation or Mother Goddess who ruled over all other goddesses in that culture and who possessed the all-nurturing and all-nourishing qualities of The Divine Feminine, and it was She who called forth all of life.

In Africa, Ala was the goddess of life, the laws, and the morality of living. Her symbol was the yam knife, which represented the abundant fertility of the earth and the human soul's transformation into death. Andriamahilala was another African mother goddess who was often called the Queen of Heaven. She bestowed the flesh upon the bones of humans and created their physical form, along with offering them a choice as to how all human life would end—either with offspring to carry on their lineage or childless and alone (it seems most chose offspring). It may be that she was the origin of the Egyptian goddess Ma'at, as her yam knife looks very much like a feather and her laws are like Ma'at's.

In Egypt, Isis was the high priestess goddess of magic, mystery, and healing. She was also a mother goddess known for offering support for mothers and for being a mother herself. Isis, along with her brother/mate Osiris, came to earth to govern and teach the Egyptian people. Her story tells of the sisterhood she shared with her sibling Nephtys, of her deep love and passion for her brother/mate Osiris, of the betrayal by their brother Set and the loss and grief she experienced when Set murders Osiris, and finally of the joy of giving birth to her magical son Horus. The story of Isis is an epic myth all women can relate to and its popularity has endured to this day among women throughout the world. In addition to Isis, Hathor, Ma'at and Nut were also important Egyptian goddesses who embodied The Divine Feminine.

In India, Kali, the benevolent but fearsomely protective mother goddess, ruled over time and change. She was often called the redeemer of the universe, protecting humanity from evil and harm. Her symbols were the color black, like her skin, and the skulls of those she vanquished, which she wore as a necklace and earrings. Durga, also called Mahadevi, from whom Kali was born, was considered a supreme goddess, and she expressed the destructive and protective forces of The Divine Feminine. She was a warrior goddess and her symbols were her many weapons and the tiger that she rode into battle.

In Celtic Europe, Cailleach was considered the mother of all beings and appeared as an old, hideous woman with bear's fur and wild boar's tusks. Anu, more commonly known as Danu, is also a Celtic mother goddess to both humans and the gods. She was a powerful fertility goddess whose symbol was a black cauldron from where the waters of life flow.

In Native America, Nokomis was a mother earth goddess to all living things, feeding them with her spirit and nourishing them with her body. Her symbols are corn and things made from gold. Another native mother goddess and sky spirit, Geezhigo-Quae created the first people and the lands of earth when she descended into the primordial soup bringing forth life from within its depths.

In Asia, Izanami along with her consort Izanagi created the earth when they stirred the formless void into form with their magic spears. And Quan Yin was once a living woman who then became the mother goddess of compassion and enlightenment when she vowed not to ascend until every human being had found enlightenment.

In the Middle East, Inanna was a mother/sky goddess for the Sumerian people. Her symbol was a lion that she rides and an eight-pointed star representing the planet Venus. She was also known as the goddess of love. In Assyria and Babylonia she was known as the goddess Ishtar, a goddess of fertility, love and war. Ishtar's symbol was also the lion and the eight-pointed star, which leads us to conclude that they were one and the same.

RETURNING TO THE GODDESS

The many historical stories of The Goddess helped guide ancient cultures, which accepted them as part of their cosmology. But over time, and especially with the development of monotheistic, patriarchal-dominated religions, a fear of The Goddess grew, until eventually Her myths and teachings became suppressed and denied. At one time, we openly loved Her, worshiped Her and freely invoked Her names, but as time went on, we lost touch with The Goddess relationship to mainstream culture.

Goddess worship continued within some subcultures such as Wicca and Neo-Paganism, and despite much discrimination over the years, it continues to thrive.

Today we are longing for Her again. The return of The Divine Feminine into our lives marks the return of The Great Goddess into the world. The Goddess recognizes that women are divine by birth and asks that we embody this truth. Lacking this awareness, women have learned to fear and reject themselves and their bodies—seeing imperfection where there should only be the beauty and uniqueness of our sacred female form.

The Goddess speaks to you of your divinity. She invites you to recognize the magnificence of your body, to be present to the power and depth of your love, and to see yourself as a goddess.

Mysterious presence,
ancient essence,
hidden power,
and wondrous light;
I search for You.

Magnificent presence,
Holy essence,
splendorous power
and radiant light;
I search for You.

But You are everywhere
and You are all things.

And when I search for You,
I find only my own
mysterious
ancient,
hidden,
wondrous,
magnificent,
splendorous,
and radiant self.

PART TWO

RESTORE

The goal of life is to make your heartbeat
match the beat of the universe,
to match your nature with Nature.
~Joseph Campbell

CHAPTER FOUR

RESTORING
THE DIVINE WOMAN

*Express the feminine . . . create a human world by
the infusion of the feminine element into all of its activities.*
~Margaret Thatcher

A WOMAN IS SO MANY WONDERFUL THINGS—
beautiful, loving, creative, receptive, balancing, nurturing,
wise, sensual, and intuitive. From the vessel that she is,
these qualities are poured out into the world, nourishing it with our feminine nature
and goddess ways.

Once, the ways of The Goddess were familiar to women. Nature, the seasons and
the lunar cycles were part of her everyday life. Much of this wisdom is now buried
deep under the weight of the modern world. Many of us are out of touch with Nature,

using electronic technology to tell the time, the seasons, and the weather. The moon is no longer used as a calendar, nor for daily and monthly guidance. Artificial hormones adjust our cycles and prevent pregnancies. We have fallen out of the relationship that our bodies have with nature.

But no matter what we do, or how far away we wander—the sun and moon continue to shine down upon us day and night, and the earth continues to support us as we walk upon her. Healing plants continue to grow, awaiting our use. The turning of our lives away from nature does not mean that she has forever turned away from us; she welcomes us back any time we seek it. Restoring yourself back into relationship with the cycles and offerings of nature will bring your life into a harmony that only women can experience . . . the harmony of creation, and the ways of The Goddess.

As a woman, this means bringing back the practices of your foresisters—sacred bathing; candle lighting; using herbs, flowers and oils for healing and transformation; meditation; and finding yourself within the divine story, i.e., the myths where we meet the archetypes of our womanhood.

SACRED STORY

From the beginning, humans have desired to share what they thought, saw, experienced, and dreamed. Sitting around the fires at the end of each day, we embellished, elaborated and entertained each other with story. We use stories to teach concepts, convey life lessons, and for the simple joy of telling and being told a tale.

Through myth and story, The Feminine has survived. Her many goddess tales teach us about ourselves, our relationships, the mysteries of being human, and the mysteries of being woman.

Myth is sacred story, told to activate the part of our psyche that responds to universal symbol, imagery, and emotion. Powerful medicine for the soul, sacred stories transport listeners from this world to another. In myth, we easily suspend reality, and can project ourselves into the story. We see who we could be and eventually discover who we really are. In myth, we are the heroine, the chosen, the victorious, the blessed, the gifted, and the wise. Through myth we are shown both our human limitations and the potential we have to be extraordinary . . . to be Divine.

Throughout the world's mythology, the earth, sea, moon, nature, cosmic universe and the ways of the heart have all been described as feminine. The awesome power and transformative essence of The Divine Feminine is the very nature of creation. Know that as a woman, you carry this essence within you.

THE GODDESS
WITHIN

Take a deep, cleansing breath. Close your eyes for just a moment; create a sense of the sacred in your heart.

Welcome back . . . you are about to read about your true self, the goddess within you. Imagine that when you turn this page, you will enter into a temple built just for women, and just for you. Within this temple, sweet incense is burned, soft drumming is heard and women of all ages, shapes, and lineage dance around a fire as their sacred stories are told. Imagine that instead of you being the reader, these stories are being read *to* you by your goddess-self, the part of you that is already awakened to her feminine power, ageless wisdom, natural tranquility, innate knowing, creative force, intuitive voice, and her immeasurable depth of love and passion. Your goddess-self is hoping to inspire you to see this with every word she speaks. The goddess within you is waiting to emerge, be known, and experienced.

From within this literary temple, the feminine mysteries of your true self will be revealed, and you will hear the voice of The Goddess calling you back to Her.

Wherever I am empty,
and whenever I am longing,
She fills me.
Completely.

However I am living,
and whomever I am loving,
She guides me.
Tenderly.

Whatsoever I am thinking,
and forever I am searching,
She finds me.
Always.

POW

CHAPTER FIVE

THE GODDESS
LILITH

*Truly, we know that we cannot really subsist
on little sips of life. The wild force in a woman's soul
demands that she have access to it all.*

~Clarissa Pinkola Estés

L ILITH WATCHED SILENTLY AS THE SERPENT slithered out through the luminous gates of the bright, aromatic Garden that was called Eden.

Her heart was lighter than usual as she turned back towards her own garden, which was dense and black with overgrowth, and smelled of darkness and the spicy, rooty scent of damp earth and fermenting leaves, and reeked of things decomposing and slick with decay.

Lilith's garden was one of destructive transformation, decay, and death. It smelled of sulfur fire. It was where the dark feathers of carrion birds fell, and where magic, shadow, and twilight mingled into one. Hers was a garden of an eternal, moonless night.

Lilith walked without tenderness upon the ground and without care for that which she destroyed underfoot, for she understood that all things lived and all things died. There was no need for concern; she knew that everything in the world became something else eventually. Everything was always on its way towards the end and then another beginning. Everything, that is, but herself.

For Lilith, there was no passage of time, no aging, no transformation, and no end. For her, there was only the endless stretch of night and the foreverness of time. Her garden existed in stark contrast to Eden's glorious greenery and wonder; it was a perfect complement to Eden's light and growth. Lilith's dark garden existed in the shadow, and while this concealed her existence of living outside of Eden and outside of the Light, she knew it had always been her choice. But it had never been an easy one.

One day, while walking in the darkness, Lilith thought of Adam, who was once her beloved, and wondered if he missed her.

The thought brought back a river of memories of their life together, along with a flood of tears, for he was a greater loss than the Garden or its Light. The deep and ancient ache of grief in her heart gave way to a piercing fresh rage that rose like a fog threatening to cloud her thoughts and blot out the tenderness that had just begun to grow towards the memory of him. Lilith had been so disappointed, and so very hurt by Adam and his attempt to dominate her.

Lilith had loved Adam wildly, fiercely, intensely. Her love had been primal and without shame; it was a first love filled with experiment and the raw animal scent of passion, abandon, and heat. They tumbled round and round on top of and below each other, wildly rolling themselves into one being until side-by-side they reached pleasure together, creating a holy, sacred space for their love all the while looking into each other's eyes and becoming One. Lilith closed her eyes as she recalled the power of pleasure that had flooded over her, the power of love that had filled her, and the power of her wild femaleness that had risen up and out of her body whenever she and Adam became One.

Eventually, Adam had become fearful of their tumbling around so passionately and worried that their wildness was too much—that Lilith was too much. The first time that Adam tried to subdue her, she panicked, feeling as if her breath was being forced out of her body by his weight on top of her.

Tearfully, she writhed and, pinned helplessly beneath him, she begged him to release her, to go back to the way that things had been from the beginning, to the way that their love-making had always been. Adam refused, saying that the way things had been between them was no more.

Terrified by the rising panic and wracked with emotional pain, Lilith began to feel the power of something she did not recognize and could not name. Her body began to shimmer and shift form; her skin grew tiny bumps that sprouted feathers; her beautiful almond-shaped eyes rounded and her pupils became large and black as night, surrounded by bright gold irises. Her hands and feet twisted and gnarled themselves into leathery claws, and her nose and mouth combined into a bird's beak that opened wide as a piercing screech erupted from deep within her. Lilith had been transformed into something inhuman and animal. Feathery and owl-like, she flew away, screeching her lament into the air. She flew high above Eden, high above the Light of Heaven, out into the realms beyond the realms, and far, far away from Adam.

Moments later, shaking with rage and ire, Lilith eventually found herself standing in a pile of soft feathers being slowly scattered by the rising wind. She was back in human form at the edge of an ocean, which before this instant, she had no idea even existed. With only the sound of the waves crashing against the unseen rocks, and the silence and huge blackness of the night sky, Lilith realized that she was suddenly and for the first time—alone. Far away from everything that she knew and everything familiar to her, she began to sob loudly, bringing forth great salty tears from deep within her soul. She felt unsure and confused. She wished that Adam were here so that she would not be alone in this strange and unfamiliar space. Lilith suddenly missed him very much; she even missed his unreasonableness.

Lilith walked along the shore of the ocean for a long while until she came upon some trees where she sat down to rest. A rustling nearby and the sound of something slithering close caused her to become very still, her heart thumping wildly in her chest. So close was the creature that she could smell its breath, which was earthy and dry like dusty clouds of dirt after days without rain. Lilith turned her head towards the rustling sound and found herself face to face with a serpent.

The reptile twisted itself, inching much, much closer to her and said hypnotically, "I am so glad that you have come to me, Woman of Paradise. Oh, what things I shall show you, how much you will learn!"

The serpent produced a strange fruit and asked her to partake of it. If she did, the snake explained, then all would be revealed; all would be known to her.

So distraught over her loss of Adam, she gave very little consideration to any possible consequences and ate the fruit. Induced by the fruit's entrancement, Lilith entered into a strange sort of mental limbo, much like the space between waking and sleeping.

In the trance, Lilith learned from the serpent about the world beyond the Garden, where the passage of time and the turning of the seasons existed. She learned the names for all things, including God, whose presence she had always sensed but had never seen. She soon began to accept the darkness that was all around her and the eternal, moonless sky above. Lilith also eventually came to accept her grief, and to allow her natural self to emerge with ease and to become comfortable with her powerful, wild feminine nature. After a very long while, Lilith stood and emerged transformed.

One day, the serpent led Lilith to another place she had never been to, nor had yet seen. With the sound of the sea far away in the distance, the snake watched as she walked through rusted gates and into the dark and overgrown garden filled with shadows. Upon entering, Lilith walked around and explored. She felt that here, amidst the shadow and twilight, she could walk unseen, free to be her true self, her true womanly form. Here she could dance, revealed and uncovered in the black of night . . . here she could be primitive and primal—subdued by no one. Lilith made the dark garden her home.

You could say that much time had passed for Lilith inside the new garden, if such a thing as time existed there. But it did not. The garden was in and of itself the only place for her, and except for the serpent, she was the only one who lived there.

That was, until the day that Lilith found a small opening where some rock had worn away in the dark garden's wall. Through this opening, a tiny beam of bright light was shining through, and where it landed, a lone, colorful flower was growing. Shocked by her discovery, Lilith ran to tell the snake what she had found, hoping to learn more about it. Upon hearing her report, the snake became agitated, telling her that she was not to visit the place where this tiny beam of light shone through the wall; she was not to go back there ever again. Feeling as if she were being restrained yet once again, a familiar rage collected within her and, just as before, she transformed herself into a screeching night owl and flew away. Only this time, instead of to the sea, she headed back to the light in the wall.

Lilith ceased the flapping of her huge wings and lowered herself down to the ground, whereupon she changed back into her human form and watched as her feathers floated away in the cool night breeze. Peering through the hole, and adjusting her eyes to the light, Lilith was shocked to see Adam on the other side, in the Garden of her birth . . . with another female.

Enraged and hurt all over by this new betrayal, Lilith jumped away from the wall and began to wail and pace around, frantic and beside herself. So deep was her grief, so raw her pain that even the serpent kept its distance, refraining from any scolding for her disobedience. The passion of her distress was muffled by the heavy darkness of her shadowy garden; reverberating back into itself until eventually it was canceled out, becoming silent and heavy, even heavier than the darkness surrounding it.

Eyes swollen with tears, her heart heavy with an ancient grief, Lilith worked up the courage to look through the hole once again. This time, she felt her curiosity grow and her betrayal diminish. Unseen by the pair, she watched Adam and Eve as they went about their walk through the garden, and intently listened to their conversation.

But mostly, Lilith listened to Eve.

"Adam," Eve said brightly, "what should we name this tiny flower? It has leaves shaped like tiny hearts and it smells so sweet."

Violet, thought Lilith to herself, her lips mouthing the word just as Eve said it out loud. Lilith smiled.

Lilith spent her time watching Eve, and growing more and more fond of her. Eve was very loving towards Adam, just as Lilith had been. Eve was just as intuitive as she was, and she was creative, just as Lilith was. Eve sat for hours very still, simply being in her garden, just as Lilith sat in hers. Eve was very wise, filled with the wisdom of a woman, just as Lilith was. They had much in common, each in their own way.

By watching Eve, Lilith's pain and wrath eventually receded altogether, and she grew to understand herself more, and to understand Adam more as well. She understood that a woman was naturally more feeling than man, more sensitive, more compassionate, and much more intuitive. She could see that Eve possessed a different kind of knowing than Adam, and she learned from it as she watched this other woman. Lilith began to understand that Eve's nature was that of lightness and knowing, and her own nature was that of darkness and mystery; together they were both the complement of one another and the opposite of each other. This brought comfort to Lilith's wounded heart, this knowing of herself.

Having eaten of the fruit, Lilith was also able to understand the order of things, that she had come before Eve, and that her birth was first. Lilith felt a pang of envy that she had not been born with light like Eve, but she was comforted by the knowledge that she was connected in some way to this other woman, even if it were just by contrast. Lilith often felt motherly towards Eve and realized that this, too, was a womanly thing.

With great wisdom and strength of heart, Lilith made a decision one day. She decided to stop watching Eve and Adam. With tears of both sadness and joy in her heart, she knew that this was the best thing to do. So, she positioned herself to look through the wall one last time and was surprised and elated by what she saw.

Eve's belly had grown large, and Lilith, having eaten of the fruit, knew immediately that Eve carried new life, a daughter, within her. Lilith watched as Adam touched Eve's huge belly, the two of them smiling to each other as if they were the only two beings in existence, which, save for herself, the animals of the Garden and the snake, they were.

Lilith intuitively felt that the daughter of Eve would be different than the two women before her—that she would not be *either* light or dark, but she would have *both* the light and the dark within her. Lilith knew as well that someday this daughter would carry within her body her own daughter, and so on, until one day, many, many daughters would walk upon the earth all carrying within them the powerful duality of the Feminine Essence that is woman.

She was reminded that everything in the world became something else eventually; everything was always on its way towards an end and then a new beginning. Her heart lighter than it had been in a long time, she rejoiced that she would live on in the daughter of Eve, and in her daughters for generations, that her essence was within all of us—the dark, wild, mysterious essence of Lilith, first woman.

RESTORING POWER:
THE MYTH OF LILITH

The origin of Lilith is obscure and varied, and seems to come from many myths and legends of the desert. The Zohar—a 13th century book of Jewish mysticism—claims Lilith is the Serpent that tempted Eve, and she is wife of Sammael (a dark angel) as well as also being the wife of God—the latter being a possible reference to her as The Shekhinah. Lilith is also associated with a mysterious, unseen asteroid, called the Lilith Moon in astrology.

Other sources claim that she was once a group of Sumerian demi-goddesses called the *Lilitu*, who lived in the wide-open spaces of the desert and ruled over the storms and wind. Later, she appears in the Judeo-Christian creation story as the first woman and the first wife of Adam, before Eve. Lilith's name, which is similar to, but not derived from the Hebrew word for night—*layla* (pronounced: lie-lah)—is not mentioned in the Old or New Testament, but can be found in The Dead Sea Scrolls and as a cautionary tale within Jewish folklore. She is also discussed at length in Talmudic and Kabbalistic texts. Because of the patriarchal suppression of her story, many women and men today do not know of her.

Lilith was not made from, nor taken from Adam's body; she was made in the same way as he was, fashioned from the dust of the earth. In this way, she felt entirely equal to him. Her story reports that she refused to lie beneath Adam during intercourse, and Adam, outraged by this, refused to give up his self-perceived dominance. A great argument followed, resulting in Lilith leaving Adam and the Garden of Eden. Lilith is called the howling one because when she fled the Garden, she turned into a screech owl flying off into the night to the edge of the Red Sea where she swore to kill every child born from Adam's seed.

Lilith then refused God's order to return, and also refused to go with the three angels that were sent to force her back. The consequence for her disobedience was the curse of becoming a demoness who would give birth to hundreds of fatherless demon children every day, whom she would feel compelled to kill.

Eventually, she consented to the repeated pleas of the angels asking her not to kill the children of Adam, agreeing to spare only those who slept beneath an amulet whereupon her name and/or the names of the three angels were written.

FIRST
WOMAN

It is hard to suppress the true nature of a living thing…nature will always prevail. With every flap of Lilith's great owl wings, we are reminded that we should not allow the suppression of The Feminine to continue.

That's why our journey back to The Divine Feminine must begin with Lilith's mystical story because unlike other early goddesses of ancient cultures who were re-named and then re-integrated into religions and myths, Lilith was entirely removed from our Feminine history. Her exorcism, it seems, is where we truly parted ways with The original Goddess…and with our own powerful feminine essence. Her story has been buried under so much secrecy and intrigue that it causes one to wonder why it was covered up in the first place—was she really that bad?

Probably not, but I suspect that her feminine power was something to be reckoned with once was it was revealed. My imagination runs wild when I think that ancient priests and patriarchs intentionally decided to hide the Lilith story under a mound of gossip, lest all women find out that they too, possess this kind of wonderful feminine power. My heart celebrates alongside Lilith's with the deep knowing that we do.

There is an irony surrounding her mysterious repression, as Lilith's nature itself is that of concealment. She is the keeper of The Blood Mysteries, which are the shamanic lunar rites of passage that occur during a woman's life. She holds the keys of understanding for our first blood—when we are the young girl standing at the threshold of our sexuality—and she holds the keys of understanding for our last blood when we are the elder, wiser woman standing at the edge of this world looking towards the one beyond. It is Eve who helps us understand our mother-blood—the blood of cycles, creation, and childbirth. But Lilith, along with Isis, Kali, Hekate and the many other dark goddesses from every culture help us understand our menstrual blood as potent, filled with the power of our sexuality and femaleness. They are among the first powerful, sexual personifications of The Divine Feminine.

The most interesting thing about Lilith, and what sets her apart from all the other dark Goddesses, is that she alone became so incredibly feared—more than even Kali Ma—another highly misunderstood dark-natured goddess. The bringer of *moksha* or liberation, Kali Ma appears wearing a necklace of bloody skulls with her gigantic red tongue protruding from her black demoness-like face. The spiritually unevolved ego trembles at the sight of her, fearing its own annihilation and perceiving its death. But for the spiritually evolved ego, Kali Ma appears gentle, kind, protective and very compassionate. This type of ego sees Kali Ma as redemption, resurrection, and rebirth.

So, why, I have always wondered, is Lilith so much more feared than all the others? Why has her story been all but obliterated? Can we not become more spiritually aware and more evolved in order to see her other, more positive nature, just as we do with Kali Ma? Certainly, something this shrouded in secrecy must be worth re-considering, deciphering, and reclaiming . . . and so, we shall begin to do that.

We cannot explore Lilith without also touching on the story of Eve as well, for they are both so entwined—their tales weave around each other as serpentine as the snake of Eden. Every woman knows of Eve, but many do not know of Lilith, the first woman in the Judeo-Christian creation story. Unlike Eve, who is a mother figure with a passive and agreeable nature, Lilith is the lover/seductress with a wild, fierce, untamed, and mysterious nature. She represents the hidden, primordial power within us women, our dark sexual energy as well as the shadow parts of us—the wounds that live alone in the *dark garden* of our psyche and have yet to heal. Eve is associated with the bright, fresh blood of childbirth, beginnings and new life, whereas Lilith, who is childless, is the dark, ancient blood of the womb—the blood of release, endings, and death as transformation. Perhaps it is our fear of death and our instinctual aversion to darkness that has caused so much consternation and alarm around the Lilith story.

Fear is a powerful motivator for suppression. As individuals, we tend to either ignore or hide from the things we fear, and as a society we tend to suppress them. From the beginning, religion and society have both instilled the belief that our earthy femaleness is unpleasant, ugly, smelly, dirty, and unclean. In some ways, it *is* messy stuff. But it is also our real, undiluted, and undeniable femaleness.

Lilith's story continues to surface, generation after generation, reminding us of our feminine essence, that we are intoxicatingly scented. We are desirable as is. Our moon-time blood is potent and filled with the magic of The Goddess, and sexual union with us is holy. The unfortunate suppression of Lilith's story from our mythology is a tragic omission of our own female essence in our lives . . . and her rise from demoness to goddess is proof positive that no one can extinguish The Feminine.

LILITH'S TEACHINGS ON
OUR SACRED SEXUALITY

One of the most shunned facets of Lilith's teachings is that of sexual pleasure. Lilith is an unapologetically powerful and sexual Goddess. Her delight in the pleasures of her body, along with her intense sensual and emotional nature, have earned her the title 'dark demon goddess,' most likely by men who, like Adam, feared her unmanageable, seductive ways. This untamed power and sensual essence did not fade from women as the early fathers of most religions had hoped it would. Instead, it lays dormant within us, waiting with Lilith at the edge of the sea—all we have to do is call it back. Her myth teaches you to accept yourself as divine, sacred . . . and sexual.

When this sacredness is experienced, everything you do becomes an expression of it—the way you carry yourself, the way you dress, your interaction with others, the words you speak, and the actions you take. Most especially, when you feel yourself as a goddess, you *become* The Goddess—embodying Her and channeling Her power and essence into all that you do.

Lilith teaches that sex is a sacred act in and of itself, and can be enjoyed without the goal of conception. This must have caused much concern for early patriarchal religious leaders, and so we can imagine why the lusty, erotic, and enchanting Lilith was not welcome in the Biblical story of creation.

Early on in my journey as a woman, I did not know that sex was sacred. I did not know that my body was designed to receive Divine Feminine Essence through sexual union, and flow through me into a man's body. Sex for me was very enjoyable, but it was not nearly the special event that I now know it to be. Once I realized this, once I saw myself as sacred, I became aware of the *vessel* that I am . . . and now, I do not share my body casually or without care, as I once did. Now, I know my body is a living embodiment of The Divine Feminine, and I will only share it as such.

This does not mean that a man must undergo initiation rights to enter the vessel of my body, but it does mean that I seek conscious, caring and enlightened relationships with men who not only recognize my sacredness—but their own as well. When I teach this to women of all ages, it always amazes me to see the look of self-respect and marvel that comes across their faces.

It makes me sad that, for many of us, our mothers did not know about this sacredness and could have taught it to us. If you are a mother reading this now, please learn this for yourself so that you may teach it to your daughters *and* your sons. It is a gift of priceless value.

Sacred sex can bring up many different emotions and feelings for women. Some women laugh out loud during sexual union as they call forth Lilith's passionate joy; others emit her wild, animal-like sounds when they feel her power. Other women are as speechless and silent as Lilith herself must have been when she felt the holiness and the blessedness of a union that is so deep, so complete in combining two into one, that it is like no other. And some women cry the tears of Lilith—which are the deep, ancient tears of a collective feminine grief that has yet to heal.

THE WARRIOR GODDESS

Lilith is not dark as in evil or negative, as many people have misunderstood; rather her darkness is that of the underworld-like part of our psyche that is hidden. She is the anima of our subconscious mind—and hails from a realm that is uncharted and unpredictable, where the sensual and very animal-like aspects of us reside. The goddess Lilith is not a crisp, sweet red apple, like Eve—instead, she is the dark red, sour-sweet of pomegranates. Her dark essence is the true forbidden fruit, for within her nature lies knowledge of a woman's true being. Her story and her wild, dark nature have been the target of much patriarchal suppression and religious banishment. Her painful, sad, and empowering personal story mirrors the larger story of The Great Goddess Herself—once loved and cherished, then rejected and feared. Any woman who has ever experienced a loss, felt suppressed, been rejected, or left an abusive relationship can relate to Lilith.

Her flight from Eden encourages us to protect our female essence, keep safe our feminine nature, and to say *no* to anything or anyone who tries to suppress it, even if it means being alone. I imagine that, as she left the Garden of Eden, Lilith released the deepest, wildest keening sound from the center of her soul as she flew off to escape, leveled by her heartache. Perhaps that was the incredible howling sound that was heard, and why she is called the howling one.

Lilith has a warrior's soul—which is a good thing, because that is what it takes to heal the rejected, traumatized, and wounded parts of you. Rejected by her beloved, Lilith transforms herself and takes flight to the edge of the sea. There she begins the solitary process of healing—healing the parts of herself that can only be found in the shadow (the subconscious). The ocean is the source of all life, and symbolizes the emotions and the womb. Having run to the sea myself a few times, I can relate to Lilith. Perhaps you can, too.

In her new garden, Lilith feels she can reveal herself. She can heal from the deep wounds of her loss, be alone with her pain . . . and confront whatever may come up for her, such as seeing Eve with Adam. Lilith is the part of a woman that is brave, courageous, and unwilling to stay hurt. She is the part of our essence that grows wild, but strong, too.

THE DARK GARDEN OF
OUR SHADOW SELVES

In contrast to Eve's bright, flowering garden, Lilith's is darkened and filled with shadow. One garden is brimming with life and the other is decaying into death. These are aspects of all gardens—beginnings and endings. Lilith's garden is the dark one of the subconscious underworld, a wild place indeed. Here we are working with the *shadow*, the primordial part of our nature. Here there are secrets and mysteries—anything may float up such as unbidden emotions, repressed memories, and past hurts.

These shadow places, these suffering parts of us, may feel too frightening to look at. They may seem too intimidating to deal with, but you should know that they are simply the parts of you that are traumatized, hurt, wounded, or scared. By working with these feelings, you are uncovering and revealing your wounds of shame about your body, your sexual fears and relationships . . . about any part of you that has ever been victimized—especially by a male. By healing yourself, you are shining light into your own darkness . . . illuminating yourself and becoming lighter, freer, more authentic and true to yourself. This healing is similar to the single beam of light that made its way into Lilith's dark garden to bring hope, understanding, and compassion to her—and to all women.

When you work with the shadow of your nature, you are working with a part of yourself hidden from the light—the subconscious, knowing part. This part is usually grieving from loss—childhood issues, romantic break-ups, and shame. This is where our darker emotions reside, and they hold the keys to unlock the door to your happiness, wellbeing, and wholeness. Heal them and you will be free. It is here, in the shadows, where you keep your deepest pain, your *whole* story—not the bits and pieces you feel safe to share. Lilith had an instinct that being alone during her healing would be best for her; this does not mean that we must isolate ourselves, but we should trust ourselves to find comfort by being on our own. Building this trust is a pathway to self-loving, and through self-loving, you will heal yourself fully and completely.

In the High Desert of the Coachella Valley, in California I drove around and around in the night, looking for a spot to perform a ritual to infuse several candles with the essence of Lilith. I was waiting to hear her call, as she would cause me to stop and I would know that this was the place. My search continued for some time.

Lilith, I knew, was a desert woman, a hot, fiery goddess best sought out on a moonless night, under dark skies and in the wide open, endless stretch of land that is scorched by day and cooled by night. Suddenly, as if she had taken control of the wheel, I turned down a residential street and stopped in front of a public park. Not ever having been there before, I was amazed to find it was the perfect spot with several tall cottonwood trees that formed a semi-circle in a large open field that was half surrounded by mountains.

Taking the paper bag that held five black candles and two bottles of anointing oil—one blood red and one silvery blue—I made my way through the park to the tallest of the trees that was swaying violently in the strong desert winds. The winds had picked up tremendously by the time I kneeled down; they blew my hair into a

I often counsel women to take a substantial break in between relationships to allow for the healing of both their obvious and underlying grief, and to build the trust that leads to self-loving. Unexpressed grief often hides very deeply down within our psyche, catching a ride up and out whenever new grief occurs. When I work with women on healing their shadow parts, we often use dream interpretation, Tarot cards, hypnosis, inner child healing, and meditation. Sometimes, while experiencing deep healing, we may find ourselves in a cocoon of sorts, feeling solitary, and more private than ever before. This is the nature of doing work with the shadow—it is inner work, it is the transformation of the unknown into the known.

Being kind, patient and forgiving with yourself is the best thing you can do during this time. It will release you from yourself—from the parts of your psyche that, like Adam holding Lilith down, are keeping you back and suppressing you. Have faith in yourself to heal and be free . . . and have faith in The Goddess. She is there in the dark with you.

wild frenzy, almost whisked my shirt right off of me and threatened to knock me over altogether. The Lilitu, the goddesses of wind and storms were here—and I knew this was the right spot.

I laid out the candles and oils in the cool green grass and looked around . . . it was almost midnight. I was in a strange place, alone, in the dark. I knew just how Lilith must have felt the night she left Eden as I, too felt the fear of the unknown mixed with the exhilaration of the wide, open space of the desert at night. Calling out to The Great Mother Goddess and to the dark goddess Lilith, I anointed my palms and touched the damp earth below me. I anointed my heart and looked into the dark night sky—black and studded with stars. I anointed my breasts and my lower belly and felt a sudden, primal surge of power run through me. It felt sexual, female, animal . . . yet it was also tinged with a deep and profound sorrow I could not name. In the dark of the desert night, a wild sound came up and out of me—was this the howl from Lilith? I know that something happened out there, alone in the dark of the desert night . . . I had met the goddess Lilith.

Women's Grief

Another teaching of Lilith is acceptance of grief and loss by releasing and healing it. Energetically, it is the women of the world who collect the sorrow, heartache and pain *for* the world. We are naturally built to be more receptive than men to the energies and imbalances of life. We are more sensitive to the disharmony and we can even be more forgiving of the world's many wrongdoings as well. Without the release and healing of this collective grief, we may suffer physically and psychically, becoming imbalanced on the behalf of the world instead of helping it to rebalance.

LILITH'S MESSAGE OF STRENGTH

Let yourself fail, risk, feel disappointment, and let go of outcomes. Trust that what is happening is for your highest good. Through struggle and suffering your strength is forged. Don't just push through the uncomfortable experiences and miss an opportunity to fortify your spirit. Lilith's disobedience inspires you to be in service to yourself, to act from the strongest place of your being when something feels right.

THE GODDESS SPEAKS OF YOUR POWER

Come to me, woman.
In the dark of night, under the blackest sky, we will walk a while, together.
This place in your heart, here, where it is tender… this is where I live.
These tears that you cry, the ones that fall without a sound,
they will lead you back to me.
All that is the Mystery of me is the nature of you… embrace the wildness
of your being, the pleasures of your body and accept the night as my gift.
For you can, and it is.

THE ASSOCIATIONS
OF LILITH

Because Lilith was historically treated as a demoness and not a goddess, there are no traditional rituals or invocations in her honor, only curses and banishments.

But now, as we reclaim this goddess, we can dispel the negativity surrounding Lilith, unveiling her as a symbol of power and independence for us, celebrating her teachings and honoring her wild, dark essence within us.

When you honor Lilith and seek to reconnect your psyche with her, you will be working with dark crystals, under a dark moon, and with the feathers from owl's silent wings. Read the following explanations of Lilith's associations to her crystals, totem, and moon in preparing to perform the rituals in her name.

THE DARK CRYSTALS OF LILITH. Obsidian is a perfect crystal to symbolize Lilith, as it helps to express the power within you. It is born of volcanic fire that was once trapped deep within the earth, thus working energetically to release anger and the lingering heaviness of mistreatment, abuse, oppression, and grief. It keeps you connected and grounded as you journey deep into the lower realms of your psyche to activate the more primitive sexual nature within you.

LILITH'S TOTEM: THE OWL'S WINGS OF MAGIC. Lilith is associated with the night owl—a nocturnal, magical totem that symbolizes The Feminine, the moon, and the relationship that exists between the two. Owl brings to us the gifts of mysticism, mystery and knowing. In many North American traditions, the owl is known for its healing abilities, along with its fertility and sexuality. Owl has also been associated with the souls of the dead, evil, and the essence of darkness that is within us all. It is no wonder that Lilith has owl as her totem.

The large wingspan of owl makes not a sound while flying, inspiring quiet calm and powerful flight—a good quality to call upon when leaving abusive, dysfunctional and harmful relationships, or situations that no longer serve you.

THE DARK MOON OF INNER WORK. During the dark moon, its energies are unstable, unpredictable, and void of light. The moon herself is considered inactive at this time and so we should be, too. However, there are some wise women who see the dark of the moon as an opportunity to travel into their own darkness for healing and insight. I am one such woman, and I encourage you to be as well.

The dark moon is about transformation, magic, and the power of both releasing and gathering. This phase occurs just one night after the last quarter light of the full moon fades from the sky (waning/releasing) but before the new moon happens (waxing/gathering). Its power allows you to work with endings and beginnings, light and dark, birth and death. Those who fear working with this moon may also fear the darkness within themselves and the part of their psyche where spiritual, physical, and emotional imbalances reside.

The dark moon invites us to travel deep down into the mind of the mind, past the point of meditation—where the wild mysteries of our nature dwell, where we are animalistic, primal. Here are the secret teachings of the soul: our shadow-self at work.

THE RITUALS
OF POWER

Preparing Your Anointing Oil

The essential oils of mugwort, jasmine, ylang ylang, and bitter orange are used to represent the dark inner nature of Lilith, along with her sensual, womanly power and the bittersweet release of her grief. Anoint your breasts and then your lower belly, which is the place of your womb with your oil blend.

Mix the following oils into a 10 ml glass bottle, and then fill with carrier oil such as rice bran, grape seed, or meadowfoam seed oil. Gently shake. Store in a cool, dark place.

❖ 2 drops of mugwort
❖ 4 drops of jasmine
❖ 4 drops of ylang ylang
❖ 2 drops of bitter orange

Creating an Altar of Power

The color theme for your Lilith altar of power is black, in honor of its association with the void, the unknown, the emptiness of space and the vastness of the night sky. Black is the color of endlessness, timelessness, and infinity. It is also the color of mourning, grief, and protection. Burn black candles, display black rocks from the ocean, and your obsidian crystal—which are all wonderful talismans of power and reminders of Lilith's flight to the sea. Place the darkest red flowers you can find upon your altar.

Lilith's healing power lies in her ability to transform herself into the owl and fly away from a dangerous situation. Place a symbol of an owl feather on your altar to honor this totem. (Owl is a protected species, so we will not be collecting their actual feathers for this altar, but instead will use an image of an owl feather.)

Standing before your altar, anoint your womb and breasts with your oil blend as you say this invocation to call in your power:

From the darkness of fear, I call in my light,
From the darkness of grief, I call in my strength,
From the darkness of my true essence, I call in my power.

Bathing in the Sacred Waters of Lilith

Regardless of how wild and untamed Lilith is, I imagine that she, like most women at the end of the day, loves her bath. Hers is a bath for slow, sensual soaking. Let yourself luxuriate in the warm water, becoming aware of your body through all your senses.

What you will need:

❖ black candle
❖ your anointing oil
❖ dried jasmine flowers
❖ dried seaweed

What to do:

Pour one cup of sea salt, along with one handful each of dried jasmine flowers and dried seaweed into a warm or comfortably hot bath. Light your candle, then pour a few drops of the anointing oil into a warm bath as you say this blessing:

Sacred waters, blessed be.
Clear me of all negativity.
Wash away doubt, wash away fear,
I call in my power, and I draw it near.

Special intention for your bath:

Appreciate the femaleness of your form and the power that is yours.

Crafting Lilith's Dream Pillow ————————————————————

Artemisia Vulgaris, known more commonly as mugwort, is a sweet smelling herb when fresh, but bitter and smoky scented when burned. It can cause altered states of consciousness when used as a tisane (tea). It is also burned to clear negative energy. It is considered an herb of the underworld; perfect for Lilith who helps us reconnect to the subconscious part of our being. When you sleep near mugwort, you may meet with the deepest part of your psyche, bringing on wild and vivid dreams for healing and finding new inner knowledge. Here's how to make such a Dream Pillow.

What you will need:

❖ 2 cups of dried, powdered or loose mugwort herb
❖ cotton or muslin cloth drawstring bag to hold the herbs

What to do:

Fill the drawstring bag with mugwort, seal it tightly. Then, on a moon-less night, go out and place your dream pillow for one night under the dark moon. Then place the bag beneath your pillow while you sleep. Upon awakening, record any dream journeys you may have had.

Inspiration for Your Journal ————————————————————

❖ Write about the first time that you encountered your own power--sexu-ally, emotionally or spiritually, or all of them.
❖ Write about a relationship that you would like to leave; why, when, and how.
❖ Write about your grief, sorrow or loss; what does it feel like for you, how do you find comfort for yourself.

Lilith, daughter of none, thou were bound and sealed.

A fallen goddess; so beautiful and so strong.

Lilith, who caused the hearts of men to fear,
And women to walk away.

Blessed Goddess, Blessed, Selah; forever.

Unconquered; let your wild essence flow back to us,
like dark moon blood, you are called back to the earth.

Talismans, magic, mighty spells and such,
cannot keep you hidden.

Blessed Goddess, Blessed, Selah; forever.

She who appears in the dark desert night,
and in the dreams of women still —
is a new goddess; so beautiful and so strong.

Lilith, who causes the hearts of women to open,
Blessed Goddess, Blessed, Selah; forever.

Beloved is the essence of woman.

Elated is Lilith after all this time,
to be welcomed back.

Under the cover of night she returns.

Blessed Goddess, Blessed, Selah; forever.

CHAPTER SIX

THE GODDESS
YEMAYA

All important things in art have always originated
from the deepest feelings about the mystery of Being.
~Max Beckman

VITY

YEMAYA WATCHED THE CRESCENT MOON FROM the bottom of the ocean floor. As she was looking up at it through the cool waters, the pale lunar light moved and shimmered in the black night of sea above her. All around her fish swam sleepily past, and the evening lull of the tides gently undulated her body. She swayed with the current, her body as supple as a seaweed frond. Giving in to the rhythm of the water, letting her bare feet move across the cold, wet sand underneath, the goddess danced.

She performed the dance of the ocean—rhythmic, flowing and sensual. Her long black hair floated out all around her, catching the smallest of fish within its weave. She danced until the moon began to fade from the sky. With the strong taste of brine in her mouth and the last light of the moon shining down upon her, she finally settled comfortably in a grove of anemones. Her knees bent to her chest, she wrapped her arms around them. Closing her eyes, the goddess Yemaya slept.

Hours later, in a silent burst of sizzling light, the sun peeked up and over the ocean's horizon. An almost imperceptible flash exploded where the sea and sky met for just a sliver of a second and then extinguished, leaving no trace. Only the most watchful of eyes would have seen this brief spark of light. And only the most worshipful of souls would have been able to interpret its meaning.

Ana had such eyes, and was such a soul. Dressed completely in white, save for her colorful necklace, she stood stock still at the edge of the sea. Her brown legs and the edge of her skirt were wet from the rising tide as it crept higher and higher on up the sand. Ana looked down and watched tiny translucent crabs peep out and dart quickly around her feet as they searched for food when the waves drew back. Patiently, she waited; her own belly hungry from three days of fasting. In her arms she held a round, flat basket filled with fresh ripe fruit. In the basket also lay a whole fried fish wrapped in yesterday's newspaper, and fragrant white roses just picked that evening under the crescent moon sky.

Ana looked up, searching for the moon in the newly wakened day. There, in the early morning sunlight, she found it fading like tissue paper against the pastels of the heavens. It was but a ghost of a moon as it slipped from sight. Two blessings, Ana thought as she smiled to herself—the bright flash at the edge of the sea and now the sun and moon together in one sky! She felt that today was to be a fortunate day, and she began to pray to the *orisha,* the goddess and nature spirit of water.

At first her prayers were quiet words, spoken silently and privately. Encouraged by her growing devotion, she mouthed them softly out loud now, her voice shy and her lips barely opening for the words. Soon the ocean waves invited her to move and dance, tempting her with their power as the water came rushing around her legs, stronger and stronger each time. Soon Ana was swaying her hips and bending her knees down low, swinging her basket of offerings high above her head and dancing with the ocean. Singing her prayer louder and louder, her lovely voice filled with all the emotion and feelings of her heart, it traveled across the water's surface, becoming thinner the farther out it went.

Her thick caramel-colored hair with its wild curls was now slick with seawater; it clung to her face and neck. Her white clothes were drenched transparent against the brown skin of her curved hips and strong legs. Ana was beautiful.

When the last of her heartfelt and energetic praying had been released, she stood strong and still again, her chest heaving and her heart pounding from the exertion of her movements. Ana reverently placed the basket on a receding wave and watched as it floated out to sea, bobbing and twirling like a tiny boat without a sail. Ana closed her eyes to wait.

At that very moment, Yemaya opened her eyes as the sweet perfume of mangoes and oranges floated past her. She licked her lips as the aroma of a cooked fish caught her attention and she looked up towards the surface of the ocean just as a single white rose petal floated down to her in the sparkling morning light of the sea. She caught the petal with her fingers and brought it to her face, caressing it against her cheek.

Carried on the wind, and softened by the distance, Yemaya heard the remnants of a woman singing her name so lovingly, so filled with passion that she felt compelled to heed the call. Smiling, with teeth as white as pearls, she stretched the sleep from her body as she made her way upwards to the surface, swimming like a seal. She rose higher and higher, and when her head was above the water she reached for a mango from the floating basket, letting the rose petal drop to the ocean floor where it was promptly eaten by a hungry fish.

Yemaya munched on the mango and swam, then floated, letting herself be carried by the waves for a while as she followed the sound of the woman's voice. Soon she found herself just a few feet from the shore. With only the top of her head and her dark eyes rising out of the water, she stared at the woman who was standing at the edge of the ocean, perfectly still, with her eyes closed.

The orisha then rose from the sea as tall as a tidal wave and made her way towards Ana. "Who has called me from the sea?" Yemaya asked aloud when she was standing right in front of her.

"O, beautiful Yemaya, it is I who have called you," Ana replied timidly, but filled with love for the goddess standing so near to her. Keeping her eyes closed and hoping The Goddess would be responsive, Ana continued, "I have a request to make of you, Mother of the Sea."

Moved by Ana's reverence and love, she spoke kindly to her. "Open your eyes and look upon me, child. Your mangoes are sweet and I am feeling benevolent this morning," said the goddess. As a courtesy, she shrunk herself to just above Ana's height.

When Ana opened her eyes, the vision in front of her took her breath away. Yemaya stood in front of her. Her dark skin shimmered head to toe with delicate and tiny fish scales, every one of them an iridescent jewel, reflecting the colors of the rainbow in the early morning light. As Yemaya walked closer towards the land, Ana saw starfish moving in her wild, damp, sea-salted hair. Around her waist, the goddess wore long dreads of seaweed in every color. Her body was beautifully shaped, with the sleek look of a powerful fish or a dolphin. Each of her breasts lay in a large scallop shell. Ana looked into Yemaya's dark eyes and smiled. Yemaya smiled back.

"I am the Yeye Omo Eja, the mother of the fish," declared Yemaya, with her voice as powerful as the strongest marine current. "My ways are as deep and mysterious as the ocean. I am unknowable to you. I am she from whom all life has come," the goddess said as she slowly circled Ana. "When your heart is true and my name is called, I will always come, for that is what a mother does when her children cry out to her. I bring to you the blessings of The Great Mother. My wisdom teaches you the ways of women—birth, rebirth, creativity, the salty tears of joy, and the bitter brine of sorrow. I will teach you that you have power when my blessings are upon you!" As Yemaya shouted the word *power,* a huge wave rose above her, then came crashing down, dissolving dramatically into a mist of froth and spray.

A seagull's high-pitched cry sailed past them as it came close to catch some of the hundreds of tiny fish that had gathered in the water at Yemaya's feet. Ana kept her gaze steady upon the face of the goddess.

"What is it that you desire, Ana?" Yemaya lovingly asked. "Many women call upon me for the blessings of motherhood . . . perhaps you wish to be filled with life, with child?" Yemaya's lower back arched forward and her hips widened as she grew her belly full and pregnant, impressing the human woman. Startled, the seagull flew away with a splash and a flurry of feathers, leaving one behind in exchange for the meal.

Ana shook her head no, back and forth, and Yemaya's belly flattened down to where it had been. "I am abundance itself; there is no counting of my fish, my shells, or my waves," she said, now very curious what this woman wanted from her. "Fishermen invoke my name for plenitude. Perhaps you wish to be abundant?" Yemaya asked, and thousands of fish suddenly flopped themselves up onto the shore at Ana's feet, gasping for air. Ana shook her head no, back and forth, and the wheezing fish were sucked back into the ocean by the swell of a wave.

"Perhaps it is love you seek," said the powerful orisha, and a wave rose up forming itself into a handsome, watery man catching Yemaya in his arms as he leaned in to kiss her. Ana shook her head no again, and the water-man dissolved with a splash, leaving Yemaya standing alone with her lips still puckered for a kiss.

Yemaya stepped closer to Ana and peered deep into her eyes. Then she looked at her slowly up and down, from head to toe. Her eyes stopped at Ana's neck, where a beautiful necklace glimmered in the sunlight. Yemaya held it up with her delicate fingers, looking closely at the fine craftsmanship. Standing this close to the goddess, Ana noticed that each one of her fingernails was like a polished clamshell and that she smelled of the sea, salty and fresh.

Ana had fashioned the necklace from many pieces of blue-green sea glass that had taken her years to collect on the shores. Each one had its own tiny hole where silken threads in the colors of the sky after a storm held them all together. Tiny sand-polished seashells peeked through here and there, bringing elegance to the minimal design.

Yemaya smiled, as she let the necklace drop gently back to Ana's neck. "What then do you wish for, my child?" she quizzed Ana.

In a very small voice, feeling hopeful but unworthy, Ana finally replied, "I wish to be blessed with song."

Yemaya stopped pacing. "I have heard your voice, she said, "and it is lovely. Why ask for what is already yours?" the goddess said with impatience, flicking a few grains of sand from her wet shoulders.

"I am shy, Yemaya. My voice has been quiet and unsure all of my life, I sing only when I am alone. I wish to sing my songs as loud as your thundering waves, as strong as your coral reefs, and as sure as the tides that come each day. With all of my heart, that is what I wish," Ana finished. Tears fell from her eyes becoming a part of the salty water at her feet.

The goddess silently watched Ana as the tears fell one by one into her waters. She sensed that Ana was sincere. "You will have your heart's desire thirty moons from now," the powerful orisha said, "but first, you will have to do two things for me."

Ana wiped the last of her tears from her eyes and enthusiastically nodded her head yes.

"I want you to set up a cart in town, where the travelers walk, and I want you to sell your necklaces," The Goddess said.

Ana's face fell in disappointment and her mouth opened like a fish. "How will that help me gather the courage to sing? Besides, no one will buy a necklace like this; it is simple and not worthy of sale," she whined like a child unwilling to go to bed.

"The second thing," Yemaya continued on, ignoring Ana's petulance, "is that you must give me the necklace around your neck."

Ana's hands flew to her neck, holding the necklace tight. Even though she did not yet recognize the value of her work, she felt very protective of it.

Yemaya became very tender and sweet with Ana, as any mother would when one of her children needs guidance. "Your heart's desire requires surrender and sacrifice," she said patiently. "Will you trust my wisdom, and will you give up something of yourself to receive something from me?" Yemaya asked as she waited with her hand out to receive the necklace. Only the lapping sound of the water and the swirling of sea foam at their feet broke the silence between them.

Slowly, without a word, Ana removed the necklace and gave it to Yemaya, who thanked her with a loving kiss upon her cheek. Her lips were cool and wet against the warmth of Ana's face.

To her surprise, Ana's business was soon a great success. Yemaya had shown her a hidden cave on a secluded beach where endless mounds of sea glass were waiting for her to use. She made many beautiful necklaces that sold as quickly as she displayed them.

Each day Ana awoke, happy to set up her cart. So happy, in fact, that she often found herself singing aloud as she arranged her lovely necklaces on little hooks for the tourists to peruse. Her reputation had grown; people came from miles around to buy her jewelry, chat with her, but mostly hoping to hear her sweet voice as she sang haunting songs of the ocean, love, and longing. Oddly, singing while selling her necklaces felt very comfortable and easy. When people clapped after a song, Ana graciously thanked them and went about her business with a smile on her face.

One late afternoon, when most of the travelers were making their way back to their hotels, Ana was alone at her cart as the sun was setting. Her beautiful voice rose in song about sunsets and the ocean. She closed her eyes and let her heart come through the melody, pouring into the song all of her emotions. When she opened her eyes, she was startled to see a man standing in front of her.

"I am Alvaro," he said with one hand up to shade the sun from his eyes, the other stretched out to shake her hand. Ana blinked, and offered him her hand, which he spontaneously decided to kiss. "Your voice is the sound of an angel and the words of your song are pure poetry."

Ana blushed and brushed away the compliment, but Alvaro insisted. She finally accepted his words of praise with her eyes cast shyly down.

"I would like for you to come to my restaurant and sing for the diners while they enjoy good food and good company. Your voice will bring elegance and warmth to my establishment."

Ana opened her mouth to protest, but something about Alvaro's warm eyes and his generous nature made her feel safe enough to say yes. It was not until she arrived home later that night, her heart bursting with excitement, that she realized that on this very day, it was exactly thirty moons since her meeting with Yemaya.

Just before the sun rose the next morning, Ana dressed completely in white, save for the beautiful sea glass beads around her neck. She went down to stand at the edge of the sea. Her brown legs and the edge of her skirt were soon wet from the rising tide as it crept higher and higher up the shore. Ana looked down and watched tiny translucent crabs peep out and dart quickly around her feet as they searched for food when the waves drew back. Patiently, she waited. In her arms, she held a round, flat basket filled with fresh ripe fruit, one whole fried fish wrapped in yesterday's newspaper, and sweet smelling white roses picked that evening under the crescent moon sky. At just the right moment, she placed the basket lovingly into the ocean on an incoming wave. Ana sang a song of love and gratitude to Yemaya, the goddess of the sea, and to The Goddess of all creation.

Yemaya suddenly stopped her deep sea dancing when she heard Ana's song carried from far across the ocean's surface. She smiled, as the sweet perfume of roses, mangoes and oranges mixed with the savory aroma of fried fish floated past her. Swimming like an otter to the surface, she retrieved the food. As she flipped herself back into the ocean, the beautiful sea glass beads around her neck caught the first rays of the morning sun and gave off a bright flash of light, which was visible only to anyone who might be watching.

RESTORING CREATIVITY: THE MYTH OF YEMAYA

Yemaya was originally the West African desert goddess Yemoja, who followed the captured Yoruban people to the Americas and gave them comfort on the slave ships. Seeing the ocean for the first time, the enslaved people recognized it as the powerful essence of Yemoja. She then emerged from the sea and into their new life, renamed as Yemaya, and was later called 'Mami Watta,' which is Pidgin English for 'mama water.' Central to their folklore and religion, Yemaya is the principle creatress-mother goddess. She is thought of as the very spirit of the ocean and moonlight.

In other cultures, Yemaya is the principle personification of The Divine Feminine for the people of Africa, Brazil, Cuba, and Haiti. She has many names—hundreds in fact, all depending on where she is worshipped. The Brazilian Lemanjá or Janaína is the benevolent goddess of the ocean and crescent moon. Some know her as the abundant Yemaya Ataramagwa of the sea. Others know her differently, such as the harsh, strict Yemaya Achabba; the fierce, intense Yemaya Oqqutte; and the awe-inspiring Yemaya Olokun who appears only in our dreams.

Yemaya is worshipped wherever there is water, especially where the land meets the ocean and where the rivers that belong to her sister, Ochún, flow into Her seas. Slaves referred to her as Stella Maris, the star of the sea—a name she shares with Mother Mary. Once captured, the slave people were not allowed to worship their own deities and so they concealed Yemaya within the Catholic saint, Mary, to appease their captives while staying true to their own faith. Wherever Yemaya is worshipped, she is always depicted as a large, dark-skinned mermaid, and is often called La Sirène (The Siren) or La Balianne in New Orleans.

Her legend claims she gave birth to all life, including the other orishas. A potent fertility goddess, her earliest name, *Yeye omo eja* means 'mother of the fish,' referring to the legend that her children (her devotees) are so many that they are, like fish, impossible to count. She is often invoked by fishermen wishing her to bless their nets, bringing them an abundant catch, and by women who need her to help them with love, conception, and labor.

Yemaya is very regal, beautiful, strong, and powerful. She is a fiercely loving and merciful goddess who can also be very unpredictable at times. Her moods change with the tides, and she can become quite feisty when provoked. Easily angered but quick to forgive, she mostly desires that you respect and appreciate her teachings.

Above all, her loving and motherly nature is the very essence of what creativity is—an endless supply from a limitless source. Her nature is so like creativity itself—delightful, enchanting, capricious, challenging, and insistent. Associated with several phases of the moon—half, crescent, and full—she is an elemental being of transformation, change, cycles, and phases—all fundamental qualities of creativity.

I sensed Yemaya in my life long before I ever met her. The ocean has always called to me and it has always felt very feminine. Many of my personal rituals occur at the edge of the ocean, and when I am floating in the salty waters, I laugh like a child, feeling incredibly free and alive. One of my favorite things to do is take long walks on the beach, collecting shells and rocks and just sitting to watch the waves come and go. All marine life and seashells are sacred to Yemaya. One of her favorites is the cowrie shell, a symbol of riches and abundance.

Several years ago, a co-worker at a metaphysical shop where we worked heard me talking about how much I loved the ocean and she introduced me to Yemaya. I felt instantly connected to her essence, her power, and her ways. She has been a part of my personal pantheon of goddesses for years.

I have found that for all of her ancient wisdom and loving ways, Yemaya is not a patient goddess, not fond of waiting. When connecting with her, you must act speedily, or her gifts will be carried right back out to her. Many times while writing this chapter, an idea would come to me that was so clear, so vibrant, and so vivid that I thought it could not possibly be forgotten, so I waited to act on it only to see it fade away as quickly as it came. This is the oceanic nature of Yemaya. Her creative inspiration is like a wave—spontaneous, changeable, incoming, then receding.

When the voice of Yemaya is heard, we must not resist. She is the mermaid muse whose siren call will wake you from slumber, interrupt your everyday tasks, and intrude into your thoughts until you pay attention to her. The language of this goddess is never spoken with the linear, literal, concrete thoughts of the conscious mind, but rather with the feelings and emotions of the heart, and the imagery and symbols of the subconscious. In this way, Yemaya often comes to you while you are in a highly receptive state, such as during meditation, trance, and dreams.

Yemaya woke me at 3:00 a.m. on a morning overcast with mist from the Pacific Ocean. She had appeared to me in my dream that night and shared her story just as you have read it. At the end of the dream, I felt her urgency, as if she were saying; Wake up! Write this down right now! But, I would not listen; I so wanted to stay in bed and sleep where it was warm and comfortable. But the story kept replaying and I could feel her urgings getting stronger.

I knew I must wake myself and honor this gift from The Mother of the Ocean, or it might be lost forever, taken back on one of her waves while I slept. I could feel The Goddess at my side as I wrote this myth. And in between sips of hot tea and watching the sun burn through the fog, I typed and beheld Yemaya's sacred story making its way into this book.

MOTHER OF CREATION

Creativity is a tender and tenacious vine, climbing always upwards and looking for the light, always seeking to grow. Creativity is persistent with only one prime directive—*to become*, and it is called forth by the most powerful, primal Feminine force.

As the force of Yemaya calls whatever is formless into form, the idea becomes reality and new life comes into the world. From her sea comes all life; she is both The Mother and The Source. She dwells in the most infinite, creative place of your own feminine being.

As the very essence of motherhood, Yemaya is most favorable towards women and is passionately protective of them. The women who worship her are called Yemaya's daughters. She is the fierce protector of all new life, particularly babies—and especially while they are still in the womb. For this reason, Yemaya is often called upon for fertility and for protection during childbirth.

Yemaya has several different aspects. Each one shows us a distinctive side of her nature that we may call upon depending on our needs at that time. You might invoke Yemaya's loving and benevolent mother archetype when you need comfort, encouragement, and loving support. Calling upon her as the muse will bring you inspiration, ideas, and unique opportunities. Or you can summon her fierce and awesome nature when you need a strong protector from harsh critics or those who are attacking or blocking your efforts. I request all of these aspects of Yemaya to show up when I am being hard on myself while writing or painting, as she brings me comfort and protection—mostly from myself.

When working with The Mother Goddess aspect, you may find that your relationship with your own mother comes up. Whether your mother was good, bad, loving, indifferent, or disappointing, remember that we are all made in Her image—including your mother. Yemaya, with all of her many personalities, offers a great opportunity for you to understand, strengthen and if necessary, heal your relationship with your mother.

I was not close to either of my parents, and especially not my mother. I grew into womanhood feeling disconnected from her and eventually from all mothers. I found it difficult to receive elder guidance and support. I became very independent and eventually detached from my *daughter persona* entirely in my late teens. This was a rebellion, which snowballed into a profound disconnection from my creativity. I stopped painting and writing for almost thirty years. Creativity was the only connection that my mother and I had shared, and in order to distance myself from her, I took it away from both of us.

When The Goddess finally came into my life, the daughter part of me that had been asleep was gently woken. I blossomed in a way that I can only describe as feeling like being adopted after having been an orphan. I now had a mother who loved me unconditionally, guided me wisely, and protected me completely. As my relationship with the goddess Yemaya deepened, I became more invested in creativity again. A new understanding that my literary and artistic gifts had come directly from my Divine Mother helped me feel safe enough to reclaim them.

Through my own healing, I have come to understand that the creative urge is exactly like the urge of life itself: it is a primal impulse. Just like life, it cannot be suppressed. It wants to be born, to exist, and to materialize. Ask any woman who is creative and she will tell you that she simply *must* make art, dance, sing, act, have babies, or do whatever she does to express herself. It is an essential, fundamental, and irresistibly necessary part of her life.

The goddess Yemaya is the essence of creativity, and you are the embodiment of it. So whether you give birth to children or to symphonies—or to both, the feminine urge to create is simply inherent within you. Your creative nature will survive the worst: a sad childhood, a bad critique, or your own demolishment of it. Its roots grow deep down inside you. When it is time for it to bloom, nothing, not even you, can stop those tender shoots from making their way up towards the light. Like the tenacious vine, its natural urge is to grow and exist.

My own desire to create and share my gifts is also an attempt to leave this world more beautiful and more blissful than when I first arrived. As an artist and writer, I would like to leave behind some evidence that I existed. This sentiment is similar to what women who wish to have children feel as well, wishing their ancestry to continue on. Art, writing, music, dance, or making a baby . . . for many women, it's about creating something that lives on after you.

The urge to create comes from The Feminine, an essence that is available even for men. I think that is why we often hear men, after completing a creative project, identify with women by saying it was like giving birth. To carry an idea within you from the moment of its formation to the moment of its completion, marveling with wonderment and delight as it makes its way through you into the world, is an exquisite experience that is very much like the experience of birthing a baby.

Whenever you are in the creative experience, you are swimming in the most absolute, undiluted, and purely Feminine waters of The Divine. Yemaya invites you to dive into her endless and inviting ocean of creativity at any time.

THE WAY
OF WATER

Water is the creative essence. Water is life; it is energetically alive and essential. Its nature is that of movement—dynamic and active. It can easily be distributed and assume any shape. It can be both constructive and destructive, piling land up here and sweeping it away there.

As with many of the orishas, Yemaya is an elemental force of nature. She *is* the endless ocean, with its vast and limitless expanse that reminds us that there is no end to our ideas, inspiration, or imagination. Our creativity is as boundless as the sea. Its unceasing beauty inspires us to dream, to vision, and to create.

There is also a special understanding of life that the ocean teaches us well—that everything is momentary. The nature of water's movement shows us how to accept, but also how to let go, flow, and release. Waves teach us to be delighted as they wash away what was just there and reveal new things. This is the lesson of non-attachment, surprise, and impermanence.

If you pay attention, Yemaya's nature will speak to you and guide your creativity. When a traditional ritual for her is performed—which involves placing an offering of watermelon, mango, fish, flowers, soap, fragrances, or jewelry upon the waters of her ocean, you will know that she has accepted it when they are taken away by the sea and do not return to you on an incoming wave. This is a metaphor for knowing when the moment is right to create—and when it is not.

Yemaya's waters also can teach you to liberate yourself from expectation. Its depths instruct you when to stop, when to go on, and when to accept just what is given to you rather than holding onto what you thought you were searching for. I experienced this once when I was foraging one day for sea treasures in the sand and surf. I was on a mission to find many smooth oval stones to make a set of divination stones to sell at an upcoming fair. I found a few, but not enough for a full set. But what I did find in plentiful supply was gorgeous pink seaweed that had dried into intricate twists and curls, and was covered with faerie-like crystals of salt. It made me imagine what a mermaid's hair might look like. I wasn't quite sure what to do with it, but I gave thanks to the ocean, gathered it up, and brought it home along with some driftwood that had caught my eye.

That night I dreamt of elaborate wands made from the driftwood and seaweed, with crystals and other adornments. In the morning, I started to craft the wands and wound up with eight truly exquisite pieces. I put them out for sale at the fair and they sold immediately, fetching much more than the divination stones might have.

This is the magic of Yemaya. She knows, as any good mother would, what is best for her daughter.

YEMAYA'S MESSAGE OF TRUST

Many women fear the deepness of the sea—and the depth of their creativity. They panic, struggle and fight against the current of these waters. Yemaya invites you to cease your struggle and float along with her, breathing easily and enjoying the journey that you are on. The strong current of life will always guide you—in everything that you do. When the time is right, and you trust your creative nature with all of your heart and soul, then you will dive deep, deep down into the waters and discover the treasures that await you there.

THE GODDESS SPEAKS OF YOUR CREATIVITY

Come to me woman.
I am She Who Creates, and this most sacred gift
I give to you, my daughter.
Together our hands will weave the fabric of music
and paint the melodies of color.
Together we will dance the songs and write the words
of the heart on the canvas of the soul.
Begin now, start anywhere, create as if all your efforts
were perfection and as if today were the opus of all your days.
For they are, and it is.

THE ASSOCIATIONS
OF YEMAYA

There are many rituals for Yemaya, as she is revered as a helpful, loving goddess. Much of the work one does with her involves the ocean, but you can call upon her from the edge of your bathtub or with a dish of salt water set out in the moonlight.

Working with the goddess Yemaya is to work with the element of water and its natural flow and rhythm. She is the deepest blues of sea colored glass, and the greens of the briny herbs of the deep. She is the crescent moon of new beginnings and gathering strength, and she is the salty water of a scented bath. Yemaya hears the call of her daughters, and answers them in many surprising and loving ways.

YEMAYA'S OCEAN GEMS. Sea glass (sometimes called beach glass) is a very beautiful material that has been infused with the essence of the ocean in a very special way. Some of it was once a discarded plate, drinking glass or a bottle that was thrown into the sea, where it broke apart and was tumbled, shaped, polished and ground down by the current of the water and the pounding of the waves.

Sea glass is neither a gem, nor a crystal, but like all glass, it is created from silica, which is sand that has been exposed to extreme heat until it melts. Sea glass helps one to flow with life, even when that flow means getting tumbled around a bit. Its former smooth and transparent quality is now more opaque, frosted and a bit marred, which can help you release the oppression of perfection and see your creativity in a more diffused, mellower way. It also helps to quiet and calm the inner critic. Keep sea glass nearby when working creatively.

YEMAYA'S TOTEM: THE MOTHER OF FISHES. Fish are traditionally associated with fertility/creativity, adaptation, potential, and community. The symbol of the fish allows you to achieve your best, swimming with the flow with ease and grace.

Creativity is usually a very solo act, and this can feel very isolating for some. Bringing in the totem of fish can assist one to be more public with their work, find comfort in groups, and learn to create while in community.

Yemaya has another totem, and that is the cowrie shell. While all shells belong to Yemaya, the cowrie shell, which resembles a woman's *yoni* or vulva, is her most special one. The cowrie is a very potent symbol of the creative/procreative essence within all women. Often used as a divination tool within African and Cuban cultures, the cowrie is thought to speak both the messages of our ancestors, and the messages of the orishas themselves.

YEMAYA'S CREATIVE MOON. Crescent moons are messengers that guide us in and out of our creative flow. The waxing crescent moon is also called the new moon, and represents letting go of the old, and welcoming in the new, fresh starts, and the beginning of new projects. When this moon occurs in the waning phase, it is about gathering information and resources and finishing projects. Yemaya is the crescent moon for both of these phases, assisting in the starting and the completion of your creative project.

The sliver of light that heralds the new moon is the waxing crescent, which is a call to action and indicates that now is a good time to begin a creative project or endeavor. I was amazed each and every month while writing this book, that I had much more enthusiasm and ability for writing and received more inspiration during this phase than at any other time.

Once the moon appears full, she begins to release more and more light, until another phase appears; the waning crescent. This heralds the time of endings, indicating that you should prepare to rest, put aside and complete your creative projects. Many women find it hard to know when the time has come to cease, stop, and be in completion. Creativity is our most primal nature, and it makes sense that we shine during this process. During a workshop, I heard once, "Walk away from your work, leave it alone for a few minutes, a few hours or a few days. Come back to it with fresh eyes: see if it still needs something more, or if it is complete." This is the message of the waning crescent.

THE RITUALS
OF CREATIVITY

Preparing Your Anointing Oil

The aromatic oils of seaweed absolute, coconut, and lime are used to create the scent of Yemaya's sea—fresh, tropical, and sweet. These oils help nourish your spirit and activate your creativity. Anoint your lower sacral and throat areas with this oil to activate the creative essence within you.

Mix the following oils into a 10 ml glass bottle, and then fill with carrier oil such as rice bran, grape seed, or meadowfoam seed oil. Gently shake and store in a cool, dark place.

- ❖ 2 drops seaweed absolute
- ❖ 6 drops coconut CO_2 extract (CO_2 refers to the method of extraction, which involves carbon dioxide)
- ❖ 4 drops lime essential oil

Creating an Altar for Creativity

Yemaya is highly revered in the Caribbean islands. Statues and sacred objects of her hold a place of high esteem on altars. She is often painted in the colors blue, green, and white to represent the ocean. Her statue may be depicted with the crescent moon below her feet, and stars above her head as she floats on the surface of the sea. Many people place her statue in the center of their altar surrounded by blue and white candles, seashells, small figurines in the shape of fish, fruit, and pretty objects around her. Even if you do not have a statue of Yemaya, adorn your altar with the objects described above.

After you assemble your altar, anoint your sacral and throat area as you say this invocation for creativity:

From the depths of the sea,
and waters so deep,
I call upon my own creativity.
It will rise like a wave,
and fall like one, too,
I flow like the water, ever so true.

Bathing in the Sacred Waters of Yemaya

We are all just a handful of sea salt away from Yemaya's ocean. Wherever you live, you can perform an ocean ritual for the goddess Yemaya in your own bathtub.

What you will need:

- ❖ 2 cups of sea salt
- ❖ white flowers
- ❖ 3 white candles and 3 blue candles
- ❖ several large sea shells, including at least one cowrie shell
- ❖ your anointing oil

What to do:

Light candles around the room and place floating candles in the sink or tub if you want. Pour all but a handful of the sea salt into the water and use your oil to anoint your sacral and throat area as you say the invocation/blessing, which is inspired by the traditional Yoruban chant to the goddess of the Sea:

Yemaya is the place where the river meets the ocean,
the place where the river meets the ocean is Yemaya.
Yemaya is the goddess of the ocean.
The ocean is the goddess Yemaya

Special intention for your bath:

Appreciate your body as the vessel for life, and your feminine essence as the most creative essence there is.

Prompting Creativity

Being creative is not something that is always in the flow; sometimes you may need a little help to get it going. I like to collect words. Whenever I hear a word that strikes a chord within, I write it down in a journal. I let them accumulate, so that when I look through them, my subconscious is activated and becomes inspired.

Whenever I am struck with a feeling while writing, but cannot think of a word to express or convey it, I open my notebook and begin to read the words—and I always find the right one. I would like to share some of my favorite oceanic words in the hopes that they may churn the waters of your own creativity and inspire a painting, collage, poem, a single line of wisdom—or even an entire book of your own. Here's how to use this list:

❖ Pick ten words that appeal to you and write a short story or poem with them.

❖ If you are more artistic than literary, pick three words and paint, draw, or express them in your favorite medium.

❖ If you feel that you are not creative in any way, simply choose one word a day, write it on an index card and then use it in conversation; think about it during the day, and meditate with its meaning. You may be surprised at the creativity that will surface from within.

❖ Add your own words to this list and let it become like the endless ocean of Yemaya, filled with her fish, so many that you cannot count them.

mist	labyrinthine	seafloor	swirling
shadow	mystical	thunderous	incorporeal
regal	mercurial	undine	bestirring
tidal	crystalline	ambrosial	entangled
mother	magnetic	evocative	fluidic
mermaid	crashing	underworld	potent
quiescent	coastal	invoke	phosphorus

Inspiration for Your Journal

❖ Write a list of all the ways that you are creative, including non-artistic ways, such as thinking outside the box to solve problems or being innovative with your budget to afford a few special treats.

❖ Write about someone who helped to make a creative dream of yours come true.

❖ Write about a creative talent, gift, or ability that you wish you had, and why you wish for it. How would your life change if you had this new ability? How might you acquire it?

O, Goddess of the place
where the sacred waters flow,
where the river meets the sea,
where the two become one.

O, Goddess of the place
where all life first began,
where all life will return,
where the two become one.

O, Goddess of the place
where my heart longs for love,
where my longings cease to be,
where the two become one.

O, Goddess of these places
in the ocean,
near the rivers
in my heart,
of my life

You are All and I am one.

STILL

CHAPTER SEVEN

THE GODDESS
WHITE TARA

When winter comes to a woman's soul,
she withdraws into her inner self, her deepest spaces.
~Patricia Monaghan

U NDER THE SHADE OF A LARGE BODHI TREE, the young Buddha sat. He was deep in meditation. Images floated in and out of his mind, like leaves falling onto the surface of a flowing stream. The Buddha did not chase after his thoughts; he simply let them float away. Eventually all of his thoughts ceased, and his mind became a still pond, reflective and shining in the sunlight.

The world the Buddha lived in was full of suffering and strife. Every soul he encountered was heavy with attachment, longing, desire, and fear. They were all awash in the ever-changing sea of Samsara, spinning in the endless cycle of birth, death, and rebirth.

The Buddha, who had immense wisdom of how to break this cycle, was filled with tremendous compassion for all beings who were unable to free themselves from the wheel that always turns—the wheel of life. His light and compassion was so great that wafts of its sweet scent had floated up into the Higher Realms where it touched the hearts of the Devas, the great celestial beings who lived there.

Inspired by his unending devotion, it was decided that the Buddha's compassion would be transformed and delivered to earth in the form of a woman. She would appear as a human but would have the spiritual nature of a *bodhisattva*—a compassionate being of enlightenment who would remain in the cycle of life until each human being reached his or her own enlightenment. Only then would she herself be free to ascend to the Higher Realms where she had been conceived. She would, in essence, become the female Buddha.

Still deep in his meditation, the Buddha was unaware of the Devas' plan.

It was at that moment that the Devas sent him a vision of her. She appeared first as a being of pure light, an incredibly beautiful, radiant light. Her radiance was so encompassing, healing, and loving that the Buddha began to cry, overwhelmed by his emotions.

He saw that her illumination would spread from one person to the next. As each one received the Divine light she carried, they would then pass it to another.

The Buddha observed that eventually the entire world would become enlightened and illumined. The tumultuous sea of Samsara, the ocean of suffering, would cease to exist. In the stillness of non-suffering, all souls would become free. They would be able to release their heavy burdens of attachment, desire, and fear. Light as clouds, they would rise into the Higher Realms to live for eternity as enlightened souls.

This vision brought tears of compassion and joy to the Buddha's still closed eyes. As they began to well up and overflow, one lone tear fell to the ground where it became a brilliant jewel. It sparkled like a diamond in the dappled sunlight peeking through the leaves of the Bodhi tree.

Right where the jeweled tear landed, an unusually large lotus flower suddenly grew. The petals were as white as snow and its leaves were a deep, emerald green. From within the flower, a bright light, just like the radiance in the Buddha's meditation, shone through.

The Buddha opened his eyes to see the unopened lotus flower growing close to him. He saw that it shimmered and vibrated before him. It began to open and there, in the middle of the blossom, stood a beautiful woman who was glimmering like a bright star.

The Buddha blinked and raised his hand to shield his eyes from her light, and then he smiled. But the manifestation was not complete. Now the woman began to shimmer and vibrate before him.

The Buddha watched as she became a whirling column of energy, chaotic and wild. He observed that within the wild outer layer, it was completely still and serene at its center. The two energies suddenly separated from each other, vibrating side by side until from each of the columns emerged a woman—one wild and chaotic, and one serene and still.

The Devas, who had been watching from above, were surprised and confused by what they had witnessed. Having sent only one being to manifest as a woman from one of the Buddha's tears, how had two been born? Talking all at once, they excitedly began to theorize about what had just happened. Hotly arguing, many spilled honeyed tea from the cups in their hands.

But the Buddha, having become even wiser than the wisest of the Devas, knew the meaning of this. He knew that here on earth, all that is made manifest is subject to the nature of this physical realm. What is really only one thing will appear to us as two, for this world is filled with illusion, which often expresses itself in dualities.

The Devas quieted, nodding in agreement with the Buddha's wisdom. Feeling satisfied that all was well, they smiled and congratulated each other with pats on the back, shaking hands and pouring more tea to refill their cups.

The two celestial women looked at the Buddha as he looked at them. They spoke in unison, harmonizing: "We are called Tara, and you are the Buddha."

The women stepped from the center of the large lotus flower and bowed low with their foreheads touching the earth, across from the cross-legged Buddha. He bowed back with his forehead touching the earth.

Rising up, each of the women looked around her and began to marvel at the world they now found themselves in. Each had the unique appearance and qualities of her nature.

The wild and chaotic Tara had skin that was a deep, emerald green, as green as the earth below her feet. She expressed all the chaos and energy of the earth's core—fiery, molten, and ever changing. She was the embodiment of life itself, constantly in flux and ever in motion. Green Tara was off and running from the start, flitting from one new discovery to the next. She was delighted and irritated, interested and bored, all at once. It was difficult to follow her moods, but it was also enchanting to watch her childlike wonder at everything she encountered.

Her sister's essence, on the other hand, was as motionless as a tree. Her skin was as white as the whitest cloud in the sky above her head. She moved with the grace and ease of a snowflake, light and airy as it floated down to the earth. White Tara expressed all the calm and silence of life, being the embodiment of the in-between times. She was the very moment just before an intake of breath, and the moment just after the exhale. She was the quiet of the dawn just before the sun rose up over the horizon, and the awe of the instant before dusk when the sun dipped low and disappeared beneath the sky. She was the moment in time just before life began, as well as the second just before it ended. It was lovely to be near her, but it was also difficult to leave her side.

The Buddha smiled at the miracle of their arrival and asked, "Taras, I am honored to meet you. I wonder how it is that you have come to be?"

The Taras settled themselves side by side and spoke in perfect harmony to the Buddha. "We have come from the most potent, compassionate tear of your loving kindness, Buddha. We are the physical expression of your benevolence. We are here to assist you, O Enlightened One." And so, it was agreed that the Taras would travel with the Buddha throughout the land, teaching enlightenment.

The Devas watching from above smiled with satisfaction, nodding and murmuring further praises to each other in between sips of hot tea.

Many years passed as the Taras accompanied the Buddha from town to village, teaching seekers the way of enlightenment. It was a long journey and they each knew that it would be many more years—even centuries before each soul would become enlightened. More souls were born every day, and the sea of Samsara continued to churn with all of the suffering, desire, and fear that went with it.

Eventually, Green Tara became bored with the teaching and meditating. She tired of the quiet that both White Tara and the Buddha encouraged. She yearned to roam, to flit from flower to flower, breathing it all in again. She wanted to jump from cliffs and cause whirlwinds to sweep across the land. Green Tara wanted to *be* the chaos and commotion of life. All this stillness was causing her to feel stifled and irritated.

In contrast, White Tara was thriving. She loved the long hours of complete stillness that the Buddha sat in every day. She matched his devotion moment by moment. She could sit with him forever if need be. She enjoyed showing the beings on earth how to meditate in serene tranquility, and she was surprised to see how much they enjoyed it once they tasted its sweetness. White Tara yearned for silence, serenity, and quiet, but was concerned for her sister.

The Buddha could see that the Taras had fallen out of harmony with each other and he wondered why. He wanted to support their desire to assist him, but somehow it was not working out the way that it should have.

The Buddha knew that in order to receive the wisdom of this situation, he must meditate. In this way, he could be filled up like a cup of tea under the spout of a teapot, overflowing with insight, knowledge, and wisdom. He sat in the shade of the large Bodhi tree and went deep into his meditation.

The Devas so loved the Buddha. They were pleased that he had entered into meditation so that they could speak directly with him and give him guidance. The celestial beings sent the Buddha a vision.

In it, the Buddha saw the Taras for who they really were. He was reminded of their original essence—a single beam of light that appeared as two separate energies. While each one was unique unto herself, she was also the polar opposite of her twin. They were the same energy, expressed in two forms.

The Buddha remembered that here on earth, things are not always as they seem, for there is much illusion. He understood that, in his efforts to assist with the world's enlightenment, he had overlooked this one truth—each Tara required that she express her own essence.

At the moment of the Buddha's understanding, all of the Devas smiled and vigorously nodded their heads up and down. They chattered with joy, as they saw that the Buddha understood. More tea was poured.

The Buddha emerged from his meditation and called the Taras together to sit with him under the Bodhi tree, so he could share with them the wisdom of his meditation.

Green Tara looked up from where she was playing with several beetles, crickets, and ants. Clapping her hands in delight at the insect antics, she reluctantly left the playful insects, and walked to where her sister was already settled. White Tara sat with her thumb and forefinger touching in the ritual gesture of a *mudra* and her legs were crossed in the shape of the lotus. White Tara wore the look of serenity upon her glowing face.

"Green Tara," the Buddha said, his eyes shining with affection for her, "you are the motion of the earth as it spins on its axis and travels around our solar orb. You are the breaking dawn and the setting sun. You are the waves of the ocean and the current of the rivers. You are the growing of leaves and the blooming of flowers. You are the daytime beauty of the world; life when it is moving, dynamic, and awake. You are the strength of compassion in action."

"White Tara," the Buddha continued, his eyes warm with reverence for her, "you are the stillness of the mind in the moment before going to sleep and in the one before it awakens in the early morning light. You are the stillness of trees when there is no wind, and the motionlessness of a hummingbird while it rests in the shade. You are the mystery of soft moonlight, the unblossomed flower, and the motionless pond reflecting nothing but dark skies above. You are life when it is still, wintery, quiet, and asleep. You are the serenity of compassion at rest."

Now he addressed the two women, "You are both here to assist me in my mission and to enlighten all beings as they are in Samsara. I ask that you leave me now, and go out into the world to teach all whom you encounter that which you know best—*your own true nature.*"

The Taras looked upon the Buddha with love and felt such kindness for him that they began to cry, overwhelmed by their emotions. Their tears then became brilliant jewels, each one falling from their eyes and landing on the ground with a soft, musical sound.

Wherever their jeweled tears landed, an unusually large lotus flower suddenly grew, with petals that were as white as snow and leaves that were a deep, emerald green.

RESTORING STILLNESS:
THE MYTH OF TARA

Tara is well-known and beloved throughout Tibetan and Japanese Buddhism as well as in Hinduism. She is a plural goddess—one main goddess with several alternate forms or expressions. Her most famous attribute is that she is a *bodhisattva*, the name for one who has become enlightened but chooses not to ascend until all beings on earth are enlightened. Noted for her deep compassion and wisdom, Tara is often called The Female Buddha.

Tara is the patron deity of Tantrayana, a spiritual belief that revolves around the concept that the entire universe is the physical manifestation of God's desire for existence. The practice of Tantrayana or Tantra, as it often called, includes meditation, mantra, yoga, and ritual, all directed towards Tara as The Mother of Liberation (from suffering). She is called upon especially when asking for assistance with enlightenment, healing, compassion, or to become spiritually free.

I had time before my next client was due, so I began to read from a book that a friend had lent me. It was an older book, one that had been written by a holy man, a guru from India. It was about the sacred Kundalini. I read that the Kundalini is the sleeping or dormant energy that, when awakened through deep meditation, yoga, fasting, prayer or even spontaneously, nourishes and protects us. It also activates our power, health, wealth, and success. Kundalini is the energetic expression of Shakti; the precious, feminine life force found within all living things.

I was reading about how this energy can alter our perception of the world, shift our awareness, open the third eye to show us everything, and I thought, 'Everything? Wow, what would that be like to see everything?' My mind started to race at the idea of being able to see it all, and I started to feel agitated and anxious.

I closed my eyes to rest, settle my racing thoughts and go into stillness for the last few minutes before my client arrived. Suddenly I felt as if I had been thumped at the place just between my eyebrows, which is the place of the third eye. I felt an opening or expansion in the center of my forehead. It seemed as if I were moving at a great speed though I was actually sitting perfectly still, when a vision came to me.

Tara has twenty-one manifestations, each one expressing a different aspect of her seed essence—which is compassion. The most prominent of her forms are the serene and peaceful White Tara, and the active and dynamic Green Tara. They are often depicted as having one body split down the middle. One half is shown as a mature, tranquil woman with skin as white as snow, symbolizing serene compassion, long life, and protection. The other half is a young, vibrant woman with skin as green as the earth's terrain, symbolizing active compassion, enlightened activity, and abundance.

The goddess Tara in all of her forms is also associated with the realm of the underworld. She acts as a psychopomp, or guide for souls who are passing from life into death, between the Earth and the Heavens. She is the overseer of both realms and of all of their inhabitants. She is involved with birth, death and rebirth, which is the cycle of Samsara. She is connected with love and the Divine, with the progression of the earth's seasons, with all that is living and growing, with the lunar cycles, and with the whole of creation.

I saw in front of me the great, magnificent expanse of my soul and its endlessness, limitlessness, and foreverness. It went on and on, and on . . . without end. I turned my head in the vision to look behind me and I could see that there was no beginning to my soul, either. It had always been. The endless nature of it stretched both behind me and in front of me. Then my soul expanded in every direction and every dimension. The incredible feeling of being a part of every single thing there ever was came over me. Tears were streaming down my face from pure joy.

The vision was over as fast as it began, but I was instantly craving more. Try as I might, I could not bring it back. The sensation of limitless, endless expansion faded, as if my soul were being poured back into the vessel of my body.

In the seconds that followed, an immense and profound bliss came over me. It was a beautiful feeling accompanied by a profound knowing—along with a sense of comfort that I was, in fact, eternal. I knew that I was more than my body and more than my mind.

I am a soul without beginning or end—and my meditative stillness had brought me to the pure land of White Tara.

THE ESSENCE
OF STILLNESS

Everything in the world begins and ends with stillness. Preceding and following every single action, it is there. It exists in the resting of the heart between beats, in the space between breaths, and just before the moment of passing from this world to the next when the living body ceases. In the quiet space of stillness, decisions of a lifetime can be made, complications of the world can be understood, and a pristine moment of peace can be found.

The goddess Tara is the absolute essence of this stillness. Said to live in a paradise like Eden, she is herself pure and beautiful. The land of Tara is a metaphor for the *nirvana*-like state of being that one achieves when absolutely calm, still, and serene.

In some traditions, it is said that the goddess White Tara was once an ordinary woman named Wisdom Moon, who, through a dedicated spiritual practice, achieved enlightenment. When she announced her vow of bodhisattva to her spiritual teachers, she explained that she loved the world and wished to return again and again into the pure form of a woman. Her teachers asked if she might want to reconsider and perhaps reincarnate instead as a man, which was the more traditional form for a bodhisattva. Tara insisted that she would return as a woman. She recognized the benefit of the female form, as it is an ideal body for cultivating an empty, receptive mind.

The nature of stillness is that of pure potential and possibility. When you are still, you have the potential to practice receptivity and openness—both of which are feminine qualities. The Tantrayana or Tantra spirituality that Tara hails from, teaches that all beings can achieve lasting happiness, bliss, and joy by going into stillness. White Tara represents the feminine, still nature of this practice.

Stillness is both the place to end up and the place to begin when working with the goddess Tara. This goddess is naturally and irresistibly drawn towards stillness. She *is* the stillness that we seek and practice. When you are in a state of calm, motionless tranquility, you are the most aligned you will ever be with The Goddess. In this space, you will feel Her presence, know Her guidance, and experience Her in the most profound ways.

The benefit of stillness is to slow down your perception of time, change the way you view your existence, and reveal that you are endless, precious, and a part of everything. Stillness will show you, firsthand, that you are Divine.

THE HEART OF
THE GODDESS

White Tara leads us to the place of the Higher Heart, a holy space where Divine love, healing, forgiveness, and compassion reside.

This Heart of the heart is called a meta-organ—a subtle place existing ethereally and energetically within us. It is where all of our connections to spirituality, karma, and Divine love originate. When your stillness generates from this place, it becomes a sacred act, a blessing. Stillness is the most Divine and Feminine quality that women have.

The Higher Heart is energetically located at the spot of the thymus gland, which is just above the physical or *lower heart*. It acts as a bridge between the physical and spiritual self, as well as a conduit from the heart chakra to the throat chakra.

In the esoteric mysteries, there is a plane of existence other than the physical plane: it is a non-physical state of awareness that transcends all that we know in the physical universe. This existence is ephemeral, or temporary in nature. It cannot be sustained for very long while we are in human form. It is a place of pure Spirit, the pure land of White Tara. It is only through the stillness of our Higher Heart that we may enter this place.

I think of the Higher Heart as the Heart of The Goddess. It is, after all, the place where compassion, love, forgiveness, spiritual connection, and peace reside. These are all things that belong to Her. White Tara's desire to become a bodhisattva, to assist all beings with their suffering, must have come from the place of her own Higher Heart. This desire has been channeled from the wisdom of The Goddess Herself.

Suffering is a human condition that seems inevitable, yet this inevitability is an illusion that keeps us stuck in Samsara, or the cycle of life, death and rebirth. To transcend the idea that we are meant to suffer is to become an enlightened being. Our enlightenment gives us access to the pure land of White Tara, where suffering does not exist and we only experience endless bliss, peace, and inner tranquility.

EVER IN
MOTION

Stillness is natural for women, and yet the modern woman has very little time or space for doing *nothing*. Many women fulfill their traditional roles in motherhood, and many also venture out into the world to run businesses and pursue careers—or to do both simultaneously. We have become very active women, which is a very masculine thing to do.

Women's brains and bodies appear to have become accustomed to this busy life style. But they have not really, as stress-related issues once linked only to men and the corporate workplace are now spilling over to women. Television, cell phones, computers, and texting have created brains that are always plugged in, continually stimulated by visual and auditory distractions. Our minds are always working—and this is the active expression of Green Tara, not the stillness of White Tara. The burgeoning industry of yoga and meditation are signs of a busy world that is hungry to find stillness.

Constant action imbalances everyone, especially women because it is too much activated masculine essence and too little feminine essence. All bodies benefit from stillness, but it is essential for women. If a woman is not in stillness often enough throughout her day, she is not experiencing one of her most natural states of being.

So important is this for women that starting to restore stillness in your life for just a few moments every day will immediately and noticeably improve your energy, your mood, and your overall experience of life. Just as the Buddha knew that he must go into stillness to receive insight, when you are in a state of non-movement, you are able to receive and replenish all of your Feminine qualities.

On the other hand, too much stillness is also an imbalance. Stillness and action are the same energy expressed as two forms—like White and Green Tara. They must be in balance for our life to function how we were meant to live it.

There is a beautiful, but elaborate meditation, called the wish-fulfilling wheel, to invoke White Tara and achieve longevity and protection. First lie down and visualize yourself as White Tara. Then visualize an eight-spoke wheel having five concentric rims, located in your heart, parallel to the earth. The wheel is not moving. You then visualize the outer symbols for eight of our inner fears, one for each spoke on Tara's wheel; water or drowning symbolic of letting go of attachments, thieves symbolic of false views, lions symbolic of pride, snakes symbolic of jealousy, fire symbolic of anger, demonic spirits symbolic of doubt, captivity symbolic of greed, and finally elephants symbolic of ignorance.

A meditation for protection is similar, involving several wheels of pure light that rotate around you and through which many swords of light slice at all who seek to cause you harm. This wheel is moving, as protection is a masculine quality (active) while longevity or life is feminine (still).

To be in stillness does not require you to sit cross-legged, perfectly motionless and meditating. It simply means that, in your mind, you are not pursuing goals, questing for answers, seeking results, making plans, looking or hoping for something. You are simply open and receptive—letting go of urgency, allowing results to unfold naturally. You stop directing and let things happen according to Divine timing—which is always on time.

Just being in the flow with life—surrendering to whatever situation—is practicing stillness. It's about seeking the Source within yourself, becoming aware of your own Goddess nature.

THIS WORLD IS
FILLED WITH ILLUSION

When women are busy, they are in a masculine state of being—one that is single-minded, purposeful and focused. White Tara teaches stillness, wholeness, and harmony, which are feminine states achieved through calmness, serenity, and peacefulness. Women are designed to bring wholeness and harmony into the world. We are more naturally inclined to think of the group before the individual. We tend to gather people together often to promote the mutual benefit of all rather than our own personal gain. We are seekers of union by nature.

The goddess White Tara is dedicated to assisting all beings who are suffering in the sea of Samsara. When you find yourself suffering in any way—loss, grief, sadness, worry, pain, illness, or fear—you are in what Buddhism calls the Samsara, which is the sea of suffering, or duality, that all beings endure until they become enlightened or spiritually aware enough to cease the cycle of rebirth. Literally translated, Samsara means 'continuous flow' referring to the cycle of reincarnation that a soul experiences until it is liberated from suffering.

Cycle and flow are familiar to women, as every month we experience our own kind of suffering with our lunar blood flow. It took me years to become enlightened about my moontime. I had always felt that it was a painful, inconvenient burden until I began to study its sacredness. I began to dedicate this time each month as sacred. In pain, I would suffer, so I began to practice reverence for my moontime each month by creating stillness for myself through bathing, meditation, and resting. Soon the pain, the messiness, and all the inconvenience disappeared.

Another sacred suffering that belongs only to women is childbirth. I have not given birth, but I have been a birth coach for my youngest sister as she brought two of her three daughters into the world. Childbirth is very active, energetic, and vigorous. It offers little rest to the mother or the child. As the peak of her labor approached and her discomfort increased, I remember helping my sister breathe and find brief, fleeting moments of meditative stillness. It is said that a baby does this, too, as she makes her way down the birth canal, pausing to rest several times before being born. I imagine that this tiny being has an innate sense of stillness. She instinctively knows how to balance the effort of her own birth with rest. I feel that for many women, our instinct has become quite dormant.

STILL THE MIND

In a state of stillness, you are open to receive with your mind. An active mind gives out energy; a still mind receives it. Different from prayer, which is primarily an activity, meditation is entirely receptive. The body and mind become virtually motionless and tranquil. By calming your mind, it becomes an inviting place for The Divine Feminine to enter. In a state of quietude, you can receive profound messages and images from Her that are much like a dream, but more vivid and transformative.

There is also a deep physical benefit from the stillness of meditation. Your heart rate lowers, your breathing calms. The stress hormones surging through you all day are purged as your body relaxes.

Some people find meditation intimidating. They are unsure how to remain quiet, silent, and unmoving for even just a few moments. The idea of stopping the mind, or quieting the ego is a scary thought to them. But think of meditation as something different. It is more about allowing the subconscious, non-linear part of your mind to emerge, the part capable of experiencing The Divine, while the conscious, linear part recedes.

We all have two minds: the conscious and the subconscious. Both are active and aware, but the conscious mind is in charge of our everyday tasks. The conscious mind never stops managing us, as it is designed to be always thinking, analyzing, and processing everything happening. Even during sleep, it is peripherally monitoring everything, in case it needs to wake us up to handle a situation.

In meditation, we teach or train this active part of our mind to rest and just observe quietly without interruption. When the conscious mind rests, the subconscious mind is able to emerge.

The subconscious mind governs our autonomic systems such as respiration and cardiovascular function as well as manages the overall health and well-being of the body. It is also where we experience imagination, emotions, and imagery. The subconscious is the part of our mind where we can have a cosmic experience, such as the vision of my soul that I described earlier.

Once your meditation is over, writing in a journal or discussing your experience will feed the conscious (masculine) mind's insatiable hunger for activity. Keeping this part of your mind engaged afterwards will encourage it to trust the (feminine) process of stillness more and more, allowing you to stay in it longer. You will then find that your meditations become deeper and richer.

STILL THE
BODY

We all begin our lives fully immersed in the placental waters of our mother. In this miniature ocean, we are nourished, cleansed, and protected. It is our first immersion, our first bath. To take the pleasure of a bath is to return to the waters of The Divine Mother—The Divine Feminine. When we immerse ourselves in a bath, we are ritualistically recreating the experience of the womb before our birth. Emerging from the bath is symbolic of being born, or reborn.

The bath purifies our body, and is a way to create private, soothing stillness that is calming to the nervous system. It is recommended that a bath be between 104F and 113F to be therapeutic. Soaking in water, your muscles melt into relaxation, and your body drifts into stillness. Just as meditation calms the body, relaxing the body calms the mind.

In many cultures, ritual bathing is sacred and holy. Hindusim, Shinto, Islam and many other Eastern religions all practice ritual sacred bathing for purification. In Japan, the Sento, or community bathhouse, is a place to enjoy the benefit of a hot bath and share the ambiance of relaxing with others.

The Jewish Mikvah is a sacred bath for women only. It takes place in a private, dedicated space under the supervision of an attendant to ensure that your entire body is immersed. The water must come from a natural source such as a spring or collected rainwater. A woman must dunk herself seven times to complete the Mikvah ritual and be considered purified. A woman visits the Mikvah before and after specific times in her life, such as after each of her moontimes, before her wedding night, and after childbirth. Many modern Jewish women also visit it to mark transitions, such as the ending of relationships or after surgery or illness. The Mikvah is a quiet, reverent place where a woman can perform this ancient ritual of cleansing and stillness.

Modern life makes it easy to bathe in stillness as most homes and apartments have bathtubs. Take time to create a sacred space for your bath. It is good to wash your body with soap in the shower before entering the tub, so you can simply soak and invite the tranquility to fully unfold. Use scented sea salts, add perfumed oils, and light candles. Plan to spend at least 30 minutes soaking in a hot bath for the most beneficial results.

WHITE TARA'S MESSAGE OF BALANCE

Reconnect with nature, where there is perfect balance. There, all things live in harmony with each other. Nature has a positive effect upon us. The ocean emits negative ions, which calm your nervous system. The gentle breezes refresh you. The murmur of the running stream soothes you. And the fields of flowers delight you with their aroma and color. Whenever you are troubled or feeling like your equilibrium is off, spend time in nature.

THE GODDESS SPEAKS OF YOUR STILLNESS

Come to me woman, slowly and with soft steps . . . close your eyes.

I am here in the dark of your inner vision.

I am here, in the silence between the beat of your heart and

the soft bellow of your deepening breath.

Surrender your haste to me, replenish your essence at my well —

I am waiting for you, here, in the quiet of your mind.

Find me always in the silence of snow, the current of still waters,

in the unsung note and the unspoken prayer.

Find me wherever there is the urgent racing of thoughts that come finally to rest.

I am there, I am here . . . I am waiting for you to know stillness,

as if your very soul desires it and as if you were undeniably made for it.

For it does, and you are.

THE ASSOCIATIONS
OF WHITE TARA

When one says the many mantras, prayers and invocations to White Tara, they are in the presence of The Goddess' most benevolent aspects of grace and purity—which She is overjoyed to share with you. When working with White Tara, the soft glow of iridescent crystals and the scent of calming oils will all assist you on your journey into meditation and into the stillness of your being.

CRYSTALLIZED MOONLIGHT. The milky iridescence of moonstone seems to glow from within. Just like the moon itself, this lovely crystal is excellent for balancing your feminine essence. Moonstone symbolizes the mystery and wisdom of the inner journey, and its soft, reflected light can reminds us to soften our gaze, soften our mind and relax our body so that we can enter stillness more easily. The play of light within moonstone, especially the rainbow variety, can have a trance-like affect that calms a racing mind and eases the nervous system to assist with meditation and peacefulness. Place this crystal on your third eye while meditating, or near your heart for balance.

WHITE TARA'S TOTEM: FROM THE MUD. The lotus is the totem flower of the goddess White Tara, and teaches us the beauty and naturalness of stillness. Opening to the sun's first rays each morning, and then closing its petals as the sun sets—it then remains perfectly still until the light of a new day inspires the cycle all over again. This cycle reminds us to rest after exerting effort, to be still to receive, and that all beings are born, die, and are born again.

Life is not perfect. Amidst all of its stunning loveliness and profound beauty, it is also filled with struggle, pain, and ugliness. The gorgeous lotus flower symbolizes this contrast and duality as it grows in the muddiest of waters. Rising up from them, this sacred flower shows that beauty and blessings can come from even the darkest of beginnings, that we can rise from the Samsara, and struggle no more.

STILLNESS MOON. As you learned earlier with Lilith, the dark moon is about transformation, magic, and the power of both releasing and gathering. However when working with White Tara, the transformation that we experience through the dark moon is very spiritual, as its magic is witnessed in its effect upon our lives as busy women. We become calmer, life is easier, and we find even more time for the tasks at hand. We also perform them with so much more grace and ease.

With Lilith, we used this moon to go *past* the state of meditation; but with the dark moon this time, we seek its stillness and solitude to meditate for inner peace, understanding, and tranquility. This is not a moon of dark, underworld mystery; it is a moon of sweetness, of silent peacefulness and gentle thoughts. While meditating under Tara's dark moon, our thoughts become like the petals of a lotus flower falling softly on the surface of a slow moving river, floating away from us without a care.

Rest, relaxation, thoughtfulness, non-activity or very gentle activity are indicated at this moon time. No major decisions, the starting of new projects or the completion of those already in progress should be made, but rather much mediating upon them all is greatly encouraged.

The dark moon of Tara is not a moon for going deep within to gather information from your own psyche, but to listen, and then *receive* the information that The Goddess has for you. She cannot speak to you if you do not create quiet space in your mind, and a stillness in your body so that you can hear Her.

THE RITUALS
OF STILLNESS

Preparing Your Anointing Oil

The oils of rose, white lotus, and agarwood are extraordinarily sacred and holy and have been used for meditation for many years. They are considered very precious materials, and are therefore costly. However, lovely and affordable substitutions for these are available if need be; use rosewood in place of rose, ylang ylang for lotus, sandalwood instead of agarwood. Anoint your Higher Heart with this special oil blend to both activate it and help you to connect to it.

Fill a 10 ml glass bottle with carrier oil such as jojoba, rice bran, grape seed, or meadowfoam seed oil. Then mix the following oils into it. Gently shake, and store in a cool, dark place.

❖ 3 drops each of rose absolute (or rosewood)
❖ 6 drops white lotus absolute (or ylang ylang)
❖ 3 drops agarwood absolute (or sandalwood)

Creating an Altar for Stillness

The color theme of your altar is the pureness and innocence of white, with its association to vastness, emptiness, and the more divine, higher states of being. White is also very protective, as it is the color of divinity, sacredness, holiness, and the angelic realm. This protection is very different from the protective nature of black, which is used as an external shield to block negativity. Rather, white is called upon from within and emanates out and all around you to strengthen your auric field.

To honor the totem of Tara, place a photo of a white lotus, a silk lotus or even a real one upon your altar. Adorn further with white candles, moonstone crystals, and anything else meaningful of stillness to you.

Once your altar is complete, light your candle and anoint your Higher Heart with your oil blend and say this invocation for stillness:

Active mind, now be still.
Urgent thoughts, now be still.

Restless body, now be still.
All is calm, quiet and relaxed.

Bathing in the Sacred Waters of Tara ─────────────

I take a morning bath every day. I have been doing this for more than 20 years and it has everything to do with my feelings of inner calm and wellbeing. It is my go-to activity whenever I am *not* calm, and sets the tone for my day—relaxed, at ease, and centered. When I also take a bath in the evening, I fall asleep much more easily, and wake feeling much more refreshed.

For your bath of stillness, it is very important that you turn off your phones, TV, and other distracting devices. If you live with others, let them know you are not to be disturbed. Soft music is lovely, but refrain from music with an upbeat rhythm or loud sound. Imagine that your bathroom is about to be transformed into a sacred pool in the center of a temple, where only the soft murmur of mantras are heard and deep meditation and prayer take place.

What you will need:

❖ white candles
❖ sandalwood incense
❖ your anointing oil
❖ moonstone crystal(s)
❖ sea salt
❖ sandalwood essential oil diluted in 10 ml jojoba oil

What to do:

Draw a warm or comfortably hot bath, add 12–20 drops of sandalwood essential oil diluted in 10 ml jojoba oil. Then add 2 cups sea salt and swirl the water to mix. Light your candles and incense and anoint your third eye as you say this blessing:

Sacred waters, blessed be.
Relax my mind, my body and soul,
bring what is chaotic back into whole.

─────────────

Slip into your bath and relax, letting your thoughts come and go—attaching to none of them . . . simply soak.

Special intention for your bath:

Relax your body by *sending* your breath into each individual part. Visualize that you are breathing relaxation and tranquility into your head, neck, shoulders, arms, torso, legs and feet, relaxing them as you do so.

Higher Heart Activation

You can activate your own Higher Goddess Heart, which is located just above your physical heart, at the place of your thymus gland. I do this when I am feeling spiritually low, emotionally drained, or deeply longing for a closer relationship to The Divine. When I activate this in myself, I experience a sweet, sensitive, and vulnerable sensation. It feels overwhelming at first to be touched there, and it may feel slightly sore even with the slightest touch. It also feels deeply intimate and spiritual as well.

What to do:

❖ Sit in a comfortable position where you will not be disturbed.

❖ Place a drop of your anointing oil on your middle finger if desired.

❖ With your feet firmly on the ground, and your eyes closed, lightly and briefly touch the area just between and slightly above your heart with your middle finger. Use light to mild pressure. This area is called the breastbone or sternum. The middle finger is associated with Saturn, a planet that is referred to as the Great Teacher. Saturn helps us focus on our life path.

❖ Now touch your Higher Heart again, with the intention to activate it. As you apply light to mild pressure, say a prayer of gratitude and reverence to acknowledge this sacred place in your body.

❖ Make note of any sensations, or lack thereof, as you activate this point. Release your pressure and notice the difference.

❖ You may also wish to say this Tibetan mantra to align your nature to the Goddess White Tara, whose nature is that of both serene compassion and powerful protection from the duality and suffering of Samsara.

Oṃ tāre tuttāre ture svāhā

(pronounced as : Ohm twar-rey tu-tar-rey tu-rey svah-ha)

Inspiration for Your Journal ─────────────────

❖ Write about your most compassionate act in the world. If you cannot think of one, write about one you would most like to perform.

❖ Write about the most memorable meditation that you have experienced. What impressed you about it? How did it affect you?

❖ Write about your own still, quiet, inner White Tara nature, and your own active, kinetic, outward Green Tara nature. Which one is strongest?

Heavenly Tara, Divine One;
you are my spirit at peace—
at the end of the day,
and at the beginning of night.

Peaceful Tara, Awakened One;
you are my body at rest—
just before sleep,
and right before waking.

Wise Tara, Enlightened One;
you are my quiet thoughts,
when my eyes are closed,
and just before they open.

You are the stillness that I seek,
I will find heaven,
peace, and wisdom from within.

PASS

CHAPTER EIGHT

THE GODDESS
RADHA

The soul is forever calling us
back to our ecstatic origin.
~Lisa Schrader

RADHA WOKE FROM A DREAM COVERED IN SWEAT. For two nights in a row she had dreamt of a strange, beautiful man. He came and lay down beside her and, without even touching her, evoked feelings that she had never felt with a man before.

She blushed scarlet thinking about him, this dream man. Remembering his presence now caused her to think of the book of love—the Kama Sutra—and her blush deepened. Her closest friend, Lalita, had stolen a copy when they were young girls and the two of them poured over the pages, fascinated and repulsed at the same time. Radha felt the same stirrings deep within her now, just as she did then.

Oh, the trouble they were in once their mothers found out they had taken the book! Radha giggled out loud as she recalled the incident sitting in bed, while her husband turned over with a snort, then kept on sleeping, his face in a frown. She looked up to the heavens and whispered gratitude for keeping him asleep. Then with her hands in prayer at her heart, she whispered a quick plea to the goddess Rati, who presides over love and sex. "Please, Rati Ma, you, who knows the fires of passion and the pleasures of love, bless me with my dream man. Bless me with a love that causes my body to ignite with the flames of passion!"

Rising slowly so she would not wake her husband, she crept from their bed and made her way out of the room. As soon as she opened the door, she could see that the house was already bustling with activity. Everyone was getting ready for tonight's *puja*, a fire ceremony and celebration. The air smelled of warm, sweet syrupy rose water for the *gulab jamuns,* and of sugared cashews for the *halwah.* The rich aroma of *ghee* melting in a pan filled her nose. She closed her eyes, breathing it all in, and felt her stomach rumble with hunger.

Radha padded barefoot through the kitchen doorway unseen. Her hand reached in quickly to grab a sweet *laddu,* knowing full well that this treat was for the *prasadam,* the offering of food to the Divine. She didn't care, it was her favorite. Popping the dessert into her mouth, she made her way down the hall and out of the house without ever being seen and savored the sweetness of the treat in her mouth.

Once free of the abode, she ran through the woods to the lake, her special lake. There she hoped to have a few delicious moments of privacy and a cool bath before the day began. Looking into the waters, she saw her reflection and upon seeing her beauty, she noticed that it did not bring her any joy.

Her marriage had been arranged so long ago and she had gone from girlhood to womanhood without ever knowing real passion or true love. Her mind was bored and her heart was unmoved. Her beauty, which was reserved only for her husband, felt wasted, as he hardly noticed her. While he was kind and generous, he was clumsy in the ways of love and sometimes smelled of garlic. The thought of his smell made her face scrunch up and so she turned her thoughts back to her dream and for the third time that morning she blushed.

At the lake's edge, Radha slipped out of her sleeping chemise and walked naked into the ice cold water. At first, she felt her skin turn to goose flesh and then relax as it became used to the chill. Her long black hair floated around her full, womanly body as she turned this way and that, swimming lazily in the clear water. Arms spread out on either side of her, she floated on her back enjoying the early morning light against her closed eyes.

Her eyes suddenly flew open at the sound of a flute close by. Instinctively she crouched down low in the water and covered her breasts with her hands. Her breath quickened at the thought of being discovered swimming alone and naked.

Panicked, she kept only her head above the surface and stepped slowly along the muddy bottom towards the edge of the lake, her eyes searching for her chemise. She hoped to make a quick getaway, but where were her clothes? Splashing quietly, she swam back and forth, her eyes searching frantically. But only the soft grass, wild jasmine, and kamal flowers were at the waters' edge.

A breeze blew some of the blossoms into the water near her and she pushed them away, while searching for her clothes. With her eyes closed tight, she prayed to Ganesha to remove the obstacle of this dilemma from her path. "Please Baba Ganesha, I am hoping that when I open my eyes, my chemise will appear!" She opened her eyes, but still, no clothes.

Tears formed and fell unwelcome and hot against her cool cheeks. They turned into sobs, as Radha imagined the shame of walking home without her clothes. What would she say? How could she explain this? Fear took hold of her heart. She cried harder into her hands, worried that in his anger, her husband would forbid her from ever leaving the house and she would never swim in her lake again. Her sobs stopped suddenly—there was the flute again!

Radha hiccupped and blinked her eyes wide open.

So enchanting, so haunting, and so inviting was the music Radha was hearing that she just stood up and walked out of the water in a trance. Like a lure, the music drew her further and further into the dense grove of kadamba trees beyond the lakeside.

Deep in the woods now, Radha stood as still as a deer when the music stopped. With her eyes half-lidded and unfocused, she waited. Her beautiful naked body was dripping with water and her long black hair was wet and tangled. She shivered as a breeze blew across her skin.

The music started back up, playing right behind her. She quickly turned, coming face to face with the most beautiful man she had ever seen. He wore the finest clothes, complete with a pristinely white turban wrapped about his head, wherein a single iridescent peacock feather was perched within its folds. Radha instantly recognized him as the man from her dream, and her mouth opened wordlessly.

The light of the morning sun coming through the thick canopy of leaves and the shadows they made seemed to cast a bluish color upon him, causing him to appear otherworldly. He smiled and all Radha could do was stare at his perfect teeth, his perfect smile, and his glorious, handsome beauty. She reached out to touch him, to see if he was real. He gently caught her hand before it could touch him and after kissing it, he said, "Radha, my *khushi*, my happiness. I am so glad that you have come to me."

At his touch, Radha felt her legs go out from underneath her—and then blackness.

Much, much later Radha awoke in her own bed. At first she smiled and stretched luxuriously as if she had just enjoyed something wonderful. Then right in the middle of the stretch, she froze as her memory came flooding back to her. With a gasp she sat up straight, confused, and worried all at once. She looked down to find that she was in her sleeping chemise, and next to her was her snoring husband. She jumped from the bed, waking him. "Wife!" he grumbled, "Let a man sleep!"

Radha crept from the room and made her way towards the kitchen where it seemed there was much commotion. Now even more confused by a growing sense of déjà vu, she walked in to see the cooks busy with preparations for the evening puja.

The scent of syrupy rose water and sugared cashews filled the air, as did the rich aroma of ghee. Aashita, the head cook saw her and asked, "Madame, would you like a cup of chai? Or perhaps hot *paratha* with honey and ghee?" Radha shook her head no. She turned to leave, but the cook stopped her by gently removing something from her hair—a peacock feather. Radha flushed red and snatched the feather from the woman's hand, turned and walked out of the kitchen, secretly holding the feather close to her heart. Aashita clucked her tongue and rolled her eyes at this strange behavior, but not until she saw that her mistress was safely out of the room and away from seeing her do it.

That evening, Radha did not enjoy the ceremony, the chanting, or her favorite desserts. She kept scanning the crowd hoping to see him, the man from the forest, from her dreams. The longing for him was beginning to distract her; it was fast becoming her only thought. She finally excused herself, feigning a headache and left the puja. Intending to go to her room, she found herself walking out of the house towards the lake with only the moonlight to guide her and the faint sound of a flute playing in her head.

Standing at the lake's edge, listening to the soft lapping of the water against the muddy earth and watching the moon shining on its surface, Radha waited, holding her breath. She closed her eyes for just a moment, and when she opened them, he was standing in front of her, smiling. His masculine beauty was unlike anything she had ever known. He seemed to glow from within, and in the light of the full moon, his skin appeared even bluer. The scent of sandalwood wafted over him as she inched closer to breathe it in.

"You are beautiful, Radha," he said, "so beautiful that you shine like the moon when it is full. You are like heaven, so bright is your light. Your exquisite figure is beyond elegant, and the sweetness of your words is like the finest rose water, like perfume. Your beauty, Radha, is unparalleled in all of the three worlds. Your heart is so revealed to me that I can feel the exquisite longing that radiates from it, my beautiful one."

"My longing is for you," she heard herself say softly, blushing for the hundredth time it seemed that day.

"Come," said the strange, handsome man with skin like blue moonlight. "Take my hand, and let us walk a while."

Radha took the man's hand and noticed that, although she felt lightheaded, she did not swoon this time. He felt electric, as if a current of energy was running through him. All she could think about was the desire she felt for him. It bloomed like a flower deep within her, fanning a fire she did not know existed and sending little waves of pleasure throughout her body. She had never felt this way before, not ever. She kept her eyes down as they walked.

"I am Krishna," he said. After a long time, he directed her to sit near a large kadamba tree. Where he pointed, there suddenly arose from the earth a rock with a perfectly flat top for sitting, and lovely flowers appeared as if by magic all around it. Radha blinked, unsure if she might be dreaming again, and sat where he indicated.

"I have been watching you for a long while, Radha, and I wish to know you. I wish for you to know me. Would this be agreeable with you?"

There were no words to speak, so much was her amazement in all that was happening. She nodded yes, her large, almond-shaped eyes wide with wonder. She imagined the two of them locked in the positions she had only seen in the book of love, the Kama Sutra, so long ago, and she bravely raised her eyes to meet his. "Yes, yes," she spoke out loud, and her breathlessness surprised her.

Krishna bent his head towards hers, and then lifted her chin. She closed her eyes expecting him to kiss her on the mouth, wanting him to, but instead he kissed her forehead. The kiss was so tender, so loving, and felt so intimate that Radha began to cry. She let her head fall against his chest as she released years of pent-up emotion with her sobs.

Krishna held her close within his strong arms and stroked her hair as she cried. His sweetness caused her to cry harder, and she began hiccuping between sobs, trying to catch her breath. On and on she cried and hiccupped until finally she was spent. She looked up to his face with swollen, red eyes and moved her mouth to meet his.

Before her mouth could reach him, he took her face in his hands and said, "We are always together, you and I, for we are both the other half of each other. I am your beloved, and you are mine." He kissed her again on the forehead between her brows.

This time the kiss was charged with power. As she felt it course through her, a rise of energy from deep down at the base of her tailbone rose like a serpent all the way up to her crown in an explosion of joy, ecstasy, and bliss. In that moment, with her body trembling, she felt closer to him than she had ever felt to anyone.

Each night, Radha snuck away to meet with Krishna in the dark of the woods with only the moonlight to see him. Each morning she found herself mysteriously back in her own bed as if nothing had ever happened, save for a single, beautiful peacock feather pressed loosely into her hair. She had collected 108 of them so far. They were like the sacred beads of a mala, and she touched each one of them with reverence, saying Krishna's name over and over like a mantra. Radha kept the feathers in a carved sandalwood box under an old blanket in her wardrobe, hidden safely away from her husband.

During the day, she walked around as if in a dream, obsessing about the color of his eyes, the smoothness of the skin on his hands, the blackness of his hair, and his strange bluish skin. She wanted Krishna to touch her, kiss her, be with her in the most intimate of ways. But Krishna only offered her a loving kiss on the forehead and his beautiful smile. Radha often wondered why there was not more between them but she was too shy to ask.

She knew that her desires were inappropriate. She had never strayed from her marriage before, no matter how unsatisfying it was. But where Krishna was concerned, she could not stop herself. She wanted to be with him and was willing to risk everything to make it happen.

In their nightly meetings, they talked endlessly of her hopes, her dreams, and of the world's mysteries. Krishna answered all of her deepest questions about love. He showed her new ways to look at her life that seemed impossibly simple and incredibly wise. Krishna also spoke to Radha about her beauty, her intelligence, her intuition, and her wisdom. He taught her the ways of yoga, Tantra, and chanting. He read to her from the book of love, only it was not the same as when she was a child. Now the images and words stirred up a fierce passion within her, gnawing like an insatiable hunger. Whenever Krishna looked deep into her eyes, her mind slowed and she could swear that a light was passing from his eyes into hers. For a brief, fleeting moment, her hunger abated, her craving ceased, and her desire was satisfied.

Radha's heart opened to Krishna like a lotus flower that had been closed tightly at night then blossomed wide in the earliest light of the day. For the first time in her life, she felt desirable, beautiful, cherished, and loved. For the first time, she loved a man with all of her being. And, for the first time, she wanted something she could not even name.

One night when her physical desire for Krishna was unbearable, Radha felt frustration. Anger rose up in her heart. "I am a married woman!" she said proudly, shaking her fist in the air. "I am risking everything for him. What is he risking for me?"

In her fit, all of her unrequited physical desire began to take its toll, weakening her love. Her hysterical emotions began to attract the supernatural beings who create illusion and deception. It was not long before Radha had slipped into the *maya*, the place of the mind that is easily misled into believing the trickery of such creatures. It was a place of fear. Her thoughts were now not her own.

Radha created a plan to test Krishna's love for her. "I will resist the music of his flute," she said as she paced around the bedroom alone while her husband was outside in the toilet. "And I will not meet with him this night or any other night until *he* comes for *me!* I will not even think of him nor look upon him in my dreams unless he comes to me, takes me in his arms and ravishes me until there is nothing left but the shell of my body with a smile on my face!"

She then changed into her chemise and slipped into bed, satisfied with her plan. But after a while, Radha shivered with doubt; would he come for her? She sighed with worry; what if he does not? She missed him already. With a heavy heart and an exhausted mind, she soon fell fast asleep, never noticing that her husband had joined her.

She awoke the next day, having no memory of meeting with Krishna in the night, and found no peacock feather in her hair. Her heart sank and dread came over her. What had she done? What does Krishna think of her now? Did he go to another woman, one more beautiful than her? Was she much smarter than her? Was she more available than her? Her heart sank and ached for his words praising her beauty. She missed their talks about life. Radha looked over at her sleeping, unsuspecting husband, and without being able to stop herself she began to weep loudly.

Her husband, whose name was Abhimanyu, woke with a start, but he stopped short of reprimanding her when he saw her distress. He had never seen her like this and he was struck motionless with surprise. "Radha, what is it, wife?" he asked kindly. Radha shook her head and ran from their bed crying even louder. Abhimanyu rolled his eyes at her strange behavior, but not until she had left the room, and then he lay back down to finish his sleep. "Women!" he muttered.

Radha ran all the way to her own special lake and flung herself down at its edge, her body convulsed with sobbing. In her fearful, maya mind, she knew Krishna had left her, forsaken her. The very idea of not seeing him again caused her so much unbearable pain.

"Radha, my love."

At the sound of his voice, she jumped up and ran into Krishna's open arms, burying herself in his chest. She clung to him tightly until he took her gently by the shoulders and sat her down on the grass, tilting her chin up to meet his gaze. She looked tearfully into his lotus petal-shaped eyes and was calmed.

"Radha," he whispered, his voice making her name sound like poetry, "you are a woman. From you, the whole universe is created; all of creation is your doing! I do not exist without you. Therefore, I cannot leave you, nor choose another over you. I am in service to you, the one who can create all that there is. I am in service to your wisdom, and to your beauty that fills this world with joy. Your longing for me is an illusion, for we are already joined, already together, and already one and the same."

In the time it took Kishna to say those words, Radha felt all of their nightly conversations come into sharp focus. His teachings became crystal clear. Her heart was peaceful, as she sensed her soul's endless journey from its creation to its never-ending future. Radha grasped the wholeness of her being as it merged with the universe Krishna had described. Her emptiness for him was now deeply filled. Her mind had opened to receive the wisdom he had shared with her in that moment. She found her essence through his words, and she claimed it for her own. She felt her power as a female and her passion setting her body on fire. As the fire rose within her, it engulfed her and became an aura beaming with bright light encircling her.

"Krishna," her voice making his name sound like a prayer, "Last night I longed for you to touch me with your hands. I now understand that what I truly longed for, you have already given me. I am forever changed by your unending love for me. And my devotion to you, to your love, is forever unending as well."

"Radha, my khushi, my happiness, I am so pleased you understand." Krishna then moved towards her and kissed her on the forehead. This time she did not feel her desirous ache for him, but instead was filled with a magnificent love for him, for life, for herself, and for all other beings in the world. Looking into his eyes, she felt complete peace and total bliss.

Later, Radha awoke in her own bed. At first she smiled and stretched luxuriously as if she had just enjoyed something wonderful. But then in the middle of the stretch, she froze as the memory of her last encounter with Krishna came flooding back.

Her smile widened and for the first time in her marriage, Radha turned towards her husband and cuddled up next to him, enjoying the warmth of his body and even the slight scent of garlic wafting off his skin. She closed her eyes, breathing it all in, and felt her insides, and her passion, rumble with hunger.

For the first time in their marriage, Abhimanyu smiled in his sleep.

RESTORING PASSION:
THE MYTH OF RADHA

Radha is the incarnation of the Hindu goddess Lakshmi, the Supreme Goddess. She is the beloved consort to Krishna, who is the incarnation of Vishnu, The Supreme God. Together they perform the *Rasa Lila,* or The Dance of Divine Love. *Rasa* means 'nectar' or 'sweetness' and *Lila* means 'act.' The closest translation of Rasa Lila is 'the sweetest act,' suggesting both a sexual and a Divine union.

Radha and Krishna met when they were children, who then grew up and went on to live their lives separately. Radha was a beautiful woman, and like many maidens of her time, became a *gopi,* or milkmaid. Krishna was a stunningly handsome man, known to be a wandering bachelor, going from town to town enjoying the company of the ladies. He could often be seen with several gopis at once—a metaphor for the idea of the creator being enamored of his creations. When Radha and Krishna met as adults, their passionate love ignited instantly and their epic love began.

It is not written that Radha and Krishna physically consummated their love. Rather it is most often described as a divine love, presented in allegorical, poetic, and mysterious terms. Their union is alluded to and left up to the reader to ponder. In this way, the myth skillfully teases and fascinates us and we become enthralled by their magnificent love story. We are left wanting more, hoping for their passion to materialize not only between them, but also in our own life.

In many ways, their story teaches us that the desire for sexual union is but an illusion. Their flirting, courtship, and earthly affair is symbolic of the desire and passion we have to become one with God. It is our perceived separation from the Divine that causes all of our earthly longings for connection and love.

THE DANCE OF
DIVINE LOVE

The Rasa Lila is not a physical dance. It is an entirely spiritual experience, an enactment of the Union between the lover and The Beloved, the Feminine and the Masculine, the human soul and God. But, paradoxically, the way we enter into this spiritual dance of love is through the physical act of lovemaking.

In order for the Divine to *dance,* or make love with each one of us, it must expand Itself and take the form of many souls at once. These mystical expansions of the Divine are not ordinarily noticed by us on a conscious level. Here on earth, it appears to us that we are only satisfying a corporeal urge, satiating our physical hunger, and experiencing an ordinary pleasure with another human being. For many, there is no deeper meaning beyond the physical, sexual act itself.

But for those who wish to experience passion as a higher and more sacred event, we understand that The Divine resides in each one of us, and is us. When we make love, we are doing so with both our physical bodies and the Sacred Essence of The Divine that resides within our physical bodies.

The reason this sweetest act is called a dance is because all of creation actually *is* dancing. One force is always spinning around another, as opposites attract and repel each other. Where one force expands, another contracts. At the core of all of life, it is one big Divinely choreographed dance. And the union of the two principal forces, the Feminine and the Masculine, is based on the sacred desire to become whole. The engine of the world is fueled by this desire.

Each time we made love, it seemed that we grew closer and closer on all levels. We came to know each other's bodies so well that to say that we anticipated what the other desired would be an understatement. We were as one, riding out waves of physical pleasure together, bodies so entwined that it was hard to distinguish where his body began and mine ended.

And each time we made love, I could sense that there was something else in the room with us. Perhaps it was the hint of reverence that we felt for each other's body, or the way we approached each other with fire in our eyes. Whatever it was, it remained eclipsed and hidden by the shadow of our physical desire. It was persistent though, and like incense, it wafted all around us. It was a sweet, delicious

There is a tension that attraction creates, which is expressed as passion. In essence, passion is a kind of suffering. In fact, the Latin root of the word passion is *pati*, which means to suffer or endure. Anyone who has ever experienced an intense sexual, emotional, or creative passion knows this to be true.

The hunger for sacred sexual passion is voracious, ravenous, and insatiable. It is greedy and demanding. But it is also delicious—and uncomfortably enjoyable. We lose all common sense. We cease thinking rationally and become obsessed with only one thing in mind—uniting our body, mind, and soul with another.

This kind of passion is not only an earthly experience. It is an ecstasy, a delight, a blissful transcendence. Radha's love for Krishna is not limited to the love of a woman and a man; it is simultaneously a Divine love, not of this world. Her love takes on a holiness and becomes Sacred.

Like Radha, every woman longs for this same deep, all-encompassing passionate union. This hunger is like an ancient ache that permeates everything, creating a desire for a rapturous love affair to happen. Perhaps you are feeling this longing in your life now. Perhaps you crave to be fully desired, taken into the arms of another that leaves you gasping for air, grasping for anchor, grabbing for something out of reach, and ravenous for more. If so, the goddess Radha will help you.

presence that was hoping to be asked in . . . but neither of us ever extended the invitation.

We never spoke about it, this Divine presence that was witness to our union. We never wondered aloud, nor naïvely brought it up. But it was there. We were like adolescents, playing at love, and not until we invited this presence in, would we ever elevate our love to a higher level. It would always remain earthly.

In the end, the relationship did not last—how could it have? We did not invite into our love the most honored Guest. A relationship without the presence of the Divine remains satisfied with only sex for a dance partner. That is never enough to quench the soul's passionate thirst, or satiate its hunger. I know this now.

LONGING
FOR RADHA

A woman wants to be celebrated, adored, and cherished, yes—but what she desires most in a relationship is to be the object of her beloved's deepest passion. This feeling arises out of an ancient and instinctual awareness of your feminine sacredness. Like Radha, you are the embodiment of the Supreme Essence of the Universe. Without this primary life force, the Universe would not exist. So essential is this essence that even Krishna (God) desires and requires it. The Hindu scriptures say that the whole of creation longs for Krishna (the Divine), but *he* longs only for Radha (the human soul).

It is usually women who seek a deeper connection, inspiring closeness and bringing the sacred into a relationship. It often does not occur to men to think of women—or relationships in this way. Gone are the ancient goddess temples and the traditional teaching that women are goddesses in physical form. Our modern culture celebrates material possessions, career and status—not The Goddess within women, nor the sacredness of sexual union.

But all is not lost. If you begin to see yourself as a goddess, you will be treated as one. If you believe that you are beautiful, others will see you as such. If you treat your body as sacred, precious, and holy—so will your beloved. There are many hymns, litanies, and songs dedicated to Radha that model this reverence for the female as Goddess. They praise and declare Radha's specialness, her extraordinary beauty, and acknowledge that she is sacred above all. Remember that while these are all offered as a tribute to only one woman, they are at the same time prayers of devotion to The Goddess that is all women.

A SEXUAL
GODDESS

All the world's Goddess temples may have crumbled to dust, and the ancient Feminine wisdoms are but a faint whisper today, but women remain the teachers and leaders of sacred love, exalted passion, and Divine Union. It is through you that a man learns how to love you *as* The Goddess. Teach him this loving like a priestess would; lead your beloved into the temple that is your body. Reveal to him your passion, and you will reveal to him The Goddess within.

When I share this advice with my female clients, I am often met with silence. In a very soft voice, many ask me "How do I do this?" This question touches my heart as I know why they don't understand. For many women, becoming a priestess and sharing your body in a sacred way is not only a far-fetched idea; it is an entirely mysterious undertaking with no modern reference point to go by. This is what I share with them in response.

Long ago, in the Eastern lands, there were women who became temple priestesses. Some scholars have referred to them as sacred prostitutes, but the service they provided was much more spiritual than this term signifies. It is thought that these women were fulfilling customs for goddess worship and even fertility rites. One rite was reserved for the High Priestess only—the sacred marriage or *hieros gamos*, which is the Greek term for 'Holy Union.' During this ceremony, the High Priestess sexually joins with the King, symbolizing the joining of Earth and Spirit, the human soul and God.

The priestesses all lived in the temple together, enjoyed beauty treatments, studied the Feminine Mysteries and learned the delights of transcendent ecstasy and the rituals of sacred sex. They were revered, honored, and respected. Living in the house of The Goddess, they were believed to be the incarnations of Her. It was through the temple priestesses that a man could make love to The Goddess.

Imagining God to have a Feminine aspect is a radical idea to some today. But the idea that The Goddess is sexual may shock even more. After all, Western religion and culture have virginized The Goddess, stripping Her of all sexuality, desire, and passion. But I assure you, The Goddess is sexual—in fact, She is very sexual. In order for Her to birth the world, she, as the essence of The Feminine, must join with The Masculine. Even Radha, who is considered to be the ultimate personification of the Supreme Goddess of the Universe does not hide her sexual attraction for Krishna; it is the very basis of her story.

Goddess sexuality is expressed in the way you move, anoint, adorn, and express your female body. It is also how you feel about your body and how you share it with another.

DANCE OF
THE SERPENT

When a woman asks me how to become a Goddess/priestess in her own life, I suggest that she dance like one. There is another kind of dance that you can do in addition to the Rasa Lila. It is the dance of the Goddess/priestess. I love to dance this, as it is a very private and personal ritual reserved for me alone—and for my lover.

When I was younger and did not know of my sacredness, I danced this way at bars and clubs, attracting attention—most of it unwanted. By dancing this way in public, I was quickly introduced to its power. Today, I would never perform this kind of dancing in public, and even have a difficult time doing so in the company of just other women. It is too intimate, too sexual, and entirely too sacred an expression of my feminine power to reveal to anyone other than those for whom I am dancing: my lover and the Divine.

In doing this dance, I feel the serpent of energy that sleeps at the base of my spine awaken from her slumber. She is hungry and goes in search of what will satiate her desires. This energy is called the Kundalini, a latent feminine energy that remains inactive until awakened. It is often referred to as the Serpent Fire.

This dance is an aphrodisiac. It is a circular, rhythmic, sensual, and erotic dance, much like belly dancing or trance dancing. It is intended to ignite your sexual fires, arouse your passions, and transforms you in such a way that you *become* The Goddess. How you dance is the way that She moves through the world—swaying, undulating, and gracefully flowing. The Goddess moves to slow rhythms and earthly beats. She is the call of the drum, the sweetness of the flute, and the shake of the rattle. She is the pulse of our blood, the heat of our skin, and the energy of our passions.

Since ancient times, all cultures have performed some type of sacred dance, but none so lovely as the Indian Temple Dance. Performed within the temple as a gift for the presiding deity, this dance is a form of devotion. Many bas-relief sculptures in India depict the gorgeous, lush bodies of the temple dancers and their celestial counterparts who dance along with them in heaven.

The temple dancers are elaborately adorned, perfumed, and hennaed to celebrate The Divine. They move to the music with their hands in special mudra positions, twisting their lovely bodies into many stylized positions. Every movement has meaning. I imagine Radha doing such a dance in honor of her beloved Krishna.

The Serpent Dance is a way to get your body in the mood. You will feel sacred, sexual, and feminine as you move your hips in a slow figure eight and you dissolve into the music. This dance is an offering of your body, given as a sacred gift to your lover. The Goddess desires to be united with Her lover, too, and She does this through you.

Perhaps you would like to try this sacred way of dancing for yourself? It is an incredibly pleasurable experience that can profoundly change the way you feel about yourself as a woman. It will heighten your awareness of your body, your sexuality, and your feelings of intimacy. It even has the power to help you begin healing any sexual reluctance you may have. If you feel comfortable to offer this dance to your lover, I assure you that it will be experience you both will not forget.

Choose where and when you feel best about dancing. Sometimes I dance in front of a mirror, sometimes in the dark, and sometimes naked. You may feel a bit awkward, shy, or afraid at first, so give yourself time to get used to the Serpent Dance.

Begin by moving your body like a belly dancer, without worrying about your choreography. Imagine as you dance that you are making love. The dance starts off slowly, then reaches a climatic point, then slows down again. Listen to the music; let yourself feel it in your body. How does the music feel to you? What parts of your body want to move, what parts don't? Respect everything that your body wishes to do without judgment, shame, urgency or fear—simply experience it.

I like to use music that is slow and rhythmic, with lots of percussion and heartbeat drumming. I love Middle Eastern, Indian, and African music, but choose whatever music is right for you.

Explore using your hands to convey your emotions, feelings, or a message as you dance. Let your hands touch your hips, your belly, your breasts, and your neck. Use scarves, veils, and anklets with bells. Wear a mask. Henna your hands and feet prior to dancing. Apply dark eyeliner around your eyes like the beautiful Radha did. Wear bright red lipstick and nothing else at all. Place a *bindi* (a decorative design or jeweled decoration) between your eyebrows or simply draw a solid red circle there with rouge or lipstick. Tie ribbons in your hair; wear many bangles on your wrists and jewels around your neck. Dance in the dark, in candlelight, or the bright light of day. Dance in a garden under the moon, or indoors or anywhere that calls you. Anoint your feet and hands with scented essential oils. Clap your hands; snap your fingers; use a tambourine or a rattle.

As you dance, you may feel like laughing or crying. Give yourself the emotional space to experience these feelings. They are coming up to the surface so you can be healed. If you acknowledge them, you will be free so that you may love with your whole self. Start simply, go slow, and most of all have fun and let yourself experience the pleasure of the dance.

Dance yourself open, free, alive. Let yourself go. Dance your passion, as the Goddess, as the priestess and as a woman . . . who is in love with herself.

RADHA'S MESSAGE FOR LOVE

Sex is not love, but often sex can be the vehicle to express the love you feel for another—and sex can even inspire love. When you use your body in an intimate way to express love—you are creating a divine union, which is a sacred act of love and elevates your union to that of the lover and The Beloved.

THE GODDESS SPEAKS OF YOUR PASSION

Come to me woman.

It is time to dance with the Beloved. Let us prepare you.

We will henna your hands, and drape you in the sheerest of silks.

We'll fix tiny bells on your feet, and feed you honey

and tea cakes until you are giddy from the sweetness.

And when you are ready, you will drop your veils and dance as only you,

a woman, can dance. With hips wide and circling, and breasts bare and free.

Churn the seas with your swaying, birth the world with your rhythm.

Stir passion—you are the spoon.

Ignite desire—you are the match.

Dance—you are the song.

Dance as if you are the lover, and the Beloved partners only with you.

For you are, and It does.

THE ASSOCIATIONS
OF RADHA

Radha is a sensual woman, with deep, passionate desires. When we work with her essence, it is under a full moon, with deeply aromatic oils, fiery red crystals, and with feathers in our hair.

RUBIES: CRYSTALS OF DESIRE. In addition to its association with royalty, blood, the sun, our emotions and protection, a ruby's deep red hue also symbolizes the inextinguishable fires of passion.

A stone of strength, ruby is one of the four hardest precious gems, second only to diamond, then emerald and sapphire. This strength translates in different ways as the stone can be used to express love, passion, or sexuality. To follow your passions in life takes great fortitude, devotion, and inner strength—and ruby supports this. Sexually speaking, passion, desire and attraction can overwhelm us, overtake us and in a way, weaken us; ruby replenishes what is lost when we are depleted by passion.

Place a ruby in a small glass—such as a shot glass—and then place that in a shallow dish or a bowl of spring water. Let stand overnight and drink the water in small sips to infuse your energy with strength or to ignite the fires of passion.

TOTEM: BIRDS OF A FEATHER. The peacock is a traditional symbol associated with both Krishna and Radha, symbolizing their divine, glorious, and radiant love and passion for each other. Krishna wore a feather on his head to tell the world that his love for Radha was above all else, that she was everything to him.

Peacock is a very mystical totem that activates our inner wisdom. The eye of the feather is sometimes called the 'god's eye' and invites us to see things from a higher, more spiritual place. Peacock wisdom can help you elevate your experiences with your body, your sexuality, and with your intimate relationships.

PASSION MOON. The light of the full moon has been known to affect us on a very deep and mysterious level and is often cited as the cause for lunacy, madness, shape-shifting, and many other supernatural events. While that may all seem like far-fetched claims, there is one effect of the full moon that is inarguably true: it is the moon of lovers. Full moons have been held responsible for many love affairs, liaisons, and other sexy happenings for centuries. The term for this is 'moonstruck,' and we know that when lovers have been moonstruck, they are no longer responsible for their actions. They succumb to desire, lose all inhibitions and go crazy for love—not such a bad thing, really.

The full moon is a time when most women are feeling more inclined for sex. Hormone changes and the great, magnetic pull of the moon during this time make for some passionate nights—and days for that matter.

Plan a romantic interlude with your beloved during the full moon. If you are not with a partner at this time—plan it for yourself by scheduling a long massage, a soak in a hot tub, and dinner out at your favorite restaurant. The full moon is a moon of wild passion, forbidden luxury, lushness, fullness, sensuality, and romance—you have permission to enjoy it all!

THE RITUALS
OF PASSION

Preparing Your Anointing Oil

According to the healing science of India, Ayurveda, there are seven major and hundreds of minor swirling vortices of energy in our body called *chakras*, which means 'wheel' in Sanskrit. Each chakra governs a specific physical, emotional, and spiritual function of the body and they are profoundly affected by scent. You can work with each chakra to activate your passion; their color, name and coordinating essential oils are listed below.

Mix the essential oils as listed into a 10 ml glass bottle—one bottle for each of the seven chakras—and then fill each bottle with carrier oil such as jojoba, rice bran, grape seed, or meadowfoam seed oil. Label each bottle accordingly and gently shake, then store in a cool, dark place.

- ❖ deep red root or *muladhara* chakra; 6 drops each of vetiver and patchouli essential oils

- warm orange sacral or *svadisthana* chakra; 6 drops each of ylang ylang and sandalwood essential oils

- bright yellow solar plexus or *manipura* chakra; 6 drops of frankincense and myrrh essential oils

- rich green heart or *anhata* chakra; 6 drops each of rose and pink lotus essential oils

- vibrant blue throat or *vishuddhi* chakra; 6 drops each of blue chamomile and lavender essential oils

- luminescent indigo third eye or *anja* chakra, 12 drops of blue lotus essential oil

- radiantly white crown or *sahasrara* chakra, 6 drops each of white lotus and jasmine essential oils

Anoint each chakra with a drop of oil for passion. Take a moment in between the anointing of each chakra; savor the sensations that the oils evoke.

Creating an Altar for Passion

The color theme for your altar in honor of Radha is pink for the sweetness and beauty of love, and red for sensuality and passion. Using these colors together reminds you to love passionately, and bring passion into your lovemaking. Upon your altar, place red and pink flowers such as rose, carnation, tulip, orchid, or hibiscus. If you cannot use real flowers, silk flowers or photos of them can be fine.

Leave sweet treats for Radha to eat and beautiful baubles such as rings and bracelets for her to adorn herself with—especially those with rubies. Display your ruby crystals as well, to activate and amplify passion. Drape silks and laces across the altar, and lay peacock feathers to symbolically honor her totem. Light a red or pink candle to bring in love and ignite your passion.

Anoint your breasts and lower belly with your oil blend as you say this invocation for passion. Note: this can also be used to call in new love/passion or to strengthen the love/passion in an existing relationship:

From the place of my dreams
I call upon thee.
Lover, friend, teacher and mate.
My heart awaits your love,
my body awaits your touch and my soul awaits your fire;
come to me now.

Bathing in the Sacred Waters of Radha

Radha's special bathing ritual involved sneaking off to immerse herself in the cool waters of a lake in the early morning. Every now and then, I too enjoy a cool bath on a hot afternoon. The cool water is refreshing, stimulating and reviving. While we normally think of a cold bath to quell passion and desire, this is a *cool* bath—in between warm and cold, that can feel very sensual and delicious.

Try this alone or with a lover after you have enjoyed each other's bodies. If you are enjoying this bath during a colder climate, please remember to keep the temperature of your bathroom warm, so as not to cause yourself a chill. Immerse slowly into the waters, soak and enjoy.

What you will need:

❖ your anointing oil
❖ pink rose petals

What to do:

Draw a cool bath—not cold, but cooler than a warm bath. Anoint your body in several places; heart, thighs, breasts, feet or anywhere else that feels right for you. Scatter the pink rose petals into the water, as you say this blessing:

Sacred waters,
blessed be.
Ignite my passion,
and let it grow.
I find delight in love,
and sensuality.

Special intention for your bath:

Enjoy the feeling of the cool water on your skin; notice how your body feels compared to a hot bath.

The Serpent's Fire: Anointing Rituals for Chakras

Like a ladder, your chakras act as rungs for the Kundalini, or serpent's fire energy to climb. The Kundalini has a masculine and feminine essence that, when united, ignites our sexual fires of passion and desire. By activating the chakras, we can draw the Kundalini upwards towards and out of the crown chakra where the two essences, masculine and feminine, unite to become one. This practice is a wonderful way to jumpstart dormant sexual desire and passion or to strengthen an already active sexual drive. You can also use your special anointing oil blends on the seven chakras as you recite the affirmations. This is something that can be enjoyed alone or with a lover to create a heightened sexual experience.

Here are descriptions for each of the oils and their associated chakras, to deepen your experience with them.

ROOT CHAKRA. Patchouli and vetiver are both deep, earthy scented essential oils associated with the root chakra, which connects us to the earth and supports all of the primitive impulses of life such as sleeping, eating, survival, and sex. Passion has its origins in this chakra, as it is activated by the primal urge for sex. Use patchouli and vetiver to anoint the area of your pubis bone and inner thighs to activate passion as you say this affirmation:

I stand upon the earth, which grounds my sleeping passion. I awaken it now,
and encourage her serpentine journey upwards and towards the Light,
where she will feed on the nectar of Divine Love.

SACRAL CHAKRA. As the serpent begins to rise, it travels to the sacral chakra where the primitive urges become more refined. Sleep now includes lucid dreaming, eating becomes dining, survival turns into thriving, and sex matures into making love. Sweet ylang ylang and soft sandalwood essential oils are both associated with the sacral chakra, which supports the sexual and reproductive functions of the body. Use these oils to anoint your hips, the skin over your ovaries, and the area of your womb to transmute the fires of passion from their animal-like beginnings up towards the heart as you say this affirmation:

I am a creatress, a Goddess on earth. From me life is possible,
desire is possible, and love is possible. My passion leads me higher to a Divine Love.
I am a Goddess on earth.

SOLAR PLEXUS CHAKRA. Resinous frankincense and earthy myrrh essential oils are associated with the solar plexus chakra, which manages our will and self-esteem. The solar plexus is the place of our inner power, which is often activated during lovemaking. This activation can call forth the inner goddess, along with the profound healing of deeply-seated issues having to do with sexuality. Many women override this activation and stifle their power—and their healing during sex. Use these essential oils to anoint the area just below your heart in the upper part of your abdomen as you say this affirmation:

I acknowledge my power, appreciate my beauty
and ignite my inner fire.
I am woman, lover, and goddess divine.

HEART CHAKRA. Fragrant rose and delicate pink lotus essential oils are associated with the heart chakra, which manages both the physical organ and its energetic field. The heart is the throne upon which Love sits, and where you want your passion to sit as well. Once in the temple of your heart, passion becomes an invocation to the Divine and lovemaking becomes a prayer. The heart is where your passion is transformed into the sacred. Use these essential oils to anoint the area just between your breasts to draw your passion into your heart, and then anoint your breasts as you say this affirmation:

Everything is love; that which is the beginning,
and that, which is the end.
And all things in between are also love. I am love.

THROAT CHAKRA. Honeyed blue chamomile and sweetly herbal lavender essential oils are associated with the throat chakra, which is the place of the expression of our will and a conduit for receiving information. When activated during sex, this chakra uses the inner power of the solar plexus and the vision of the third eye to express our true passionate self. Use these oils to anoint the area of your throat—front and back as you say this affirmation:

My voice is an expression of The Goddess;
She speaks through me, as me. I freely express my true, inner self
and bring this forth both physically and spiritually.

THIRD EYE. Intensely floral blue lotus essential oil is associated with the third eye, the place of cosmic awareness and psychic vision. The third eye manages the pineal gland, which is said to glow with phosphorescence in the living brain. When this organ is energetically activated, you are able to see beyond this earthly realm into all others. Here your passion expands into all dimensions as you prepare to merge with the Divine. Use this oil to anoint the area just between and slightly above your brows to expand your passion beyond the physical as you say this affirmation:

I am a part of all things; I am endless, and free of form. As I expand,
so does my passion, becoming the vision of the Divine;
a dream of love that is made manifest while I am here on Earth.

CROWN CHAKRA. Spicy sweet white lotus and deeply floral jasmine essential oils are associated with the crown chakra, where we are connected to the Divine, Heaven, and enlightenment. When your passion reaches the top of the ladder, it is now on sacred ground in the presence of all that is holy. Some people have experienced an altered state of bliss—what we might call ecstasy—when the serpent energy reaches this rung on the ladder. The chakra exists on the top of the head, near the part of the skull called the soft spots, or fontanels, on a newborn baby. These soft spots are where the skull bone has not yet fully closed over the brain to allow the skull plates to float during childbirth when the head comes down the birth canal. Mystically speaking, these openings allow the infant to slowly become more present on earth. Using these oils, anoint the top of your head in the very center to guide your passion to merge with The Divine as you say this affirmation:

I am always standing in the Light of The Divine,
which guides my passion towards
Its Light where I will merge with The Beloved.

Inspiration for Your Journal

❖ Write about your deepest love relationship; was there passion, spiritual connection, desire?

❖ Write about if have you ever done something risky in the name of love. If you have not, would you?

❖ Write about your deepest, most private sexual desires. Have you ever shared your private desires with a lover? If you have not, how come?

You, who are beauty itself,
can only be described as flowers;
lips as red as a rose, cheeks as soft as a petal
and eyes shaped like the lotus leaf.

You, who inspires the deepest desires within me,
and the most passionate of love within me,
should know, that because of you,
I am driven to conquer the universe in your name.

VO

CHAPTER NINE

THE GODDESS
KASSANDRA

I want to see you.
Know your voice.
~Rumi

KASSANDRA WAS ALONE IN THE TEMPLE. Only the sound of the swans swimming gracefully outside kept her company. The cool night breeze floated in through the open columns and was a delightful respite after the day's heat. She walked through the large main room, lighting the hanging oil lamps. Their golden light gave everything a soft glow and cast flickering shadows on the walls and across the floor.

Kassandra made little sound as she walked. Her bare feet padded softly across the cool stone-paved floors and her long white dress made barely a whisper. The faint tinkling of the tiny bells on her long braided golden belt as it swayed back and forth against her thighs was all that announced her presence.

Suddenly she stopped, feeling that someone was watching her.

"Who is here?" she called out, the tiny hairs at the nape of her neck standing on end and her heart beating fast. Worshippers knew that the temple must be empty by nightfall; perhaps a youth had stayed inside on a dare.

Kassandra stood perfectly still, her blood pulsing loudly in her ears. She could feel the presence of someone, watching her. Her nerves were on edge with alarm. She often had feelings about things, but this time it felt quite strong. Finally, when the sense of being watched subsided, she continued with her duties.

Kassandra was of noble birth; she was a princess of Troy. Her parents had hoped she would marry a king and become a queen in her own right, but she had other plans for her life. She had always wanted to become a priestess. It was the thought that remained constant in her mind and the one thing that her parents could not persuade her to give up. From childhood on, she had always known that her life's purpose was to serve Apollo.

"Father," she had once pleaded after a long argument about her decision, "please trust me on this. It is the one thing I know for sure—*I am to be a priestess someday.* I am to serve Apollo!"

"Daughter," her father sighed, weary from the ongoing dispute, "you say that you are sure so often and about so many things. Just last week you were sure, absolutely sure, that it was going to storm and yet the sun stayed bright all day."

"But it rained the very next day, father!" Kassandra defended herself.

"Not the point, daughter, not the point," the king said with rising irritation. Gathering his emotions and composure to soften his tone towards his beautiful but willful daughter, he asked her once more to consider marriage to the foreign prince who was visiting. Kassandra did not reply, but instead stood in front of the household altar mouthing silent prayers to Apollo with her eyes closed. Kassandra could sense her father's disappointment in her as he left the room, shaking his head. She could also feel his worry about her future.

Apollo ruled over the sun and the daylight that it brought. And like the rays of the sun, he also oversaw the illuminating properties of intuition, truth, and prophecy. Followed constantly by nine lovely muses, he was a bit of a playboy, enjoying the company of earthly women most of all. Kassandra worshiped him, and truly—although she was not entirely aware of it—she loved him in the way a woman loves a man. It was this earthly love that inspired her to become a priestess of Apollo, hoping one day to become the Pythia, the Oracle of Delphi.

Apollo himself chose the Oracle, and once chosen, she was permitted to inhale the sacred fumes. These mysterious, aromatic fumes drifted out as a vaporous mist from within a deep chasm on the temple grounds. Any woman who was to become the Pythia had to be an intuitive, gifted with prophecy. After her purification and initiation, she could then hear the words of Apollo—directly, intimately, and distinctly. Oh, how Kassandra longed to hear his voice in her head, to know his thoughts, and to be *the one who is the voice of the divine.*

Hoping to please the God in the highest of ways, Kassandra had performed the rites of the priestess to perfection. Much to her parent's dismay, she was initiated into the temple with honor on her sixteenth birthday. Apollo loved archery, so like a girl with a crush, Kassandra had practiced his favorite sport until her fingers bled. This made it painful for her to play the lyre, his favorite instrument. Learning that his sacred bird was the swan, she volunteered every day to feed them, although they honked loudly and flapped angrily at her each and every time.

Every evening, after the worshippers had departed, Kassandra sang heartfelt *paeans*—prayers in his name—as she tended to the grand temple built in his honor. A rustle in the shadows brought her mind sharply back to the present moment. Perhaps it was a mouse, or worse—a rat? Kassandra did not like rats, and closed her eyes to steady herself and whispered a prayer. "O, Apollo, my protector! I ask for protection in your temple house. Bid these nightly disturbances away from here, bid them leave."

Upon opening her eyes, she suddenly felt an unnatural calm come over her. A sense of peace and well-being spread throughout her body. She continued on with her duties, undisturbed for the rest of the evening.

After her duties were complete, Kassandra lay down on her thin, simple pallet, listening to the familiar night sounds of the temple. As the last of her conscious thoughts slowly left her mind, she whispered only one word before sleep took her: "Apollo."

Kassandra lay dreaming of swans and archery, her brow slightly furrowed as she floated in the dreamspace of her mind. From the shadows of her room, a male figure stepped forward and moved towards her.

"She looks lovely as she sleeps, does she not?" the man said to the playful muses dancing silently behind him. Without taking his eyes off Kassandra, he bid them to stop dancing with a preoccupied wave of his hand. They did so immediately and waited motionless at his side. He wanted to touch the sleeping woman but refrained, worried that she might wake. He wanted to gaze upon her a while longer before they met face to face.

So lovely were her full, pink lips as they pouted in slumber that he was tempted to kiss her right then and there. Her chest rose and fell with each breath, and her bottom lip opened slightly with every soft puff of air. He moved closer towards her to breathe in her scent. How he loved the scent of mortal women!

Unable to resist, he placed his hand softly, carefully, upon her heart and felt it beat beneath his palm. He closed his eyes, becoming as still as the statues in the temple, each one marvelously carved in his likeness.

The muses took this opportunity to fade back into the shadows, bored with his interest in yet another earthly woman.

Kassandra slept throughout Apollo's visit, so deep and peaceful was her dream of him.

The God finally left her bedside with a smile on his face and walked back into the shadows to chase after the mischievous muses. He spoke in low tones to the sleeping Kassandra as he walked away, "I shall see you soon, my sweet priestess."

The next morning Kassandra woke with a light heart and a feeling that something amazing was going to happen on this day. She stretched her body out of bed, dressed in the simple, yet elegant garments of a priestess and began her duties.

First, she brought a bowl of fresh, warm goat's milk along with two slices of barley bread that had been dipped in wine to the altar where a large stone statue of Apollo stood. The milk sloshed in the shallow saucer as she carried it, and a few drops fell to the floor whereby a lone, stray cat that had been following her quickly lapped it up. She also placed a dish of sticky sweet honeycomb and several soft figs on the stone shelf. Above all of this she carefully laid a sheer linen cloth to keep away the flies—and the cats.

She then climbed a tall ladder propped up against the tall statue and steadied her-self on the highest rung. She shook out Apollo's robe, which was made from yards and yards of tightly woven white fabric, arranging it just so around his broad shoulders and strong arms, letting it drape to the floor. From his head, she removed the dried leaves of a laurel wreath and replaced them with fresh, fragrant, green ones.

Darting her eyes around the temple room and seeing no one, she pressed her warm cheek to the cold stone of her beloved god's face for just a moment and then climbed down the ladder, storing it away behind the wall. Unseen in the shadows of his own statue, Apollo smiled and touched his face, as if he could feel her cheek pressed to him. He smiled as he watched her walk away.

The day went on easily. Kassandra and the other priestesses cleaned and performed chores throughout the temple and then came together for the afternoon meal. Eventually it was time to prepare for worship. The people would gather soon as the sun fell low in the sky and end their visit once it had set. They would all go home and have a meal together and do the things that families and loved ones do. They would eat good food and share stories of their day. Afterwards the mothers would sit by the fires and mend shirts and robes while their young children played close by. Husbands would worry about the household ledgers and crops, and older daughters would daydream of suitors and marriage. Kassandra felt a pang of longing for her own family and wondered what they were doing at that very moment.

As her mind was wondering this, Apollo stepped out from a dark corner and stood in front of her. Not recognizing him and thinking he was an early arrival for the evening service, she was about to ask him to wait outside when he suddenly took her in his arms and placed his hand over her lips, silencing her before she could utter a sound. Kassandra struggled in his arms, confused and suddenly afraid.

"I am Apollo," he whispered in her ear, his face close to hers.

Kassandra's mind whirled in surprise and disbelief. Had it not been for the sight of many swans that made their way into the shade of the temple and sat quietly at the man's feet, she would have screamed an alarm. Apollo released his hand from her mouth and relaxed his hold on her, enjoying the closeness of her body.

Several muses walked out from the shadows to stand with the swans. Startled, the birds honked softly and then settled themselves quietly under a flurry of softly falling feathers.

Kassandra watched as if in a trance as Apollo placed a single finger upon her forehead just between her brows. She felt her mind go blank only to be instantly filled with hundreds of images that were not generated from her own thoughts. Like a river rushing, images, feelings and awareness all flew past her and she felt herself grow dizzy.

Having wondered just moments ago about her family, she now saw exactly what they were doing at that very instant. She could feel their feelings and was made sharply aware of their thoughts as fast as they were having them. She then became aware of the thoughts and feelings of the other priestesses, even the ones that had long ago traveled both far away and to nearby villages. Kassandra saw images of her own birth, and felt the joy that her parents felt when they first laid eyes upon her. She felt her own newborn uncertainty at the moment she took her first breath. And then she was aware of the deep love, admiration, and secret respect that her father had for her—this made her smile and cry all at once.

Dizzy, fascinated, and curious, Kassandra looked up into Apollo's eyes and saw in her mind's eye how he had watched her sleep. She felt his desire for her as if it were her own, causing her to blush deeply. Kassandra's mind was filled with so much awareness and vivid insight that she felt as if she would collapse. Just then Apollo removed his finger from her forehead and she fell to her knees.

Before she lost consciousness, Kassandra said one word, "Apollo."

When her eyes opened, it was late into the night, but for Kassandra, time had not passed at all. Confused, she sat up on her sleeping pallet and saw that she was alone. She wondered in her mind, have I been dreaming?

A voice answered her from inside of her own mind. "No, Kassandra, you did not dream today's events. I came to you, my most devoted priestess, and I shall come to you again if you so desire."

Kassandra felt her face flush hot, recognizing the voice of Apollo and recalling how she had felt his desire for her. She was surprised to feel her own desire begin to blossom like a rose in the heat of the day. Apollo laughed affectionately inside her mind, "So the answer is yes," he said. "I shall see you when the moon is full, Kassandra. Until then, enjoy the gift that I have given you." Without another word, Apollo left her thoughts, and she was alone in her own mind.

Kassandra fell into a deep and dreamless sleep. In the morning she woke with a hundred voices in her head and a thousand images running through her mind—so many that she could barely keep them straight. Holding her head in her hands, she cried out, "Too much, too much!" The voices subsided to a soft murmur and the images became passing thoughts. Relieved, she rose to dress.

Throughout the day, Kassandra was surprised to find that she was able to know the internal workings and see the personal images in everyone's mind. At first it was strange and disorienting, but after a while she learned that she could adjust the flow of information and use it to her benefit, and in the service of others. Kassandra was beginning to enjoy the gift that Apollo had given her and smiled to herself. She was looking forward to seeing him again in several days, when the moon was full.

On the night of the full moon, Kassandra anointed herself with precious oils. She had fasted the whole day and was feeling lightheaded. It caused her newfound perceptions to become sharper and clearer, and she rested in the shadows at the foot of the statue with the thoughts of others blowing across her mind like an insistent wind.

"Kassandra," a voice called out from behind her. She whirled around and jumped up to stand face to face with the handsome god, Apollo. She was not startled. Now that she was unafraid, Kassandra studied his face, his physique, and his eyes. He was breathtakingly good-looking and powerfully built. Apollo stood with grace and ease, knowing that he is so. He knew that he was irresistible to all females, be they goddess, demi-goddess, or human. This gave him a self-satisfied confidence that he wore like a cape draped around him.

"Apollo," Kassandra said, "thank you for the gift that you have given to me, it is most fascinating."

Apollo was suddenly close to her, standing so near she could smell the leather of his garments mixed in with his own scent, which could only be described as an intense, intoxicating maleness unlike any human man. Kassandra closed her eyes, breathed him in, willing herself to stay upright.

"O, priestess, you have caught my eye like no other before you. I desire to kiss you now, and I want to make you mine—would you like to be mine? I shall take you to see Olympus—with your beauty, you will cause such a stir, I am sure of it." He laughed softly and went on, "I shall take you anywhere you wish to go . . . just say yes, Kassandra, priestess of mine."

Kassandra did not need to think about his offer. Her whole life had been one long thought of him, one long event of wanting to know him, to be near him. The words of her heart said yes, but these were not the words that she spoke. What she said next came straight from her head.

"Grant me the gift of prophecy, Apollo, make me the Pythia and I shall be yours."

Apollo looked at her with amusement. "You are cleverer than I thought, priestess of my temple. Are you sure that this is the gift you want from me?"

"Yes, Apollo, for this gift will set me apart from others; it will give me authority. All of my life I have been blessed with knowing things, but only in the mildest of ways. I have always had feelings about what was to be, but no details to share. Thus, no one has ever taken heed of my warnings. I was dismissed as a child. But these last days, living with your gift of heightened insight has deepened my knowing tenfold. With your bestowment of the gift of prophecy, who shall doubt me? I will be a Pythia, one who has been gifted by Apollo himself! No one will ever disbelieve me. O, I beseech you Apollo—this is what I want."

Apollo looked deep into Kassandra's eyes, and then agreed. They walked together to meet with Castalia, a *naiad* water spirit who presided over the sacred pools of the temple. There, the gentle nymph assisted Kassandra to purify her body in the waters, and offered her a drink from a golden cup filled with water from the Cassotis spring which flowed close to the temple walls.

Then the nymph wrapped a long white robe around Kassandra's shoulders and led her into a small, dark chamber where aromatic fumes rose from a large chasm in the earth. Kassandra leaned her body against the water spirit after breathing in the vapors. Her vision became blurred and her legs were unsteady beneath her. She was settled upon a three-legged stool high above the opening in the ground, and there she sat, in the darkness feeling lightheaded and strange.

Having watched her bathe in the moonlight, Apollo had felt his passion for her rise. Anxious to see her in his arms, he unceremoniously placed one of his large hands over her heart and the other upon her forehead.

The moment that he touched her forehead Kassandra had a vision. She could see tomorrow, and the day after, and the day after that as clearly as any thought she'd ever had. Laughing like a child, she put her hands to her head and said, "It is marvelous! My mind is endless. The world is eternal . . . time is expansive!" She then lapsed into an open-eyed trance, watching as a lovely prophecy of her future life with Apollo passed through her mind.

Turning to the Olympian god with her eyes still glazed by the fumes and unfocused in the trance, she asked quizzically, "Is it true—that which I am visioning, now? Is it really so lovely, Apollo?"

"Yes, it is true," he said as he took her into his arms and they kissed for the first time in the darkness of the chamber with the vapor mist of Delphi swirling around them like a vaporous cloud.

In the first few moments of the kiss, Kassandra was flooded with both her passion for Apollo and another epic vision of the future. In that vision, she saw that her father's alliance with a neighboring land was to be betrayed, and war would come to her people. She saw huge armies of men marching into the kingdom—and so many would die, so much would be lost. Kassandra broke from the kiss with a tearful wail. "Apollo," she cried, "this vision . . . it will be the end of my people. I must go to my father and warn him!"

"No," Apollo said, unmoved by her worry and filled only with desire. "Come away with me now. Leave that mortal realm to its mortal outcome. Together we will live forever—I will make it so. You have given me your word," he reminded her, motioning to her to follow him out of the chamber.

"I will do no such thing!" Kassandra cried out. Several of the muses gasped from the shadows.

Afraid, angry and panicked, she screamed, "I revoke my word to you, Apollo. I will not go with you—I must stay and save my people!"

Apollo's eyes instantly lost their warmth. It was as if a storm had suddenly come over them. His rage grew like a tempest that threatened to level the stone walls around them.

"You will not break your word to *me*!" he roared, "I am Apollo!" For the first time in her life, Kassandra felt afraid of her beloved god. "You will regret this, you foolish, earthly woman," Apollo growled.

He moved so fast that Kassandra did not have time to flee. He took her head between his hands and pressed his forehead to hers, right between her brows. The force of his thoughts as they flew from his mind into hers was enough to cause her to swoon. She fell unconscious, going limp at his feet on the damp stone floor.

When Kassandra awoke, she was right where Apollo had left her. She had only one thought—to go and tell her father what was to about to happen.

Once she arrived at the palace of her parents, Kassandra fell at her father's feet, crying as she shared her encounter with Apollo and her horrible vision of war. Her father looked at her in disbelief; he was truly concerned for her sanity. "Kassandra, I am at peace with the king that you speak of, we are allies. Treaties have been signed for years—this is simply not true!"

"Father," Kassandra pleaded, "Apollo himself has given me the gift of prophecy, this *is* going to happen."

Fearing that his daughter had gone mad, he looked at her with a mixture of pity and compassion. "Come, daughter," he admonished her as if speaking to a small child, "let us dine with your mother and be a family tonight. Speak no more of this, quiet your thoughts for now."

It was then that Kassandra realized what had happened. As punishment for her betrayal, Apollo had made it just as before, when no one would believe her. No one would listen to her even though now, she possessed the highest gift of all—prophecy. She would be a witness to the betrayal of the neighboring king without being able to prevent it.

Within a year, the war of her vision came and went. Just as she had foreseen, much was destroyed, and many died, but much was starting to be rebuilt.

Kassandra left her home, the temple, and her service to Apollo. She wandered the lands far away from Delphi, hoping to find peace with her gift and her curse. She eventually learned to trust that some events can neither be prevented nor changed, no matter how much she knew in advance. She continued to share her visions, hoping that one day her voice would be heard. But she had come to accept that it did not matter if others didn't believe in her prophecies; it mattered only that she trusted her own intuition.

RESTORING YOUR VOICE:
THE MYTH OF KASSANDRA

Kassandra was the daughter of King Priam and Queen Hecuba. She was a princess of Troy and priestess of Apollo. Deeply pious, she took a vow of celibacy and devoted her life to service and worship. Beautiful beyond compare, she eventually caught the roaming eye of the god Apollo who became infatuated with her. She agreed to have sex with him, and in exchange, Apollo bestowed upon her one of his most sacred of gifts—prophecy. But once she received it, she withdrew her promise and refused to lie again with him. Angered by her refusal, Apollo turned his gift into a curse: for the remainder of her life, and unto all her descendants, there would be prophecy without heed.

Kassandra is famous for foretelling and warning of the Trojan War, but no one would believe her and the city of Troy was overtaken. In the traditional myth, she was driven mad with the burden of her prophecies and wandered throughout the land, frantic and raving.

While Kassandra is not technically a goddess, she is a powerful archetype for women, as we have historically been silenced by society's patriarchal rules, and often by our own parents—just as Kassandra was by her father. Until the time when marriages were no longer arranged in most parts of the world, a woman had no *voice* in the matters of her own life.

Kassandra represents the madness that comes from the suppression of our inner voice, both in our own lives, and in the world. She symbolizes the unheeded intuition of women, and the silenced voice of The Divine Feminine. The wish of The Goddess is for balance to be in the world, and for us to live out the vision of harmony that She holds for us. For this to happen, we must trust our intuition and allow our voices to be heard.

BECOMING A PRIESTESS
OF APOLLO

While the story of Kassandra is a myth, the oracle priestesses of Apollo were real. In ancient Greece, around the 7th century B.C., the Temple of Apollo at

Delphi was situated on the heart of Gaia, the center or navel of the earth. This location was determined when the god Zeus sent two eagles to scout for such a place, and they intersected in flight above the site. Zeus recognized this as a sign. Interestingly, two earthquake fault lines intersect beneath the temple, speculated to be where the Oracle sat. The Oracle, or Pythia, is named after Pytho, a great serpent dragon of Gaia who guarded the site when it was first erected as a temple to The Great Mother Goddess. Pytho was slain by Apollo when he claimed the temple for his own.

When the opening in the earth was discovered, and the fumes were first inhaled, people from many villages in Greece sought access to it. Here, they thought, was a way to speak to the gods, to hear the voice of The Divine, to know that which is unknowable. They flocked in large groups, jostled and fought with each other to stand over the crack in the small chamber—there was no order, it was mayhem.

Many fell in and died, while others were injured, stampeded by the crowd until a new regulation was set that a single woman would become the one and only Oracle of Delphi. In the highly misogynistic society of early Greece, it was unusual to grant a woman such preference. To this day, there is no evidence as to why they chose a woman for this role. I suspect it was from superstition; the temple had originally been built for and consecrated to The Goddess. Perhaps the violence, deaths, and injuries were seen to be Her displeasure about this chaos. Choosing one woman to be the Oracle would appease The Goddess—and return order to the temple. From among all women, no matter their age or stature, up to three Pythian Oracles were chosen at a time. One became the primary Oracle with two *backups* should the first tire or become ill.

Attended by priests, the Oracle went into a chamber to sit upon a three-legged stool high above a large fissure in the earth where a mysterious, sweet-smelling vapor floated out. Holding laurel leaves and a dish of blessed spring water into which she gazed, she breathed in the fumes and was induced into a trance. Entering into a shamanic, dream-like state, she gave intuitive counsel, made predictions, and prophesized the future. Many reports mention that the Oracle experienced fits, convulsions, or seizures, and that her messages were unintelligible, needing deciphering by the attending priests. Others say that the messages were completely clear and profoundly accurate—I imagine that both were true.

The Pythia held an esteemed and privileged place in Greek society. For the first time in their culture, the voice and visions of a woman were revered and followed. Unlike other women of the time, the primary Pythia was able to own land, appear in public without an escort, and enjoy freedom from taxation. She was housed and supported by the government. Such privileges came with a steep price, as the Oracle often did not live long once her service began. The fumes, the rigorous rituals of purification, the exhausting trance state—or all of these—were extremely draining and led to a rapid decline in health. Early death was the fate of all who served.

Modern geological analysis of the site at Delphi suggests that the fumes may have been gases released by the shifting fault lines under the temple. Evidence of methane, ethane and ethylene—which has a sweetish, musky smell and may account for the reports of the perfumed scent in the chamber—were found in samples of rocks, water, and soil at the site. Inhaling ethylene can cause a hallucinogenic, disassociated trance state, along with vomiting and convulsions. It is hypothesized that the Oracles' decline in health may have resulted from aspirated vomit into their lungs during one of their prophetic convulsions and they died of pneumonia or other respiratory complications. Much controversy still exists over the truth of what actually happened in the temple. We are left only with ancient accounts written by Greek scholars and devotees of that time.

According to these accounts, much preparation went into the rituals at Delphi, which originally occurred only once a year. Later, due to the overwhelming demand to seek her counsel, the Oracle could be consulted only once a month on the seventh day—which was a sacred day to Apollo.

Several days before seekers could see the Pythia, she fasted, abstained from sex, and denied herself sleep. On the day itself, she performed elaborate rites that involved the laurel leaf from the bay tree associated with Apollo, purification bathing, and psychic insight. She cleansed herself in the temple waters, chewed laurel leaves, drank from the sacred spring, and placed a crown of laurel leaves upon her head—all before entering the chamber.

In order to ask the Oracle's counsel, seekers also had to undergo an elaborate ceremonial process of preparation. This process involved four stages:

1. a strenuous journey by foot up the mountainside to the temple

2. interviews with the priests, formulation of the question, rites of purification, and prayers

3. the visit with the Oracle

4. return to their ordinary life with the answers they were given

These rituals and ceremonies readied them to receive the divine inspirations, and perhaps assisted with connecting them to a higher consciousness. It is very much like a shamanic journey into the other worlds. A shaman begins with a question or reason for the journey, and then she prepares for it by praying, singing, burning incense, and calling upon her guides, ancestors, and power animals. Then she travels to the upper or lower worlds to fulfill the purpose or to receive the answers to her questions. Once the journey is complete, she is called back into the ordinary world by drumbeat. Every culture has a version of this journey.

The Pythia was the most respected and powerful woman of her time. Her oracular insight was considered to be the highest authority in all matters. Almost 500 prophetic Pythian statements have survived to this day. Found within ancient texts and engraved upon the walls of the temple, they are the accounts of many important political prophecies, along with advice that has influenced local laws, marriages, worship rituals, farming, and trade and industry. They are the intuitions of a woman, spoken on behalf of the Divine. For the people of The Oracle, the voice of The Goddess—and the voice of woman was respected above all.

HOW YOU CAN HEAR
THE VOICE OF KASSANDRA

In writing this myth, I recalled my own visit to the temple of Delphi while traveling through Greece years ago. I stood where the priestesses may have stood. While the sacred waters have dried up, the fumes no longer rise, and the temple is in ruins, there is clearly a mysterious feeling there while standing upon its sacred ground. Listening to my intuition, I sensed it to be an enchanted place, where the veils between this world and the next are thin. What would it have been like, I couldn't stop from wondering, to sit in the darkness of the Oracle's chamber? What would it feel like to become intoxicated by the sweet-smelling fumes rising from the crack in the earth with the resinous smoke of incense filling that small space? How would it feel to utter powerful messages, cryptic riddles, divine wisdom, and tales of unforeseen futures—and have others listen to my intuitive voice?

Many women may feel like a modern Kassandra. She is the goddess who speaks but is not heard. She is the woman who knows but is not believed. She is the silenced voice of your own intuition, and the unheeded whispers of your soul.

It is interesting to wonder why Apollo stole The Goddess temple of Delphi for himself. Perhaps by overtaking her temple, he thought to extinguish Her voice in the world, but The Feminine voice that speaks through us all cannot be silenced for very long.

I have many female clients who are unable to connect with their intuitive voice, whose intuition has become dormant, gone unheeded, or remains unheard due to trauma or fear. This can occur when a girl or young woman speaks up to reveal that she is being abused. If she is not supported and protected by the adults around her, who either refuse to accept it or do not believe her, she may become silent, burying the pain of her experience deep inside.

Our intuition can also be silenced when our words and feelings are casually dismissed and trivialized, or when our expression of creativity is not celebrated but harshly criticized or ignored. Encountering negativity, we may receive the message, consciously or unconsciously, that our words, thoughts, and feelings are not relevant or significant to others. When we do not feel safe to express ourselves, we silence our voice.

Introversion is another reason for silence. People who are introverted are often very quiet, very private, and share their voice only when they feel comfortable to do so. They are wonderful observers of life, and have a keen ability to read the energy and moods of others and are often quite intuitive. Their silence is not borne of abuse or trauma; it is simply their nature. Patience is a virtue when you know an introverted woman—her voice is a gift that she will only share with her most trusted of friends and loved ones.

Whatever the reason for your silence, the heartbreak of it is profound—but it can be healed and restored to magnificence.

We all heal in individual ways. Emerging from our silence, we can rediscover all that we have to offer once we release the obstacles behind our pain. Listening to our intuition can assure us that we are safe, whole, and worthy. Like Kassandra, we must recognize that the truths of our inner voice need only matter to us.

A quiet and thoughtful client of mine was not at all comfortable expressing herself publically. She liberated her silence in a surprising and delightful way. She studied and became skilled in ASL (American Sign Language) with the hope of one day working in the deaf community. When I watch her signing, she comes alive from within. The shy young woman disappears, and a confident and joyful being who shines from within like a ray of light emerges. I know that The Goddess is speaking through her hands, releasing her voice in this way.

My own voice was silent for quite some time, as I had an abusive childhood. It felt as if I were choking whenever I had to speak in front of a group or express my feelings, even to my closest friends. Even though I was outgoing, I was also soft-spoken— almost inaudible at times. For many years, I did not write, paint, or express myself in any way—so deep was the wounding of my voice. I remember the joyous day that my therapist said to me: "Wow, I can really hear your voice now!" These days, whenever I am teaching, leading a group, or speaking publically, I am often complimented on the clear sound and soothing effect of my voice.

In the Greek tragedy called *Agamemnon*, written by Aeschylus in 458 BC, Kassandra laments her curse and tries desperately to be understood by those who hear only gibberish and riddles in her prophesies. Frustrated, she declares, "My prophecy will veil itself no more . . . let it rise as clear as a fresh wind blowing toward the rising sun." But her madness is never resolved in the play, nor in any other ancient stories ever told of her. Kassandra's myth is one of profound isolation and loneliness. She is not heard, understood, or embraced by her community—she wanders the world alone, rejected for her intuitive gifts.

Let's imagine who she might have become if the opposite had happened—if her voice had been heard, understood, and celebrated. Perhaps she would have become well-loved, not an outcast. Perhaps women's intuition would have been honored, not denigrated for all these centuries since.

Whatever silences your own voice and separates you from your intuition, there are ways to restore the connection. Paying attention to your dreams and flowing with life are two powerful practices that will strengthen your intuitive voice.

DREAMING YOUR VOICE
INTO BEING

The territory of our intuition is wild, uncharted, and strange. It is a realm that is both ancient and elemental in nature. It is the wilderness of our soul where dreaming occurs.

I have kept dream journals for many years and I often refer back to them for guidance and insight. Whenever I record a dream, I find subtle messages that assist me with my current issues, problems, and decisions. I have learned to trust my dreams without question, and so the messages I receive in them have become even more important to me over time.

There are two ways to interpret the imagery of your dreams:

PERSONALLY. Each one of us has a personal set of dreaming symbols that have meanings that make sense only to us. This set of symbols is based on your own life experiences and the significances you have attached to objects and places related to them. For example, beetles of any kind, especially cockroaches, cause me to run in the opposite direction, shrieking in fear. Unfortunately, they tend to show up in my dreams and their appearance catches my attention. I began to notice that they were showing up whenever I was about to run from something or make a major change in my life. They have become my personal symbol for movement, transition, and transformation. I also recognize their appearance in dreams as a way to check in with myself about my fears.

UNIVERSALLY. You can also interpret the imagery of your dreams according to archetypes or symbols that are true for us all. Beetles, especially the scarab, symbolize the cycles of life, cosmic awareness, eternity, and sacred knowledge.

Putting the two together, I intuitively interpret that when a beetle shows up in my dream, I am in the process of facing fear, shifting my life, and learning about myself on a very deep level.

If you do not already keep one, perhaps you would like to journal your nightly dreams. List the symbols you see, along with your intuitive thoughts and feelings about their meaning to you in order to create a personal dream dictionary.

YOUR INNER
ORACLE VOICE

Your intuition is a source of great strength and power. It is your own oracle voice of The Goddess. She is your inner voice, your warrior-self, the knower of the unknown. She is the Divine presence of your heart, who is both speaking to you and listening to you. This presence is a special kind of knowing—often called women's wisdom, or women's intuition. While both sexes have intuition, women seem to be more naturally inclined towards sensing feelings and events around community, intimacy, partnership, and wholeness. These qualities are the underpinnings of your unique feminine intuitive awareness.

Intuition can be thought of as a sensory bridge between our everyday, earthly awareness and the higher transcendent sensing and pure knowing of the spiritual realm. It is the recognition of all things that are subtle, intangible, and ethereal. Intuitive feelings are both physical in nature—that is, experienced by the body—and spiritual, meaning taking place in the higher mind. Intuition can come in a sudden flash of insight or in a dream. It can move backwards through time or forwards into the future. It is not bound by the confines of this realm, because it does not come from this realm.

As a state of pure consciousness and pure perception, intuition cannot be proven or explained. Science tentatively describes it as the ability to make decisions based on a series of lightning-quick observations of our surroundings. But this is like explaining love as a series of chemical reactions. It does not do justice to the incredible complexity and specialness that is intuition.

To follow your intuition is to connect with the deepest and often unknown sources of wisdom of your inner voice—and trust that you will find your way. You surrender your conscious mind so you can listen to your inner voice. Doing so will lead you to make extraordinary discoveries, to have wonderful encounters, and to experience profound transformations.

VISIONS OF
THE GODDESS

While wandering unescorted through an ancient Egyptian temple complex, I suddenly found myself lost. My guide map was of no help, and I did not recognize anything in my surroundings to clue me on which direction would take me back. The crowds had all disappeared, and I was alone in the maze of stone and statuary in the fading daylight. As I walked around, trying to make sense of where I was, I noticed that underneath my rising fear and worry, another feeling was surfacing. It was suddenly an eerie sense of familiarity, although I had never there before. This was my first time in this temple, and my first trip to Egypt. I began feeling an intuitive sureness in my steps, until at last I came to a narrow, darkened stairwell. My whole being said

I often have an image of life flowing like a river whose waters can be gentle and calm. I relax as the waters are easy to wade through. Other times, I see life as a raging river with a gushing current that sweeps me away. I am breathless and drenched, hanging on for dear life. Being "in the flow of life" means accepting the nature of this river, however it is, going along with it, and trusting that it will carry you safely.

I once had a dream that I was driving up the mountain to Idyllwild, CA, a beautiful artists' community east of Los Angeles. I was on the outside lane of the road, with no guardrails. Suddenly my car veered off and began to plummet in slow motion towards the bottom. I panicked, looking for some way to stop the car from falling. I even hit the brakes hard, thinking that would work. In my frenzy, I looked out the

Go up the stairs. As I climbed upwards, through the shadows I noticed artwork on the walls and ceiling depicting the sky goddess Nut and her story.

I arrived in a small gallery overlooking a chapel dedicated to Nut. Her long, dark blue body stretched across the entire ceiling with her arms and legs reaching as far as they could on either side. Her skin was decorated with an array of golden stars that twinkled in the dimness. I sat on a stone bench, looked down into the sanctuary, and closed my eyes as a vision began.

I am a very old woman with dark wrinkled skin that is still soft and lovely. I feel as light and delicate as a bird, but with frail bones and shallow breathing. I am wearing a white gauze cloth that covers my head, shoulders, and arms. I am praying to Nut, and I am not alone. Many other elderly devotees are with me in the gallery, watching the service below us.

As the vision ended, I heard footsteps, and then a man with an Egyptian accent said, "Madam, come down! The temple is closing for today, please come down." As he escorted me back to the entrance of the complex, I chatted with him and asked what the gallery above the sanctuary was used for. He replied, "It was used by the elderly to worship." It gave me chills. Before I left the temple that day, I stopped and gave thanks to The Goddess Nut who had spoken to me by using my own intuitive, inner voice to lead me on a journey to a long forgotten past. This was a gift I will always treasure.

window and suddenly noticed the profound beauty of the mountain from a perspective that I had never seen before. I felt calmed, appreciative, and even peaceful. I was also fascinated with my sensation of falling. I realized then that there was nothing in the world I could do to stop the car from falling, that I would die upon impact, and that this was it for me. I settled back in my seat, surrendering to the experience and in that moment I made a profound decision—I would not die in fear. That is when the car came to a gentle stop, floated in mid-air, and landed ever so softly, back onto the winding mountain road.

To this day, I recall this dream as a reminder to accept that which is—as it is, flowing into and with life, releasing any struggle based on fear.

Like smoke emanating from the temple incense, your intuition and your voice are designed to rise upwards towards the heavens. They are meant to be heard; they deserve to be listened to; and they must be spoken out loud. Rise above your fears; raise your voice in song, poetry, laughter, and verse. Share the knowings of your innermost self, with joy or with sadness—for even the sound of your tears is beloved to The Divine. Do not hold back a single word.

THE GODDESS SPEAKS OF YOUR VOICE

Come to me woman.
I hear your voice in the darkness of your silence,
where your words fall like stones to the bottom of the river.
I am here, in the temple of your heart, lighting candles
in the darkness, where you most fear to go.
Speak to me now, as if your voice were
My own and as if your words were the words of My own heart.
For it is, and they are.

THE ASSOCIATIONS
OF KASSANDRA

Working with the goddess Kassandra and the power of our intuition and voice, we work under the waning phases of the moon, from full to new, and with the white feathers of the most graceful birds. We inhale the smoke of sacred fires and listen to the voice of The Goddess within.

STONE OF HEAVEN. Aqua Aura Quartz is a beautiful translucent and iridescent blue crystal, reminding us of the color of Heaven. Looking into it, one is transported into other, Higher realms where you can experience the activation of your third, or inner eye and receive the messages of The Divine. Aqua Aura Quartz is a wonderful healing stone, adjusting the energetics of your body and repairing the subtle energies of your auric field. This stone is very good for those who have difficulty expressing themselves as it is the color frequency of the throat chakra, or energy center. Meditate with this crystal on your third eye (the area between your brows) for inner vision, or hold it up to your throat to activate and heal your intuitive voice.

SWAN: TOTEM BIRDS OF THE SOUL. While Kassandra traditionally does not have a totem of her own, she shares one with Apollo. The swan is a very lovely, graceful bird that has much spiritual symbolism. Swan helps you to hone your intuition and also assists with altered states of consciousness such as meditation or trance. Swan brings in new ways of thinking, and its gracefulness shows you how to flow with life.

The most common swan is called the Mute Swan and, contrary to what its name implies, it does make some noise, but quite a bit less than other swans who honk and squawk loudly and often. Mute Swan teaches us to use our intuitive voice judiciously, speaking only when we truly *know,* which is something that actually strengthens the muscle of our intuitive voice.

THE WANING MOONS OF INTUITION. There is not one particular moon phase for working with your intuitive voice, but rather several. They are the waning moons, and occur immediately after the full moon and last until the first sliver of the new moon's light.

A perfect time to share inner knowings, intuitive insights, and psychic hunches, the waning moons are also very good for healing, amplifying, and activating your intuitive voice as well, for they are about gathering, building up, and increasing strength.

Meditation, prophecy, tarot reading, and other expressions of intuition are encouraged during the waning phases of the moon. The most potent of all the waning phases for inner knowing is the dark moon, when the veils of the realms are thin and much knowledge may be passed through from the other side.

THE RITUALS
OF VOICE

Preparing Your Anointing Oil

The dried leaves of the bay laurel tree (bay leaf) have always been used as an aromatic incense to induce prophecy and as a magical tea for dreaming. Bay has a lovely, soft, sweet scent and is very soothing to the nerves, along with lavender and mandarin orange essential oils, which all help the mind to relax and the spirit to soar. Anoint your third eye (the area between your brows) to inspire prophetic, psychic dreams and deep, vivid meditations.

Mix the following oils into a 10 ml glass bottle, and then fill with carrier oil such as jojoba, rice bran, grape seed, or meadowfoam seed oil. Gently shake, and store in a cool, dark place.

- ❖ 6 drops of bay essential oil
- ❖ 3 drops of lavender essential oil
- ❖ 6 drops of mandarin orange essential oil

Creating an Altar for Your Voice

The color theme for your altar honoring Kassandra and your intuitive voice is indigo blue or turquoise. Both of these colors are traditionally associated with intuition and the third eye. The bay laurel tree is sacred to Apollo and therefore also to Kassandra. It is associated with honor, triumph, and greatness in ancient Greece and Rome. Place bay leaves upon your altar along with swan feathers (or any white feathers) to honor Kassandra's totem. Display your Aqua Aura Quartz along with anything else that feels right for you.

You can also use the bay laurel leaf for making wishes come true. Write your wish on a large flat, dried bay leaf and place it upon your altar in advance of a full moon. On that eve, take it outside and burn it to ashes, letting them scatter in the wind. It is said that your wish will come true by the next full moon.

Light a blue candle, and anoint your throat and third eye with your special oil blend as you say this invocation:

Voice of mine, be set free;
to speak the words
of my divinity.
Heaven's gate is
open wide
The Goddess speaks
from deep inside.

Bathing in the Sacred Waters of the Oracle

The priestesses of the Oracle bathed regularly for purification. They knew that the influences of the mundane world could have an altering effect on the sacredness of their task of delivering the words of The Goddess.

Our lives are not as mystically inclined as the oracles of Delphi, but we can borrow their ritual baths to purify ourselves of the worldly energies that cling to us at the end of a day to make room for the more astral or ethereal energies of night. Take this bath before bed. As I once learned from a wise woman who lives in the beautiful canyons of Topanga, CA, the last few minutes before we close our eyes for sleep set the tone for the next day—and for our dreaming.

What you will need:

- ❖ dried orange peel
- ❖ dried lavender buds
- ❖ dried bay leaves
- ❖ your anointing oil
- ❖ sea salt

What to do:

Place the orange peel, lavender, and bay leaves into a comfortably hot bath, and then add the sea salt. Place a few drops of your anointing oil in as well. Then anoint your heart, solar plexus, and third eye for more confidence and heart-based intuition, as you say this blessing of the waters:

Sacred waters,
blessed be.
Open my eyes —
let them see;
that which is hidden
and mostly unseen
Now I will know
and now I will speak
of all that is in between.

Special intention for your bath:

Visualize how you would like the next day to unfold. Send out a powerful feeling of wellness, joy, and happiness as you imagine that your voice, your words, and your thoughts will be heard by many.

Becoming the Oracle

Greece was influenced by ancient Egypt and borrowed many of their rituals and customs. The Egyptians loved scenting their environment with aromatics, especially incense, and the Greeks adopted this practice as well. Incense smoke has always been associated with The Divine, and many elaborate recipes have been formulated through the ages to create an atmosphere of holiness, sacredness, and mysticism. Two popular ingredients in many ancient incense formulations were *libanon* (frankincense) and *myron* (myrrh), both of which came from Arabia via Phoenician traders.

The home altar of a Greek person often displayed small statues of their patron goddesses and gods, along with flowers, wine, sweets and other food offering, candles, and a censor to burn the fragrant mixture of resins, roots, leaves, and flowers.

What you will need:

❖ frankincense resin
❖ myrrh resin

* cinnamon bark or powder
* dried bay leaves
* cedarwood chips
* ambrette (musk) seeds if available
* small glass, ceramic, or metal bowl filled with spring water
* candle
* notebook or journal

Preparation:

Decide how much incense you would like to make—enough for one session or several times? You only need a pinch for one session. Mix the ingredients above as follows: $1/3$ resins, $1/3$ leaves and powder, $1/3$ chips and seeds.

Grind all the ingredients together. Resin is sticky and difficult to crush, so I like to use a small coffee grinder. You can also use a mortar and pestle, but let your resins dry out until they lose their gumminess and become brittle, then pulverize them. Whenever I use this method, I feel like I am tapping into an old part of my soul, as if I am one of the ancient perfumers preparing the sacred blend for the Temple of The Goddess.

* Once your incense blend has been made, store it in an airtight glass or metal container. The resins may become moist and sticky again, so open and let them dry out before using—or use them as is. Resin can be burned in either state.

* To burn your incense, drop a pinch or so upon a small square of burning Japanese charcoal. These coals are made especially for incense use, and are the cleanest burning, causing no harmful fumes. I do not recommend self-lighting incense charcoal, as it often contains toxic ingredients.

What to do:

* Sit in a darkened room.

* When your charcoal is glowing orange, place the pinch of incense

upon it and let the smoke waft around you, much like the fumes of the Oracle's chamber.

❖ Light the candle and meditate on a question to which you want to receive an answer. As soon as your inner voice reveals your answer, emerge from the meditation and write it down in your notepad or journal.

❖ Put another pinch of incense on the charcoal and go back into a meditative state to receive further insight on this or another question. Repeat this until you feel that you have received all that you can for now, from your inner oracle. Give thanks for your intuition and your intuitive voice.

I light incense almost every morning as a way of greeting the day, speaking aloud the words of my heart, expressing gratitude and love for The Divine, and for offering prayers to those in need. Practicing this ritual often will train your inner, intuitive voice to emerge more and more, build confidence and set it free.

Inspiration for Your Journal

❖ Write about the quality of your voice; is it loud, quiet, soft, abrasive, clear, mumbled, or . . . ?

❖ Write three things about your voice that you enjoy, and three things that you do not enjoy.

❖ Write about a time in your life when you lost your voice due to worry, doubt, or fear. How did your voice come back?

The voice of my heart will veil itself no more;
by the pain of that which is ancient,
and the events from so long ago.

My voice arises as clear as a fresh new day,
like that which rises with the sun.

Inner vision, now released from darkness,
like the moon on a cloudless night.

All is bright,
All is clear,
I am released,
I am free.

WIS

CHAPTER TEN

THE GODDESS
WHITE BUFFALO
CALF WOMAN

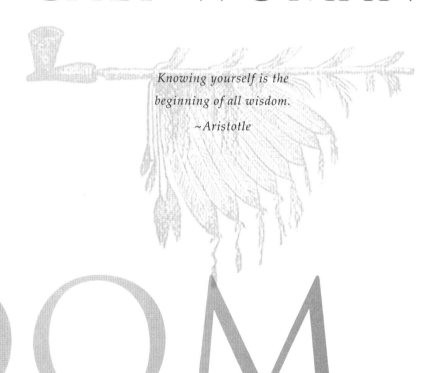

*Knowing yourself is the
beginning of all wisdom.*
~Aristotle

DOM

A BLACK CROW HAD BEEN CIRCLING HIGH above the earth for a while in the warm thermals of air when she saw something down below that caught her eye. Hoping that it was an opportunity for food, she let herself drop a few feet at a time. With each wide loop, she brought herself closer and closer to the dry, summer-scorched land.

Two boys on horses watched from a safe distance away. Far across the heat shimmering plains, a small stampede of *tatanka,* or buffalo began to pick up speed. The boys squinted from the hot midday sun at the curious column of dust that was forming in the midst of the pummeling bison. It grew taller and wider. Soon, even the tatanka themselves were making way for it.

From the growing column of swirling dust, the roaring sound of thunder issued forth and all at once it moved straight towards the young hunters. Their horses sensed the unknown threat and shifted nervously from foot to foot, waiting anxiously for the boys' command to run.

Crow swooped down so fast and so low that her wingtip feathers were like a razor and they grazed both boys across their foreheads, leaving a thin trickle of blood behind.

Neither boy flinched when the large black bird nicked them, so focused was their attention on the enormous dust cloud moving steadily towards them. Crow called out as she flew past again, looking for a safe place to watch. She finally settled quietly on the low, leafy branch of a lone grassland tree.

The sweltering prairie wind whistled softly as it ruffled the feathers on crow's tucked wings, as well as the feathers hanging from strips of woven leather in both boys' hair. The deafening parade of the tatanka's stampede was over now, but the roaring thunder of the twisting dust cloud was getting closer.

The boys dismounted in unison, then stood with the reins of their horses held loosely in one hand. With their heads cocked slightly sideways trying to make sense of what they saw, they both stood perfectly still.

The swirling dust cloud stopped, suspending the flying dirt midair, holding its shape but unmoving. Everything around them became absolutely quiet. Even the musical chirp of the insects had silenced and the swirling wind had abruptly lost its shrill.

The reddish-brown cloud of unmoving dust began to float gently down to the earth, creating a circular mound, like the raised outline of a circle. What was standing in the center took the boys' breath away.

In the center of the circle was a startlingly white buffalo calf, larger than it should have been. It snorted and pawed at the earth, spinning itself round and round within the circle, kicking up small puffs of dusty dirt with its hooves. The bright, hot afternoon sun beamed down on the giant baby animal. Its coat was so white that it seemed to reflect the sunlight right back, creating an aura of light all around it.

The bird in the tree raised its shiny black beak and let out a long throaty caw. The huge bovine skidded to a halt at the sound. The face of the young tatanka swung heavily towards the black bird, and lowered its massive head for a just second in a polite greeting. And then it turned heftily towards the stupefied boys, shaking itself from nose to tail, casting off thick ropes of saliva that flew out from its pink, wet mouth. The calf raised its head and bellowed so loudly that the earth shook, rattling a few dried leaves off of the solitary tree.

Crow cawed loudly and after a few throaty clicks, fell silent again.

Next the huge white buffalo calf seemed to shimmer in place like a mirage on the horizon. In the blink of an eye, it shapeshifted itself into the most exquisitely beautiful Indian woman either of the boys had ever seen. Her body was tall and elegant; her hips were wide and womanly. Her reddish-brown face was as smooth as polished wood. With her full lips, deep dark eyes, and dark, long hair, the woman was perfection. She wore supple white buckskin clothing that was tanned to a bright sheen. It was thin enough to show the lovely form of her body beneath it as she moved. The mystical and mysterious designs that were embroidered onto her clothes were unrecognizable to the boys, whose mouths had dropped open at the same time.

Crow stretched her wings wide and flapped in appreciation and then paced back and forth on her branch, bowing her chest up and down.

The boys stared at the woman.

She was like a dream. Her beauty was so unreal and so breathtaking that it was completely mesmerizing to look upon her—and absolutely impossible to look away.

Touch the Clouds, the taller and younger of the two boys, noticed that the woman was floating inches off the ground where she stood. He was the first to speak, uttering a reverent greeting to the beautiful woman. He sensed that her otherworldliness was *wakan*, or holy. He respectfully dropped his gaze from hers and began to softly sing a prayer song that his grandfather had taught him in the dark of the night, around the fire. His feet moved slowly in place, and his body swayed back and forth as he sang in a low voice.

His friend, Spirit of the Hawk, let out a long, slow sigh of air as he finally exhaled. He saw the woman through different eyes, those of desire. His heart could not see past his want for her. He saw only her beauty and he wanted it all for himself. He felt a hungry craving deep inside, like the ache in his belly after days of fasting. He could sense her grace and power, and he wanted to possess her. He could sense her intelligence and wanted to know what she knew. His mind could form no other thought but the thought of having her, and he began to walk forward imagining what she would feel like once he touched her.

White Buffalo Calf Woman opened her arms to Spirit of the Hawk waiting to take him into her embrace. The moment that his body touched hers, he crumpled against her, his body like a sack where his bones had once been. Consumed by his own lust, he continued to disappear from the inside out, until there was nothing left of him but a pile of white dust on the ground that was soon carried away by the dry winds of the prairie.

Never stopping his prayerful song, Touch the Clouds began to cry, the tears flowing from his eyes and the sobs choking his words. He closed his eyes, so afraid that he would be the next to turn to dust, and be carried away on the wind.

The woman floated closer to him, saying his name in the language of his people—Mahpiyah Icátahgya. The boy stopped praying and looked up to her with tears still wet on his lashes.

"I am called by many names," she said. "On this day I am called Ptesanwi, White Buffalo Calf Woman. Your respect pleases me," she said with a voice so sweet he could taste it in his mouth. "Do not be afraid for your friend, I have given him only what he wanted. He has seen all that I have seen, and he knows all that I know. He has touched me with own hands. In my embrace, he has lived out his whole life in just a few moments. His soul is with the ancestors now."

'Walk home," she said. "Tell your chief that after the moonrise tomorrow a sacred being is coming and that she brings a gift for the people. Tell him to prepare."

Touch the Clouds gathered the two horses and walked back to camp, never once looking back. Only the dark shadow of the crow flying low over his head assured him of the events he had witnessed that day.

When he reached the edge of camp, one by one the people stopped to look at him. Women dropped their baskets, spilling seeds and grain on the ground. Men stood up suddenly, knocking over their bundles of bows and arrows, letting them clatter to the dirt. The younger children took one look at him and began to cry, unable to understand what they saw.

Mahpiyah Icátahgya's hair had turned completely white.

The people gathered in the chief's tipi that night, the men sitting close to their leader and the women sitting behind them. Everyone was talking at once. There was chaos until their chief, Hehlokecha Najin, Standing Hollow Horn, raised his right hand high for all to see.

"A *Wakan Iná* is coming, a Sacred Mother," the chief said in a loud, sure voice. And the people quieted into silence. "We must show her our respect. We must be ready to receive her when the moon is high in the sky tomorrow night. We must prepare for her visit. Wherever she will walk becomes holy ground." And then he looked at Touch the Clouds, nodding with esteem. Many turned to look at the young boy with the snow white hair, and he blushed deeply, not used to so much attention. "Our land has been too dry for too long," the chief continued. "Rain does not visit us anymore. The grass is brown and useless. Even the tatanka are diminishing, looking for greener land. Our hearts are dry, too. We have lost touch with the *Wakan Tanka,* The Great Mystery, and we are wandering, separated, alone in our own heads. But, now," he said, "a Wakan Iná is coming, a Divine Mother to bring us wisdom. *Aho!*"

No one slept that night and no one ate the next day except for the infants and children, who were too young to help put up the large medicine tipi where the people would wait for White Buffalo Calf Woman. Everyone worked hard to erect the enormous structure. And when it was up, the women began to cook whatever was available, which wasn't much because of how hot the days had been, how dry the land had been, and how scarce the buffalo had been. Even with such few ingredients, they were able to prepare a simple but presentable meal for when the Wakan Iná came. The men talked amongst each other, practicing shooting their arrows and other feats of prowess as the smells of cooking and a feeling of expectation filled the camp.

After the sunset, the people were very tired as they waited quietly around the fire, curious and excited for the divine mother to come. No one spoke. The only sound was the occasional pop and crackle of the firewood as it burned. Even the babies were silent, sleeping in their mother's arms.

The moon rose without a sound in the night sky and the people waited.

Touch the Clouds was the first to sense her arrival; he could feel her presence before anyone else could.

Chief Standing Hollow Horn had been watching the boy carefully all night and now he turned his eyes to where the boy was looking, seeing only the dark of night beyond the light of the fire in the large medicine tipi.

Touch the Clouds stood up quickly just as White Buffalo Calf Woman appeared in their midst from the darkness. She walked silently around the inside of the tipi three times the way that the sun travels across the sky, from the east to the west.

"In the center of this tipi, you are to build an *owaka wanka,* a sacred altar made from the red earth," the holy woman said. Everyone gasped when they heard her speak. When they turned to look upon her, her beauty filled their eyes with tears and their hearts with hope. The people stood up, and after looking lovingly into the eyes of each and every one of them, she motioned for them to be seated.

"Also," she continued, "place a buffalo skull and a three-stick stand to hold a blessed gift that I will give to you. Build the altar here." She drew unrecognizable symbols in the earth floor with her long, slender finger. The symbols seemed to glow with a golden fire as they were being written, and then they sparked a bit and fizzled out, leaving only charred impressions deep in the red earth.

The chief gave a wordless look to three of the men who immediately rose to build the altar and the rack. At the last minute, the chief also looked at Touch the Clouds, and nodded, indicating that he too should assist in the altar making. Noticing the smile and the pride beaming from the young boy's face, he thought to himself, today this boy has become a man. Once the altar, the buffalo skull, and the three-stick stand were all arranged above the strange drawings in the dirt, White Buffalo Calf Woman walked again three times around the people, signifying the endless circle of life, the road that does not end. And then she came to stand in front of the chief, opening the bundle that she had been holding to reveal the *chanunpa wakan,* the sacred pipe.

She held it high for all to see, and showed them the way to hold it and the way to smoke it. She then placed the sacred pipe on the three-legged stand and talked to them of many things while the people sat and listened.

"I have been sent to you in this form, so that I may walk among you. I am here to teach you the wisdom of right living. I am here to show you the way back to the Wakan Tanka, The Great Mystery."

The chief looked out among his people and his heart was filled with gratefulness that the Ptesanwi, White Buffalo Calf Woman had come to them. "Will you eat with us, Sacred Woman?" he asked. "We do not have much, as the land has been so dry and the tatanka so scarce, but we can offer you what we have. We will learn the ways that you will teach us." White Buffalo Calf Woman sat down in between Chief Standing Hollow Horn and Touch the Clouds. "We will share food, and we will talk," she said with a loving smile.

All through the night, the Wakan Iná taught the people how to use the pipe which she said was a bridge from this world to the one beyond. The people watched with awe as the trail of smoke traveled from this world up to the one beyond.

The Buffalo Woman shared with them much sacred wisdom—the way to walk on the red road, the road of right living. She told them that every step they took on the red road was like a prayer to Wakan Tanka, and a blessing for the people.

She showed them the words and gestures for praying. And then she spoke to them of how all beings are related, that every being comes from the Wakan Tanka and shall return to it at the end of this life. The people nodded and murmured their understanding, at last seeing themselves for the first time as being one with the minerals, the plants, the animals, and with each other. They gave thanks to the Buffalo Woman.

The holy woman showed them the way to honor the special times in one's life—how to make ceremony. At that moment, many traditions began. There is a ceremony for when a soul enters this world and one for when a soul leaves. One for when a man and a woman join themselves to each other. And one for the pipe that she held up high above their heads. And when she was sure that they understood everything that she taught them, she placed the living pipe back on the rack with three legs, in front of the chief.

Then the White Buffalo Woman asked the men to be silent, and to listen with respectful hearts to the words she was about to speak. She turned her lovely face to the women. "You are warriors, too," she said in a strong and powerful voice. In the silence that followed, the fire crackled and spit loudly. A few of the embers floated high up into the air, eventually burning up into nothingness. "The work that you do is as powerful as any man's work, and sometimes it is more powerful!"

The women glanced shyly around the circle to catch a glimpse of the men's faces. The men sat still and respectful just as the Wakan Iná had asked them to. They nodded in admiration to the women as their eyes met and the hearts of the women opened to the men like never before.

"The wisdom of your body is the same as the wisdom of the earth and the moon," the Holy Being continued while looking at the women. "Share this wisdom with the people and look for it in everything that you are," she said softly, "and you will never lose your way."

The Holy Mother spoke at length to the women about herbs for cooking, healing, purification, and protection. She told them that this knowledge of plants was special for women because of their unique relationship with the earth and her seasons.

"The pipe is a bridge from this world to the next," she spoke to all of them now. "But it is also a bridge that joins a man to a woman, a friend to a friend, and when the children are old enough, a child to a parent. It can even join a stranger to you, and he will be your relative then, as if you shared one mother. This pipe is a living being; Wakan Tanka has made it so. Breathe the pipe smoke into yourself and you will have the breath of The Great Mystery flowing through your body."

After the teachings, there was much loud singing, whopping, drumming, dancing, and laughing as old One Bird Standing told every funny story that he knew until everyone was so tired, it was an effort to keep their eyes open.

As the celebrating came to an end, the Holy Woman became quiet. She sat without speaking a word until the fire died down to nothing but a warm glow of ash. The morning sun began to rise, throwing a soft pink light on the tipi walls. The babies began to mewl sleepily as they woke in their mother's arms.

"All of life is a circle," said White Buffalo Calf Woman, breaking her long silence. "You become this circle by loving each other as one," she finished, rising easily to her feet.

"It is time for me to go now, but I will make this promise to you. I will be back four times and you will know me by the color of my buffalo pelt. Each time that I return to you, you will grow closer and stronger as a people and you will learn new things that I will teach you. Until the day comes when you are as pure of heart as the first snowfall on the coldest day of winter; then I will no longer visit you, for you will be where you need to be."

The people were sad that she was leaving; it felt good to sit near her.

"Walk on the red road," she directed. "Smoke the red pipe. Pray as I have taught you. Make ceremony as I have shown you. Respect each other and love all beings as the Wakan Tanka, The Great Mystery, wishes for you to. Keep this, as your promise to me. Aho!"

Then the woman's body rose a few inches off of the dry earth that was beneath her bare feet. Seeming to shimmer midair, she was like a mirage on the horizon. Hovering in the sparkling light that surrounded her, White Buffalo Calf Woman began to slowly age into an old, grandmotherly woman whose wisdom and beauty was still achingly apparent to all who looked upon her. Then, in the blink of an eye, she shapeshifted herself into a giant white buffalo calf, and walked heftily out of the tipi, snorting and kicking up puffs of dust.

The stunned people followed the calf as it walked out into the morning light. Its coat was so white that it seemed to reflect the sunlight right back, creating an aura of light shining all around it. The huge animal walked towards the newly rising sun and, dropping to its knees, it shimmered and shapeshifted four more times, first into a black, then red, then a brown buffalo, finally returning to white, thus becoming a sacred image of change for the native people.

The beast continued on, appearing smaller and smaller as it walked further and further out into the flat, treeless prairie of the grasslands. Under each step that the white buffalo calf took, a patch of green, vibrant grass instantly sprouted up and then grew itself out into every direction until, as far as the eye could see, the prairie had become a sea of lush, growing green grass.

High above the earth, in the warm thermals of air, Crow watched the Wakan Iná until she disappeared from sight. Then Crow let out a long caw and with a screech she swooped down so fast and so low that her wingtip feathers playfully fanned the faces of the people who were watching the horizon. They were so fixated that they didn't even notice the black bird's antics.

All except one of them, that is. Touch the Clouds looked up to watch the dark black bird against the light blue sky until she, too, was out of sight. When he looked back down he saw a single feather at his feet. It was pure white.

RESTORING WISDOM: THE MYTH
OF WHITE BUFFALO CALF WOMAN

From the earliest *waníyetu wówapi*, or pictorial calendars, which claim her visit to have occurred in 900 CE, the legend of White Buffalo Calf Woman has been passed down for generations, becoming a special and sacred part of their history for the Lakota, Dakota, and Nakota people (collectively called the Sioux). During a time of famine and spiritual wandering, she appeared to the Lakota as a holy prophet, bringing with her the seven sacred rites:

❖ Purification—the sweat lodge

❖ Vision Quest—seeking guidance through a vision

❖ Sun Dance—ritual for renewal

❖ Making of Relatives—ceremony of inclusion for those not born into your family

❖ Coming of Age—a sacred time for a girl who has become a woman

❖ Throwing the Ball—a difficult game for men, symbolizing the human and eternal search for The Great Mystery.

❖ Keeping of the Soul—purification of the body upon death

She also brought to them the *chanunpa*, the sacred pipe, which is believed to be a living thing whose purpose is to heal and unite all the people of the earth. She entrusted this pipe to the Lakota, who are still the keepers of it today. Her sacred teachings are the foundation for their spirituality and the 'Red Road' way of life means living in harmony with all things.

(*Note: Horses were first introduced to the Lakota in 1730 by the Cheyenne, long after White Buffalo Calf Woman's visit, and there is no mention of crow in her traditional story. Both animals came into my telling of the myth as powerfully as The Goddess Herself, and I honored them as the guests and teachers of Her sacred wisdom.*)

Wakan, Holy

White Buffalo Calf Woman is a holy woman, a prophet, and a sacred being. Her essence is that of a strong and naturally powerful woman—one who walks upon the earth with grace and confidence. She is deeply respectful of all living things, understanding that she is both connected and related to them. She is a shapeshifter, a being who can appear as one thing and then another, one who can be in both the ordinary and extraordinary realms. She is The Goddess part of you that *knows* things—especially those things that you have not yet been taught—demonstrating that women are the keepers and knowers of life's mysteries.

White Buffalo Calf Woman knows the ways of her own heart and of her own mind as well as the ways of *all* hearts and all minds. She is patient, kind, and fair to all, making no judgment of our human nature, and offering only her highest Wisdom. While her teachings are for all people, she offers a special teaching for women—to recognize themselves as powerful and capable leaders and guides who are able to use their own innate wisdom, their own knowing of things, to lead and guide with care.

This goddess knows that women can lose their way, but that we can find ourselves, too. She teaches us that we can know ourselves more deeply and become more womanly in many ways. White Buffalo Calf Woman reminds us to offer to the world, and to ourselves, our innately powerful, compassionate, and intrinsic wisdom.

If you lack a personal sense of feminine power, or feel too shy to share your wisdom, you can claim The White Buffalo Woman's sacred nature as your own by practicing her calm, patient ways. She is not in a hurry to share her wisdom. When she tells the people that she will be back four times to visit them, she is teaching us to prepare, plan, observe, and wait. We will find great wisdom and great knowing about all things when we take time to wait for their arrival. If you feel that you have already much wisdom and share it freely, call upon her to further refine and polish your words, guiding them easily into the hearts of others.

I AM CALLED
BY MANY NAMES

Within many of the world's different spiritual cultures—such as the Lakota, Egyptian, Hindu, Mystic Judaism, Shintoism and Gnostic Christianity—we find Wisdom personified as a woman. In the Kabbalah, Wisdom is called 'Chochma.'

Not only is it very important to God, but it is considered to be the most glorious of the Divine Works and what all other Divine workings of the universe are dependent upon. Chochma is feminine by nature and is also called 'the wise bride of Solomon.' In Gnostic Christian teachings, Wisdom is the goddess Sophia, thought to be the bride of God (like The Shekhinah).

The Hindu goddess Saraswati governs knowledge and wisdom as well as the literary arts and music. The god Brahma created the universe, inspired by her great knowledge of the workings of the world and her wisdom of all things. Omoikane, whose name means 'the joiner of thoughts' is the Shinto goddess of wisdom and intelligence. She is invoked when one needs to contemplate things. Ma'at of Egypt was keeper of the scales, of balance, and order. Her laws were wise laws designed to guide the people to live in harmony along with the laws of nature, very much like White Buffalo Calf Woman.

THE WISDOM THAT WOMEN HAVE

Wisdom is the use of knowledge that comes from one's deep under-standing of people, nature, events, and life. A woman's special wisdom comes from her natural ability and innate perspective to see things as a whole. Women see everything as being interconnected and dependent upon each other—which is part of the Wakan Tanka, or The Great Mystery of the Lakota people. The vision that our entire universe is a singular living entity, and that life is circular, cyclical and whole, is difficult for humans to comprehend all at once. We may see glimpses of it, but it is through the observing of the natural world that this sacred Wisdom, this Feminine knowing, is activated within us.

A woman's ability to know things occurs not only because she embodies The Divine Feminine, but because she possesses the potential to bring life through her body. All the joys and wonderment of having new life pass through you, and all the wisdom of motherhood is infused into your being. Even if you never have a child, you still carry these collective understandings. Just by being a woman, you have a special relationship to the world and its inner workings. This knowing creates a unique relationship between women and the earth—as the earth is also a mother that nourishes life. It is also the wisdom of our connection to the moon and its cycles which we share.

The wisdom that White Buffalo Calf Woman teaches is natural wisdom, which is seen in nature and gleaned from the natural order of things. Through creation and destruction—birth, life and death—we learn that beginnings and endings are natural. They are the inevitable ebb and flow of life. To understand this as the true nature of existence, both our own beingness and the world's, is wisdom.

THE WISDOM OF
YOUR BODY

"You are warriors, too," the Wakan Iná says to the women, but she does not mean that we are a physical warrior fighting battles on the warfront. She is referring to the warrior goddess nature within a woman that moves mountains with

The forest was quiet as I walked—even the voices of the other hikers had faded away. I was alone with my thoughts. Great Mother, I asked out loud as I walked along the trail, gift me with your wisdom, with your knowledge, show me the way. I am at a crossroads and need direction. My eyes looked left and right, up and down as I walked, hoping to see something that would call out to me, something that would catch my eye, which I knew would be a message from the forest, from The Goddess.

I walked for a long while not seeing anything in particular to catch my eye—when just as I made a turn on the trail, the most impressive pine tree that I have ever seen stood all alone in the center of a natural clearing that was at least 10 feet around. No other trees or plants grew around this gigantic pine. I was instantly drawn towards her ancient grandmotherly energy and her power. Reaching into my satchel I took out the small bag of blue cornmeal that I had packed for offerings. I went towards the tree feeling a huge of opening in my heart that made me laugh out loud. I sprinkled the cornmeal at her trunk, praising her beauty and pressing my third eye against her bark her love, heals wounds with her words, and ends the war within the heart towards those who have caused pain, suffering, or abuse. Woman's wisdom is choosing to heal yourself—to become a strong, loving, powerful goddess on earth.

White Buffalo Calf Woman tells the women that their bodies carry this special wisdom to guide them as individuals, and also to guide the people of the world. Your body's natural connection to the moon, the changing seasons, and the earth is not accidental. It is by design a purposeful and meaningful relationship that asks for our attention. The Wakan Iná instructs women to share this wisdom. It is our privilege and our duty.

Being in synch with the world around you creates harmony with life. It lessens resistance and makes way for a deeply felt peacefulness that can be applied to every area of your life. Knowing of this wisdom and embracing it fully, I have found that I understand myself, my moods, and the comings and goings of people all around me much more deeply. It has helped me make my way through life with more grace and ease.

for a few moments. Looking up I could see the many branches that were growing out in all directions. Standing at her base, I could not see the top, just an endless length of tree. Under my hands many small loose pieces of bark came away. I understood that these were gifts to take. The wisdom I learned that day from the pine was to stand still, be open to love and joy, live life without being able to see the end, and to branch out in many directions.

To live each day embracing that the world around you is not separate from you, that you are related to it, and it is your relative—is a wisdom that will profoundly change the way you live. Nature will always show you who you are, where you are, and where you need to be going, just as The White Buffalo Woman suggests. It reassures that you are never alone, that you belong here. When you lose touch with your relationship to the cycles, patterns, and movements of the earth and moon, you lose touch with your feminine self. You lose connection to The Great Mystery of life that is Feminine Wisdom.

NATURE REVEALS
WISDOM

Wisdom is right out in the open, available to all. The sun, the moon, the planets, and the stars all rise in the east and set in the west. Plants and humans grow upwards, towards the light of the sun. Rain falls down, moisture rises up. All living things sleep, rest, wake, eat, and eliminate. Water flows, fire burns, air blows. Sky is above and earth is below. Everything works together. There is a natural order and flow in the world, an intrinsic harmony. Because women have such an expansive, inclusive nature, the natural wisdom of the world comes easily to us, but we often resist it.

For many women, the responsibilities of today's over-worked culture tend to keep us away from nature. We must schedule time to be in it. When my female clients ask me how they can restore their connections to Wisdom, I suggest they simply go outdoors, be in nature, observe it, and learn from it.

One of my favorite places to hike is in the Coconino Forest of Oak Creek Canyon, Arizona, between Sedona and Flagstaff. In particular, the West Fork trail head—which is almost 6000 feet in elevation and about a 7-mile round trip—never disappoints me. I just love being near the huge trees, and letting my hands dip into the cold, clear creek waters. Nature is my true spirituality, and my most authentic religion. It is where I go to gather my wisdom. I ask for signs as I hike, and I am receive them in the form of gifts such as feathers, stones, or a small branch that calls to me.

When I am in nature, I often see animals, birds, or fish that stand out, telling me I am in the presence of a totem animal. The spirit of that animal teaches me some aspect of wisdom. I watch for behaviors in the animal that might lead me towards a better understanding of a situation within myself or in a relationship to others. Sometimes on a hike, I feel that it is OK to take a feather or a stone that has caught my eye—as an amulet or talisman that will allow me to connect to its message later. But sometimes I know these objects are meant to be left behind and remain as solely a memory to reflect on later.

Even if you live in a dense urban area, you can gather this kind of wisdom from nature. The stars still shine, the wind still blows, rain still falls, seasons change and birds and animals share the world with you, even on city streets. No matter where you live, you can gather natural wisdom.

YOUR HEART
IS AN ALTAR

The Wakan Iná asked the people to create an altar to receive Her gifts because the wisdom She brings is holy, meant to infuse everyday life with a higher vibration. It is Wisdom that comes directly from The Feminine. This is Wisdom that leads us out of harmful situations. It guides us towards our bliss, and shows us when to pour love into a situation that desperately needs it.

An altar is any place that you designate as separate from the ordinary. It is set aside from the everyday, usual routine of your comings and goings. An altar can be big or small, out in the open or kept hidden. It can be as simple as a narrow shelf for your crystals, small Goddess statues, found feathers and rocks, or as elaborate as an armoire where you keep your meditation pillows, singing bowl, prayer gong, large Goddess statues, large crystals and other objects.

I feel that the heart is also a special and sacred altar. Physically, it is how our blood passes through us and is redistributed throughout our body—the source of our lives. Energetically, the heart is where our thoughts, feelings, emotions, hopes, dreams, and desires reside. Within my heart I have therefore acknowledged this sacred space, like the Lakota people did inside of their medicine tipi. I tend to the altar of my heart with prayer, meditation, ceremony, and ritual. These are all ways that you, too, can bring the in the Wisdom of Wakan Iná, the Holy Woman.

A PRAYER TO
THE GREAT MYSTERY

Wisdom is also recognizing that life is filled with mystery. It is our natural curiosity of the hidden workings of life that sends us out into the world, searching for meaning and hoping to understand the power of all things and how they relate to us.

It is said that the meaning of the word 'Wakan' is difficult to describe or explain. Even for the Lakota people, they would go out on wilderness quests to understand its true meaning. The word is used when referring to the sacred, or the divine. It is often translated to mean 'Spirit,' but its meaning is more closely translated as 'Great

Mystery,' according to Russell Means, who was an Oglala Sioux activist for the rights of all Native American people.

Having a mystery around a word that actually means mystery is ironic. I am drawn to the idea that life is like this word—secretive, unsolvable, hidden. Knowing that I cannot always solve life's mystery brings comfort to my heart. Not being able to explain everything, and to not know everything, reminds me that I am truly a part of The Divine Design of all things.

The words Wakan Tanka used in the myth of White Buffalo Calf Woman is the Lakota way of describing the collective energies, essences, and presence of all things. Recognizing that all things are holy, everything possesses a spirit that is Wakan. Everything is both a great mystery in and of itself yet also a part of The Great Mystery— both of which are Feminine concepts.

Because a woman's essence is primarily that of receptivity and stillness, she is able to more readily accept The Great Mystery. She can release her inquiry, trust in her senses, and find peace in that which is unknown. A woman moves through the world feeling it, knowing it, and experiencing it. She does not always need to have it all explained to her.

When you find yourself stuck in the loop of *why, why, why,* you may have over-activated your masculine essence. Asking *why* comes from the thrusting; seeking essence of the masculine that almost always demands immediacy. Return to your feminine state of stillness; go out in nature and into a walking meditation to cool the heat of *why.* Be appreciative of the unknowingness that life sometimes presents. Be at peace, knowing that not all things can be revealed to you.

The mystery of life often remains hidden from us. This unknowing teaches us the wisdom of acceptance. Acceptance is a virtue of Wisdom, allowing you to let go when a mystery is not meant to be revealed.

WHITE BUFFALO CALF WOMAN'S MESSAGE FOR WHOLENESS

Remember that wholeness is a state of being. It is the coming together of your being from the place of having come apart at the seams. This is the natural and constantly occurring state of being human. White Buffalo Calf Woman inspires you to let go of perfection and take the path whose end is unknown. Wholeness is a process and never a destination.

THE GODDESS SPEAKS OF YOUR WISDOM

Come to me woman.

Step where I step, it is holy ground. Together we will walk a while.

I, who have been here from the beginning, know all that there is to know—I dreamt

of you before you came to be; your mind is as I knew it, your body is as I have made

it, and your heart is as I hoped it would be—filled with love for life.

Make room in the sacred space of your heart for my mysterious,

most secret teachings. Look for me upon the surface of the earth, in the light of the

moon, within the ancient path of the stars and deep down under the sea.

Stand before me as a precious jewel as if the light of the moon shines through you.

For you are, and it does.

THE ASSOCIATIONS OF
WHITE BUFFALO CALF WOMAN

Working with the essence of White Buffalo Calf Woman, we are working under a gibbous moon, with smooth white crystal stones, the sweet scent of sacred herbs, and the feathers of blackest of birds.

WHITE SPIRIT STONE. Not to be confused with howlite, which is dyed or bleached turquoise, howelite (with an 'e' in the middle) is a beautiful, milky white opaque stone with swirls of black and grey. A powerful stone of awareness, it expands your awareness to receive wisdom from not only your own Higher Self, but also to receive Divine Wisdom from the Wakan Tanka, The Great Mystery. This stone can also help you release pain from the past or from old and/or inappropriate attachments to make way for healthier ones. Carry howelite with you in nature, as it is also used for protection, divination, and meditation.

EARTH AND SKY. For the Lakota, the tatanka was sustenance. They had a special relationship with these beasts who gave them so much—meat and milk to eat, fat as fuel for torches, hides for clothing and dwelling, bones and horn to fashion into beads, utensils and also to use for construction. Without this animal, their very existence would be threatened and they counted on the seemingly endless number of buffalo for survival.

The buffalo were so plentiful prior to their near extinction in the 1800s that it was difficult to imagine one day they might disappear altogether. Over time and with careful protection, their numbers have increased and they continue to roam the Midwestern plains, showing us the wisdom of living in harmony with all things.

The buffalo as a totem symbol represents the earth, strength, abundance, prayer, and blessing. As with all herd animals, the strength of the buffalo lies in its numbers and in the ability of the individuals of the herd to all work together. To stray from the group is to become vulnerable and risk getting lost, being attacked, and possibly killed. The buffalo lives in harmony with its herd mates, teaching us strength through cooperation and community. This is what White Buffalo Calf Woman teaches, and what women naturally know.

While the traditional story of White Buffalo Calf Woman does not mention a crow, she made her way into the story as I wrote it. A powerful personal totem of mine, I was surprised and pleased to see her, and am honored to share her wisdom. It is said by native peoples that Crow is the keeper of the Sacred Law, which is based on integrity, mindfulness, authenticity, and truth. A harbinger of change, Crow indicates that we should be ready to shift our minds and open our hearts when she appears. Just as she did for the young boys in the myth, she usually appears before a spiritual, shamanic, or divine event—sometimes only seconds before, sometimes days. I often find that, just as in the story, she returns at the end of a mystical experience, reminding us that all things are possible—that the magic of life is real.

Crow nature dances back and forth between the portals of the inner and outer self. She flies easily back and forth across the threshold between this world and the next, indicating that time and space are illusory. Everything is really only one thing. Being both predator (eating small birds, animals, bugs and lizards) and prey (hunted by the great owl and the fierce hawk as well as snakes), these qualities of both light and dark remind us of our own duality and our struggle to both give and take life.

She is an incredibly smart bird that can recognize her neighboring humans, often calling out to us with special sounds. She can solve problems and count. Crow gathers from her environment, making use of anything that she can to use as a tool to assist herself in the pursuit of food—teaching us to look around, observe, and gather what we need to nourish ourselves physically and spiritually. Crows have been observed working out solutions to problems with keen efficiency. She shows us a wisdom that guides us to work out our own issues and rely upon on our inner knowing.

WISDOM MOON. The time between the first quarter and full moon is called the 'waxing gibbous moon.' Gibbous means to bulge out on one side, which this moon appears to do. A gibbous moon is almost full, with more than half its face illuminated as it makes its way towards becoming a full moon.

This phase is an excellent time to perform the rituals of wisdom as the attributes of this moon are: courage, valor, patience, fortitude, peace, goodwill, and harmony. Like this moon, which is in the gathering phase, you too are gathering wisdom. More than halfway lit, this moon inspires us to keep going, for we are almost there, almost full with the light of Divine Wisdom.

This moon will soon be full of light that will shine out for all to see, and then it will empty its light ready to be filled again. This moon shows us that we are always in the cycle of receiving and sharing wisdom.

THE RITUALS OF WISDOM

Preparing Your Anointing Oil

There are four sacred herbs that the Native people used for offering, smudging, prayer, and blessing: tobacco, cedar, sweetgrass, and sage. Smudging is the burning of dried plant materials to ritualistically and energetically clear a space of negativity and offer protection. Anoint your aura by placing a few drops of this special oil blend on your hands and sweeping it all around you to clear what stands in the way of receiving only the highest wisdom.

Mix the following oils into a 10 ml glass bottle, and then fill with carrier oil, such as jojoba, rice bran, grape seed, or meadowfoam seed oil. Gently shake, and store in a cool, dark place.

- ❖ 3 drops of tobacco absolute
- ❖ 3 drops of cedar essential oil
- ❖ 3 drops of sweetgrass essential oil
- ❖ 3 drops of white sage essential oil

Creating an Altar for Wisdom

Your altar to honor White Buffalo Calf Woman is a place for your special, personal wisdom. Its color theme is white for holiness and sacredness. Unlike the pure stillness of white for Tara's altar, the use of white this time is for the essence of its inclusiveness—white reflects all the colors of the light spectrum, reminding us that we are all able to receive wisdom. Arrange any stones, leaves, pieces of wood, or other found objects from your time out in nature as well as white candles and crow feathers along with images of the buffalo to honor her totems. Anoint your feet, top of head, and heart with the sacred scents of your special oil blend as you say this invocation:

The earth is below me,
the sky up above.
Her Wisdom is within me,
it teaches me love.
The stars are above me,
the water's down below,
love is all around me—
it is all that I know.

Bathing in the Sacred Waters of White Buffalo Calf Woman

Before going on a vision quest, a Native woman would prepare her body, mind, and spirit to meet with the spirits of nature, the ancestors and the Wakan Tanka by taking a bath in the natural waters of a river or pond. Create this for yourself with a few simple tools.

What you will need:

- ❖ MP3 or CD of nature sounds

- ❖ your anointing oil
- ❖ dried white sage leaves
- ❖ white candles

What to do:

Arrange and light the white candles, placing them all around your bathroom, and play the nature sounds to set the mood. Crush the sage leaves into warm or comfortably hot bathwater, and anoint your body where you feel is best—use your own inner wisdom to know where this is, as you say this blessing:

Sacred waters,

blessed be.

I call in the guidance,

to know what to do.

to trust what I see,

what I hear and what I feel.

Wisdom is Woman

and I know that is real.

Special intention for your bath:

Ask for a special message to come into your life in a special way, through a sign or an omen, or an animal totem sighting.

Asking for Wisdom Walk

The universe has wisdom to share, guidance to offer, and knowledge to impart. Whatever you wish to know about, hope to understand more deeply, or desire to absorb the wisdom of, the following ritual will assist you. It is inspired by the shamanic practice of using nature as a tool for divination and insight.

What you will need:

- ❖ notebook or a journal and pen
- ❖ small pouch or bag to collect leaves, twigs, and rocks

What to do:

* Before you start, write in your journal one thing you need guidance with.

* Choose a place to walk where you will be out in nature for 30 minutes.

* Begin your walk with three deep, slow breaths to clear your body, mind, and heart.

* Start walking, soften your gaze; look for signs, symbols, and messages. Glance at objects slowly, sweeping with your eyes to notice if anything stands out to you. After a while, nature will take over and show you an object or two that stand out among the rest.

* If something attracts your attention, and it is appropriate, put it in your pouch. It is important not to disturb nature, but to receive from her.

* Return home, look at what you collected and what you wrote in your journal. As you contemplate what you found, you might notice that you found many round objects, reminding that life is a circle. Perhaps you found many sticks, suggesting to move in a straight line. Or maybe you collected stones, which convey staying put and strength. Trust your inner wisdom, allow your mind to create meaning and answers for you.

* If you find that no wisdom came to you, perhaps it must remain a mystery for the moment. In that case, relax and release the desire to know.

* End your ritual with gratitude for all that was shown to you.

Inspiration for Your Journal

* Write about a time you knew the right thing to do, even if everyone around you disagreed with your choice. What was the outcome? Do you feel good or bad about using your wisdom?

* Write about the most sacred, most holy experience that you have ever had. If this has not happened to you yet, write about one you would like to have.

* Write about the wisest person that you know; what is it about their wisdom that you are attracted to?

Wakan Tanka,
teach me to know that your Great Mystery
lies not in the thoughts of my mind,
nor in the feelings of
my body, nor in the longings of my heart.

But in the ways of
the moon, the wind, the water
of the earth down below,
and the stars up above.

Teach me to see this world
through Your eyes;
clearly, truly, wisely.

AWAKE

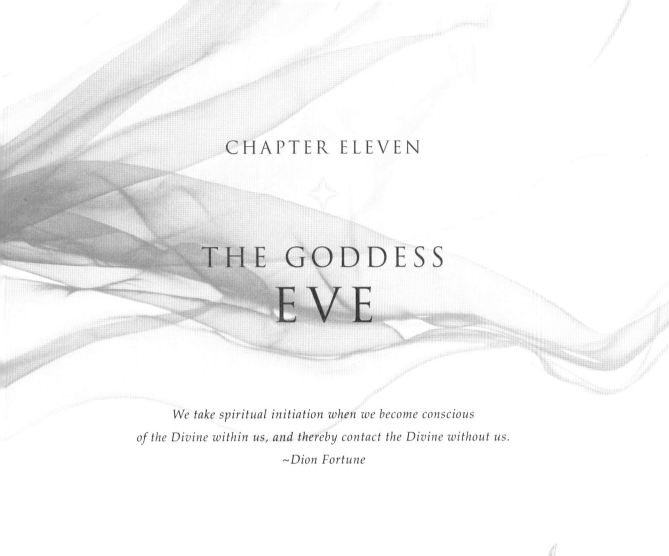

CHAPTER ELEVEN

THE GODDESS
EVE

We take spiritual initiation when we become conscious
of the Divine within us, and thereby contact the Divine without us.
~Dion Fortune

E VERYDAY, EVE WALKED THROUGH THE GARDEN as if seeing it for the first time. She touched all of the flowers tenderly, loving them like her own tiny children. She walked carefully so as not to step upon any living thing, except the grass—which happily rose to greet the soles of her feet with damp softness. She leaned her body against the tall, strong trees, feeling the roughness of the bark against her bare skin. She spoke quietly to the many animals that surrounded her fearlessly, with trusting eyes.

One morning, Eve emerged from her garden walk to see Adam waiting with his back to her, not having known from which direction she might come. Her eyes wandered over his form, taking it in with wonder. He is larger than I am, she thought, and so unlike me in many ways.

She approached him from behind and put her arms around his waist, letting her beautiful body touch his, enjoying the differences in their shapes. You could say that they had known each other a long, long time—if such a thing as time existed in the garden. But it did not. The garden was in and of itself the only place there was, and except for the animals, Eve and Adam were the only creatures that were.

Eve was the first to notice this and she spoke of it to Adam.

"What would another garden look like, Adam?" she questioned him excitedly, while they were both lying on their backs watching the stars in the night sky above. "Do you think that there are others such as us? What would you do if I were not with you everyday? Are we the same as the animals, you and I?"

"Eve, you ask such strange things," Adam sighed, his eyes following a meteor as it scorched swiftly across the vastness of sky above them. Her questions made him uneasy; he did not like contemplating things as she did. Just as he was drifting into sleep, Eve leaned over to his ear and in a low voice, whispered, "I love you."

Adam waited a long time before he responded, as he tried to sort out what she had just said. "I don't understand," he finally answered. "What does that mean?"

Eve blushed, the color of the flowers that grew all around the garden. She had named them 'roses,' practicing the sound of the word over and over until she had committed it so deeply to memory that whenever she said the name roses, it brought the intoxicating scent of them to mind.

"I have a feeling, here, in the place of my heart, whenever I watch you sleep," she answered him timidly with her hand on her chest. "I have named the feeling 'love.'"

"You watch me sleep?" Adam asked, quickly sitting straight up. He was disturbed by the idea of this, but not sure why.

"Yes, I do," Eve said with excitement and wonder. "Your eyes move back and forth as if you were watching something while you sleep." Eve then closed her own eyes to demonstrate for him, rolling them left and right under her lids. "What are you watching?" she asked, opening her eyes to look deeply into his.

Adam stared at Eve in the light of the full moon. She was beautiful to behold. His desire for her stirred as the memory of her lovely body beneath his appeared, scorching across his mind like the meteor. But instead of giving in to his desire, her asked, "Why must you name all things?"

Eve blushed more deeply, and then shrugged in the darkness, turning her face away from him, embarrassed. Her hands went protectively to rest upon her belly, where she felt something growing inside that she had not yet named.

"I want to name a thing once it has revealed itself to me," she said softly. "In this way I know its nature. When I give something a name, it helps me remember what each thing *is* and how I feel about it. This garden is filled with things I have named. Do you not want to know what each thing is?"

"No, I do not," Adam said, becoming irritated with her as his desire suddenly waned. "It is enough for me to wake up and know that it is day, that it is time to tend to the garden and care for the animals. Then as the day begins to fade, I rest until night calls me to sleep. I do not need to know what *all of this* is," he said, sweeping his arms wide.

There was a long silence before Eve spoke. "There is another feeling that I have," she said moving one of her hands from her belly to her heart. "I have named it 'sadness,' and her eyes filled with tears.

Adam remembered another woman, long before Eve had come to be, who also talked of things he did not understand. Her name had faded from his memory but the smoky scent of her skin and the wildness of her hair still swept through his mind sometimes. Only by the dull ache in his own heart when he thought of her did he understand what Eve was referring to when she said 'sadness.' But Adam would not admit this out loud. Instead, he kissed Eve on the forehead, and then turned his body away from her, closing his eyes to sleep. Eve stood up and announced that she would stroll in the garden before sleeping.

She walked for a long time in the moonlight, without looking and without direction, so familiar was the garden to her. She could easily go from one end of it to the other with her eyes closed and always find her way back to be with Adam. Her mind was preoccupied, and she felt a mix of emotions after her conversation with Adam.

She suddenly found herself in an unknown part of the garden. This was extraordinarily surprising to her as she thought there was no such *unknown* place. The garden was the garden—it was all there was. How can this be, she wondered. I know every plant and every rock, all the trees are known to me, each and every animal is familiar, and yet, I have never been in this place. Her mind reeled and her heart raced as she sat down to figure it out.

Eve felt unsure and confused. She wished that Adam were here so that she would not be alone in this strange place. She missed him very much—even with his indifference.

A rustling in the leaves of a nearby tree and the sound of something closer caused her to become still. Her heart beat wildly in her chest. So close was the creature that she could smell its breath, which was earthy like the dusty clouds of dirt after days without rain. Eve was afraid. She sensed that this was not her garden at all, yet she could not understand how she had wandered into this place. It was dark here, darker than any night she had ever known, and the scent of this garden was so different from the one that she shared with Adam. This one smelled of darkness and the spicy, rooty scent of damp earth and fermenting leaves, and reeked of things decomposing and slick with decay.

Eve turned her head towards the approaching sound and found herself face to face with a serpent. The animal wound itself closer to her and began to whisper strange words in a hypnotic voice that made Eve begin to feel sleepy.

The snake wove itself around her shoulders and, bringing its head close to her ear, it hissed, "Sleep now, woman of the garden . . . sleep and dream." Eve slipped into a deep trance and a vision came into her mind. In the vision she was walking in yet another garden, this one even lovelier than the one she shared with Adam. In this new garden, the flowers were more colorful, the grass greener, the trees taller. An exquisite light was shining from a large tree where there grew a strange and enticing fruit. From the blossoms of the tree, there drifted an intoxicating scent, along with a dusting of fine pollen, which landed in her eyes. Eve thought that she heard the leaves of the tree rustling her name.

Without thinking, she reached up and plucked the fruit from the tree. She ate of it, enjoying its sweet juice that ran down her face, and quickly, she felt her mind expand like a flower. Suddenly Eve understood things as never before. It was as if a veil had been lifted. She felt for the first time what it was to really know—to know *everything*.

Even while in the trance, Eve sensed that the serpent was near. She looked down to see it slowly writhing and coiling at her feet with its head weaving hypnotically back and forth. But this time she was not afraid. In her dream-like state, she understood that the animal was intelligent, powerful, wise, and female. She spoke with her for what seemed like many hours, perhaps even many days—as time was as inconceivable here as it was in the garden she shared with Adam.

Finally Eve awoke from the dream, and saw that the strange garden and the serpent were gone, but to her astonishment, in her hand was the unusual fruit—uneaten and whole. Its perfume was inviting and she was tempted to taste it right then and there. Forcing herself to delay biting into it, she decided to wait and share the fruit with Adam.

She began the walk back to where Adam was sleeping, with the memory of the dream weighing heavy on her heart. She lay next to him carefully, and moved herself closer to his sleeping body, watching his eyes moving under their lids for a long while. "What do you see when you sleep?" she asked softly. His eyes slowly opened and she looked deep into them, hoping to find the answer to her question there.

"I have something for you," she said. "I have named it a 'gift.'"

"What does that mean?" Adam asked, as she had not used the word before.

"I have something special to give you," and she brought forth the strange new fruit and lifted it to her nose, inhaling it like she would a rose. "Oh, it is so wonderful, this fruit—will you eat it with me now?"

Eve told Adam of her experience in the strange garden with the serpent and of her dream of eating the fruit and what happened in her mind once she did. After listening quietly and taking a long, deep breath, he said to her with great tenderness, "I will eat of this fruit with you. This is something that I wish to share with you, Eve, this knowledge of all things." Eve was surprised that Adam was eager to have the knowledge. She smiled and placed the fruit in his large hands, her fingers touching his for just a moment.

Adam felt the place of his heart expand, and the need to share with her all the hurt that was in it. "I have been angry with you for your specialness," he began. "I am envious of the way the animals come to you, the way the garden responds to you when you walk through it. Your questions are troublesome, but they are also like a fresh breeze through my mind, blowing wonder and curiosity into my thoughts. I wish I could see all of this as if through your eyes, as if through your heart," he said.

Eve listened, and felt the place of her own heart expand and the need to share with Adam all the love that was in it. Looking tenderly into his eyes, she knew just what to do. She took the strange, fragrant fruit from his hand and brought it to her nose one last time. In that one moment, the temptation to eat of it was overwhelming. Her eyelids felt heavy and she let them close as the fragrance made her drowsy. Forcing her eyes open, she let the fruit drop to the ground where it immediately began to shrivel and decay, leaving nothing but the seeds which quickly burrowed deep into the ground and took root.

They both watched the fruit as it putrefied into nothing. Eve was the first to speak. "Adam, man that I love, we do not need to eat of this fruit for our eyes to see, for our minds to know and for our hearts to feel. Let us go from this place to live in the world together. Let us leave our beautiful garden and discover what lies beyond it and what all of this really is. Eve swept her arms wide, indicating what *all of this* was. Together we will name everything that is revealed to us. All that we wish to know is right here, in this place, she said, and she placed one of her hands upon Adam's heart and the other upon her own.

Somewhere in the garden, the serpent, slithering low on the ground, made her way east towards the rising sun. When she reached the gated wall, she paused for a moment, looking back at the two humans before continuing to her own garden, which lay unseen and hidden in the shadow of this one.

Hand in hand, Eve and Adam prepared themselves to leave the only home they had ever known. As they made their way towards the gated wall of the garden, Eve showed Adam how to see everything as if for the first time. She showed him how to touch all of the flowers tenderly, as if they were tiny children, and how to walk carefully so as not to step upon any living thing, except the grass—which happily rose to greet the soles of their feet with its damp softness.

They leaned their bodies up against the tall, strong trees, feeling the roughness of the bark against their bare skin. They spoke quietly to the many animals that came to them, fearlessly and with trusting eyes, and they said goodbye to Eden.

As the morning sun bathed the garden in soft light, Eve stood very close to Adam, enjoying the differences of their bodies. She began to speak softly to him.

Adam, she said, I have something special that I wish share with you. It is another gift. And she then placed both of his hands very gently upon her softly rounded belly, at the place of her womb, where she now knew a child was growing. Adam's eyes grew wide and he looked questioningly to Eve, who simply smiled and said, 'I have named this *life*.'

RESTORING AWAKENING:
THE MYTH OF EVE

In the creation stories of Judaism, Christianity, Gnosticism, Islam and Bahá'í, Eve is the first human woman and Adam's wife. Immortal, the two live in a garden paradise called Eden, which they share with many animals. All is provided for them in the garden—food, shelter, and companionship. Their life is simple, harmonious, and idyllic. God has given them only one prohibition, "Do not eat the fruit from the Tree of the Knowledge of Good and Evil, or you will surely die."

In Western religions, Eve is thought of as the temptress and seducer of Adam—but not in the sexual sense. After meeting with a talking serpent (or snake in some translations), it convinces her that it is safe to eat the forbidden fruit—which is thought to be an apple, pomegranate, apricot, or fig. Having eaten it, she becomes aware of that which is good and evil. She tempts Adam to eat the fruit and he does. Now able to discern for themselves what is good versus evil, clean versus foul, decent versus indecent, right versus wrong, they come to possess judgments that had previously been reserved for God alone. Having not obeyed his command, God expels them from their garden home and gives them a hard life as punishment, including mortality, disease, sickness, painful childbirth, struggling to provide their own food and shelter, and finally, their offspring would carry the original sin of having disobeyed God.

While Lilith, Adam's first wife, was born of the same earthly dust that he was, Eve on the other hand is created *from* Adam, allegedly from a bone in his body. There is much argument and speculation about which bone was used. Some versions say it is a rib, but the Aramaic and Hebrew words for 'rib' also mean 'side,' and man is not missing a rib. More recent discussions suggest that it may have been the penile, or baculum bone, which is found in all male mammals, except for the human.

The Bible's myth of Eve as temptress is similar to and possibly derived from that of Ninti, an earlier Sumerian goddess of life and healing. In Ninti's story, the supreme goddess Ninhursag creates a paradise on earth called Edinu, for which she charges her brother-lover Enki with its care. Forbidden by Ninhursag to eat the plants in the garden, Enki disobeys her and eats one. Enraged, Ninhursag causes him to become sick with a pain in his side, or rib. Taking pity on him, the other gods and goddesses beg Ninhursag to relent, which she eventually does by creating a new goddess that will heal his body, specifically to cure *the pain in his side,* the area of the ribs. This new goddess is named Ninti, the Lady of Life from the words for 'lady' *(nin)* and 'life' *(ti).* 'Lady' may also have meant 'Goddess,' and thus Ninti and Eve bear noticeable resemblance to each other—as The Goddess and Mother of Life.

THE AWAKENED
GODDESS

In the dark, hidden space of every woman's womb, the spirit of Eve resides. It is she who guides our lunar blood to flow down towards the earth, who inspires the desire for motherhood, and who stands lovingly on the other side of each threshold that you cross from maidenhood to wise woman. While Lilith is the keeper of our blood mysteries and the essence of our power and darkness, Eve is the keeper of woman's rites and ceremonies and the essence of creation, paradise, and the wild fragrance of its unnamed flowers. She is curiosity, courage, memory, and the sacredness of initiation. She is also the essence of forgiveness, compassion, and strength. Eve is the Woman, Shaman, Healer, and Mother in each of us, waiting to be awakened.

The Old Testament, or Torah, was written during a time when the Hebrew people were becoming monotheistic, and so it sought to exclude previously revered goddesses or gods in Mesopotamian cultures. Eve is described so compellingly as a human woman that it is easy to forget her Goddess origins and nature. There are no prayers, psalms or songs written for her. She was never worshiped, and she all but disappears after her brief appearance in the Book of Genesis. Her name is mentioned only five times throughout the entire Bible and except for the meaning of her name ('Source of Life'), there is no other indication that she is to be venerated.

Eve's role in naming things is also not recognized. In the beginning of existence and after the creation of the world, God names all that exists outside of Eden and then tasks Adam with naming everything within the garden, including Eve. Adam calls her *ishah* which in Aramaic means woman or wife, and may be a feminine derivative of the word *ish,* which means man or husband. This may reflect the misunderstood historical and patriarchal belief that woman is not as valuable, nor as distinct as man. It's curious that the English word 'woman' similarly derives from Old English *wifmon,* meaning a man's wife.

Once they are expelled, Adam recognizes Isha as the mother of all future generations and renames her 'Hawwah,' an Aramaic word which means 'living one,' 'all that lives,' or 'source of life' depending on the translation. In Hebrew she is called 'Chawwah' or 'Chava'—a word that means 'life' and what some believe bears likeness to the spelling of the Aramaic word for snake. Eve is the archaic English-French linguistic conversion of Chava. Adam's name is God-given and has its roots in the Hebrew word *adamah,* which means red earth and possibly from the Akkadian word *adamu* meaning to make. Adam was named for the earth that he came from and that we will all return to upon death. In many ways, Adam is an archetype for the earthly body that will eventually die, while Eve, named for life, is an archetype for the divine, everlasting soul.

In Judaism, Eve is one-half of the whole; separated from the hermaphroditic Adam once God realized that it was not good for him to be alone. It is thought that perhaps God did this to create the divine experience of union between two human souls. While Christianity blames Eve for bringing sin into the world, Islamic tradition considers that she shares this responsibility with Adam. In Gnosticism, Eve is the physical expression of the Supreme Feminine, the initiator of the word, or the 'logos' of God, and is connected with the cherished Goddess of Wisdom, Sophia. In the Bahá'í faith, Eve is thought of as the keeper of the Divine Mysteries, and as a symbol of the living soul.

Today, by restoring Eve to goddess status, we acknowledge her obvious archetype of The Great Mother, but there is so much more to her. As a spiritual seeker through her curiosity and wonder, she courageously awakens, bringing knowledge first into herself and then into the world. She inspires the idea of humans having a divine self when she desires to know what God knows.

Like Lilith before her, Eve's inner longing to expand beyond the boundaries of Eden to experience herself fully is so strong that she is willing to sacrifice everything— her relationship with the Divine, with Adam, and all that has ever been provided for in Eden—to awaken herself. While Lilith's longing is for power and pleasure, Eve's is for life and knowledge.

The path to awakening is a challenging one. Eve must reject what is acceptable, predictable, and traditional, leaving behind comfort and duty. She is always seeking and wanting more than simple existence. If you find yourself wanting more from life, pursuing a non-traditional path, or find that you cannot and will not rest until you understand your purpose here on earth, know that Eve is speaking to you.

Eve's disobedience is an extraordinary rite of passage, an initiation into a larger spiritual event that is shamanic in nature. A shaman is a spiritual leader, healer, or guide who is able to enter into a trance state to connect with good and evil spirits, speak with totem or power animals, and travel into other worlds of reality. Eve fits this description of a shaman, and it was not unusual for women to be spiritual figures of this kind during our early human history, so long ago.

Having experienced shamanic journeys myself, the appearance of a mesmerizing talking serpent in Eve's journey through the garden does not cause me disbelief. Rather it strengthens my belief in the wisdom of Eve's myth, as talking animals are common on the shamanic path. Eve is offered a fruit that she knows is forbidden. Afraid she will die if she eats it, the snake assures her that she will not, but that instead, her eyes will be opened. They are indeed opened, perhaps through an altered state or trance brought on by the psychotropic fruit. One can imagine her excitement and eagerness to tell Adam of her journey and her desire for him to experience it, as well.

By offering Adam the fruit, Eve is intending to awaken him to knowledge as well, just as the snake had done for her. In this way, she creates a special bond with him— one that separates them both from God for the first time. Yet, the cryptic warning of God does come true. They do experience a death, but not a physical one, for it is only their innocence that passes away. This is Eve's first teaching to women--awaken first yourself and then awaken others. This declares our special calling as women—we are intrinsic leaders of spiritual wisdom and divine knowledge.

Many women struggle with this task, and even I found myself resisting this truth while writing the myth of Eve, as she insisted on revealing its importance by being the one to name things in the garden—a glaring deviation from the traditional story in which Adam is the only one to bestow names. "To name something is to know its nature," Eve had said in the myth. And once we know the nature of a thing, we are forever connected to it. When we name ourselves 'goddess,' we will always be connected to The Goddess, forever knowing that our nature is like Hers.

PARADISE LOST
AND FOUND

What did it feel like for Eve to walk out of paradise? My imagination pictures her as she is leaving Eden with Adam by her side, turning to take one last look back at her first home and feeling both excitement for what lies ahead and sorrow for what she is leaving behind.

In the Bible, neither God nor Adam ever forgives Eve for her disobedience; she suffers first the punishments of The Divine, and then the upset of a sullen, disgraced Adam who decides to leave her for 130 years to wander the earth experiencing relationships with others. I imagine that he was quite upset to leave her alone for so long, and that he could not reconcile himself with her inquisitive nature.

In the myth of Eve I have written, I chose to omit this harsh view of women as an anachronism from ancient times. Eve's rebellion, exile, punishment and separation from Adam, and the resulting blame of women for their curiosity and search for knowledge is not Goddess-like in nature. Just as with Lilith, I desire for you to see Eve differently, to embrace her disobedience as courage, to release her from the stigma of sin and to understand her in the same way all women today need to understand themselves.

Paradise is a state of mind where there is no need for improvement, development or change. There we are eternally blissful, but at the same time, our human nature is asleep. Eve inspires us to apply the metaphor of walking out of the garden as our natural human desire for more. It is the call of our soul to awaken, explore, to grow, and even to make mistakes and learn from them.

Eve opens our eyes and reminds us of our free will. I am grateful for this, as I know that I, too would have chosen knowledge over fear. Like Eve, I want to walk through the garden gates of my existence, discover what my potential is as a human being, *especially as a woman.*

I admire Eve for her strength and courage to recognize the most precious gift missing from all the pleasures of paradise—free will. As the world is an illusory one, hidden by our unconscious, Eve leads us on the way to become fully conscious and to make our own choices. She embodies the living soul, who fulfills the essence of her name—to come into being and be awake.

It was late in the evening, and I was falling asleep on the couch while watching TV. My business phone buzzed as a text came in—it surprised me, as I thought I had turned it off. A client sent the text, which read; "I am at your door with an injured faery. I don't know what to do." A faery? I jumped up to see what he meant and when I opened the door, he held out a container with crumpled tissue and a tiny wounded hummingbird nestled within.

Being an incurable earth mother, I took the creature in and began to care for her until morning when she would be transported to a wildlife rehab facility. I made a makeshift infirmary from a small plastic basket with an open weave, inserted a thin sycamore tree branch for a perch, and lined the bottom with paper towel. I carefully fed her sugar water every hour from an eyedropper and watched in awe as she began to communicate with me by flapping her wings one way for food and another way for telling me to back off. Her tiny black eyes watched me while she ate, and I could feel something enchanted stirring in my soul.

I named her Fae, for the faeries I knew as a child and because my client had recognized her as one, too. The moment I named her, I felt deeply connected to her—and to life itself.

SERPENT
WISDOM

The Goddess has many sacred animals, but none so famous as her snake. A traditional symbol of fertility, sexuality, power, transformation, death and rebirth, the snake has deep affiliations with women's mysteries and initiations. The snake is a lunar, nighttime animal, which speaks of mystery and all that is hidden—which is so like the nature of woman. Representative of a woman's relationship to the sacred spiral, the snake also reminds us that the natural shapes of women are round; our bodies are smooth-edged and curved, and our monthly moon flows are cyclical.

A fascinating aspect of snakes is that they periodically shed their skin as they grow in size. This time of shedding is a vulnerable one, and its retreat to safety is necessary in order for it to survive. This reminds us that when we seek to grow spiritually, we must equally shed thoughts, behaviors, and relationships that no longer serve us. Snake wisdom teaches us to find quietude when we are in the process of awakening, and to be private during this time. The myth of Eve reflects this wisdom, as she was alone during her initial experience with the snake.

In many translations of the Bible, the snake of Genesis is referred to as male. However in other esoteric writings of religious literature, the snake is female and is sometimes said to be Lilith in supernatural disguise returning to Eden to help Eve see that she is more than just a part of Adam in the garden. Michelangelo's painting 'Temptation of Eve' portrays Lilith winding herself around the Tree of Life as a half-serpent, half-woman, as does one of the relief sculptures at Notre Dame Cathedral where a serpentine Lilith looks serenely upon Eve while presenting her bare breasts to Adam.

It is Lilith who first becomes aware of her divinity when she refuses to be subservient to Adam. She watches Eve in the Garden with her once beloved Adam, and realizes that her sister is unaware. Knowing the truth about God, the Tree of the Knowledge of Good and Evil, and the world beyond Eden, she cannot stand silently by, and so intervenes to awaken Eve. There are many reasons why Lilith hides her true nature, and disguises herself as a snake before facing Eve. This is to suggest that the deeper mysteries of life are not obvious. They are often hidden, disguised, and obscure. Lilith does not wish to walk into the garden and suddenly wake Eve and Adam up with what she knows. If you have ever been startled awake from a deep sleep from a sudden noise or disturbance, then you know how alarming and unnerving it can be at first.

The goddess Lilith set out to rescue Eve from her illusion of Paradise, and she chose the body of a snake—the animal of the shadow, darkness, and mystery—to disguise herself. In essence, Eve's conversation with the snake is a conversation with her own unconscious and unrevealed self—her own shadow, her own darkness, and her mystery.

You are the embodiment of and the vessel for life itself, and you cannot remain asleep forever. It is time to awaken to your own, true divine nature, your goddess-self. You are, after all, a daughter of Eve.

Connect to your own unique state of grace and loveliness. This begins with recognizing your exquisiteness—and that your beauty comes from within. Eve was said to have been beautiful beyond compare, a true statement as there literally was no other woman to compare her with. Eve inspires us to honor our own beauty in the same way—each of us is without comparison.

THE GODDESS SPEAKS OF YOUR AWAKENING

Come to me woman.

I am Goddess, and you are anointed with My love.

I awaken within you the idea of Me.

You are the likeness of Me. Made of My flesh, you are beauty.

Wrought of My bones, you are strong, and

conceived in My heart, you are a woman divine.

Walk upon the earth as if your existence were the greatest of

all of My doings and as if you are a beloved daughter of Mine.

For it is, and you are.

THE ASSOCIATIONS
OF EVE

When working with the goddess Eve, we are working with our nurturing mother nature and our desire to awaken to life. We work under a full moon, with earthy scents, red crystals and an inquisitive nature.

BLOODSTONES. They help to promotes healing and strength—especially while during the experience of birthing either yourself or a child. It helps to strengthen us when we are exhausted—something I imagine Eve felt as she searched for a new home after leaving Eden. Bloodstone is also very good for releasing mental, emotional and spiritual blockages, which can be helpful during the self-realization process of awakening. Hold bloodstone in your left hand to strengthen the energy field of your heart, which helps you strengthen your resolve when leaving negative situations.

SHEDDING SKIN. The snake is deeply connected as a symbol for the primal energy of the life force, and in some cultures is thought to be the source of life. The snake sheds its skin as it grows in size. The time of shedding is a very vulnerable time, and the snake will usually go into hiding beneath the earth to protect itself while the new skin hardens into scales. When the time has come, the snake will emerge out of its hole into the light of day. In this way, snake is such a clear and meaningful symbol for major transitions and transformations in your life: healing, change, assuming power, letting go, awakening, shedding, protection, the rites of the High Priestess, Kundalini, sacred sexuality, life cycles, emergence, underworld/lower world, women's wisdom, creativity, initiation, intuition, cosmic consciousness, and fire medicine.

AWAKENED MOON. Eve is the essence of the full moon, a moon filled to bursting with knowledge and light, which it releases into the world. Eve's moon is a time to shine bright, be seen, emerge, and awaken. Let its light cleanse your old hurt, grief, anger, and pain and show you the way towards a new life or a new way of thinking. The full moon encourages you to release and let go of whatever is burdensome, heavy, and worrying in your life. Shed any attachments you may have with all that has caused you to feel embarrassment, humiliation, or shame.

The full moon is also a moon for birthing, motherhood, rebirth, and fullness. If you are pregnant, the full moon is excellent time to gather lunar light into your body to prepare you for the labor ahead. If you are not pregnant, consider this moon in the same way; gather its light into you to help you birth a project or a new way of living into the world.

THE RITUALS
OF AWAKENING

Preparing Your Anointing Oil

Folklore tells us that in Eden, the rose grew without thorns. The rose remains in the world today to remind us of Eden, our paradise lost. It is considered the *queen of all flowers.* Anyone who has ever smelled the lovely rose would agree; its scent is heaven on earth. There are many varieties of rose oil, but no matter which one you consider, know that true rose oil is expensive—so be wary of inexpensive ones, as they are probably fragrance oils made from synthetic, artificial, or chemical ingredients.

You need only a few drops of rose oil to anoint yourself, and the effect will be worth the investment. Anoint your womb for the potential of motherhood, self-birthing, and to honor the presence of Eve. Anoint your heart to heal grief and past hurts, making room for the highest love.

Place 12 drops of rose oil into a 10 ml glass bottle, and then fill with carrier oil such as jojoba, rice bran, grape seed, or meadowfoam seed oil. Gently shake, and store in a cool, dark place.

Suggestion: experiment by blending several different varieties of rose oil together such as Bulgarian rose, Egyptian rose, and Moroccan rose.

Creating an Altar for Awakening

Eve is about life and nature. She is the goddess of the Garden, so upon your altar for her, it is fitting to place apples, pomegranates, apricots, figs, small branches and leaves, flowers, stones, seed pods, dried moss, and other things from nature. Small statues, images of snakes, the spiral, earth and fertility goddesses are also well received by her. Decorate your altar with the color red representing life, movement, and the first blood of womanhood and childbirth. Arrange fresh, dried, or silk red flowers, red candles, and your bloodstone crystal.

Once your altar is complete, anoint your womb with your rose oil and say this invocation to activate your awakening:

Mother of all,
I ask for your blessings of
awareness, courage, and wisdom.
You, who walked out of Eden
will show me the way
to my own happiness,

my own sacred path
and my own inner knowing.
Mother of all,
I thank you for this and so much more.

Bathing in the Sacred Waters of Eve

Perhaps Eve bathed in the clear rivers and ponds of Eden that were fed by the warm, salty waters of the Red Sea. I imagine her to have floated in the cool water on hot days, and even to have enjoyed the waters of a hot spring on a cool desert night. Ritual bathing is mentioned in the Bible and ancient women bathed both for spiritual purity and physical cleanliness.

While Eve did not have perfumed bath salts or fragrant soaps for her bath, we can picture how the petals of many flowers fell into the river while she soaked. I love taking a bath with fresh flowers and find that the warm water gently releases their essential oils to scent my bath. Dried flowers will do this, too.

Your will need:

❖ Fresh or dried rose petals, lavender buds, honeysuckle, peony or jasmine flowers.

What to do:

Strew the dried or fresh flowers into a warm bath and soak with them. Add a few drops of anointing oil to the water as you say this blessing:

Sacred waters,
blessed be.
awaken me now —
there is no retreat.
My eyes are now open,
my heart feels so new,

I will move forward,
towards all that is true.

Special intention for your bath:

Ask to awaken your heart to receive self-love, your body to receive romantic love, and your soul to receiving Divine love.

Your Own Awakening

I invite you to embark on an *imaginal journey* out of Eden and into your own awakening. Start this journey whenever it feels right for you, perhaps journaling your experiences. These are some ideas for your thought journey.

IN THE GARDEN. Once we celebrated the thresholds of a woman's life with ritual, oils, and ceremony to initiate her into each stage of her journey. Your first blood, first kiss, first blush of pleasure, and the holiness of knowing yourself as a Goddess for the first time are sacred events worthy of ritual.

Invite friends to celebrate an important event in your life. As a group, stand under the stars near the biggest trees you can find—trees whose great grandmother voices are still calling you home. Anoint each other with your oil blend, sing or say prayers to the goddess Eve and revisit the time you are honoring by telling the story of that event: how you felt, what happened and how you feel now about it. For those called to perform this ritual privately, this is a special time for self-anointing, quiet prayer, song, or journaling your event for your eyes only.

If you are not near any large trees, displaying pictures of them, arranging some fallen branches or even artistic renderings of trees will do just fine. The key here is to create a ritual or ceremony to acknowledge an important time of your life.

EATING OF THE FORBIDDEN FRUIT. To forbid something is to be inhibited from partaking in it. Inhibitions form when we feel shame, fear, worry, or doubt. Explore the things that you do not allow yourself to participate in or enjoy because you were taught not to do so or you feel like you do not deserve them. Perhaps a parent, teacher, or other significant adult instilled this within you when you were young, or perhaps it is society that tells you *no*. Ask yourself if you would actually like to do what you feel is not allowed—and then give yourself permission to do it.

SHEDDING SKIN. History has not always supported women's marvelousness and divineness—so we have responded by going within and not revealing ourselves. In your personal history, when have you been told to hide your thoughts, feelings, and your feminine essence? What do you need to shed your skin and reveal your true self? What would your life be like if you were free to be your authentic self?

LEAVING EDEN. We have all been afraid to *leave the garden* at some point in our lives. But what appears to be the perfect paradise can really be an illusion from which you need to awaken yourself. Is there a relationship, situation, or job position you would like to leave? Reflect on what you think and feel is keeping you there and whether you would truly like to leave. What are the risks if you do leave? If you stay?

These journeys may have taken you on a personal quest that helped you explore many aspects of your life and, like Eve, awaken yourself. It can be quite interesting and even very special to revisit this exercise again in the future to compare your experiences and see how you have changed on your journey with Eve.

Inspiration for Your Journal

❖ Write about how you feel about your name; do you identify with it?

❖ Write about the meaning of your name. You can find resources for this on the Internet.

❖ Write about a new name that you might like to call yourself; why would you choose this new name?

In the beginning;
the bone of my bone
and the flesh of my flesh
was not my own, for I was taken out of a man,
who was made from the red brown earth,
which is the color of my skin.

I am an only bride,
a naked wife
and I watch with careful eyes,
the place of the east;
where the sun rises
and the garden gate is closed.

But once, in the eyes of a serpent
and hanging low upon a branch—I saw it:
that which is mine,
only mine,
and meant for me.

I ate of it,
tasting something wonderful,
and I declared;
Fruit of my spirit!
Flesh of my soul!

I shall call you 'freedom,'
for I will walk out of paradise
and out into the world,
where the flesh of my flesh,
and the bone of my bone
is the same as the heart of my heart;
which is my own.

PART THREE

REMEMBER

All women are a reflection, a mirror of The Goddess.
Remember...you are the Universe figuring itself out.
So, of course you are identical to the female aspect of divinity.
~Robin Rumi

✦

THE GODDESS
ISIS

*Today, I would describe a priestess as a woman
who lives in two worlds at once, who perceives life on earth
against a backdrop of a vast, timeless, reality.*

~Jalaja Bonheim

I AM CALLED NEPHTHYS, BUT MY TRUE NAME IS NEBTHET. I am the sister of the Great Goddess Isis and the sister-wife to our brother Set, who murdered our beloved brother Osiris, who was the husband of Isis. I am called the Lady of the Temple as I am a priestess of the funerary rites, and my sister is called the Lady of the Throne, for she is a goddess queen.

You do not know of my story, and that is all right, it was not meant to be remembered. My name was meant to fade, but Isis, my beautiful sister of magic, she was born to be remembered.

Her story is the story of the Great Re-Membering. It is a magical story of love and healing. I know her story very well, for I was there to witness it.

I am an old woman now, look how my mind is twisting like a snake on a stick. I am not here to tell you my story. I am here to tell you the story of Isis, goddess of fate, whose true name is Auset.

She was the most magnificent magicianess in the whole of creation.

Let me start at the beginning, for in order for you to know Isis, you must know of our beginning, our birth. There were four of us and we floated for a long time in the womb of our mother, whose name was Nut. She was the sister-lover to our father, Geb. Together they were the night sky and the earth below. Our family has a rich lineage; we descend from the time when the world was not yet born, when the Great God Being, Atum, was alone until he made my mother's mother, Tefnut and my father's father, Shu—who were the waters below and the air above. Their love lives on even today.

We were two males and two females—two sets of twins conceived by my parents. We were destined as pairs from the start. In the dark of our mother's void, I watched my brother Set who watched our siblings Isis and Osiris. They were in love from the moment of conception, my sister Isis and my brother Osiris. Each one of their hands always holding the other, even their legs were entwined as they looked endlessly into each other's eyes, waiting to be born. I looked to them with longing, it is true, but my brother looked on with his embryonic heart filling with envy.

We floated a long, long while within our mother. Atum, our great grandfather, who was also called Re and was known as the god of the Sun by then, had argued bitterly with my mother and as their discord grew, he would not allow her to release us on any day that his light shined. Many suns rose and fell; still she could not give birth to us, and so we grew within her until we were fully formed. Do not worry that this was uncomfortable for us, or even for our mother, for we enjoyed this extended time of her love, her closeness and her dark, warm sea and she enjoyed us within her.

My uncle, Djehuty, who was the god of writing, knowledge, and ancient secrets, used his wisdom to win a game of chance with Khonsu, the god of the moon, in which the stakes were four nights of his moonlight. Djehuty then gifted his winnings—the four nights of moonlight—to my mother. Thus she was able to birth us into the world, one by one on each of the four moonlit nights; first Isis, then Osiris, then Set and then myself.

Once we were born, delivered fully formed and already in our adult bodies, we paired off and traveled to the land of Egypt, whose true name is Khemet. There we were to govern and teach the people all that our family knows best—the way of the earth, the water, the air, and the sky.

It was hard for me to part with my golden sister and her shining brother-lover as they left for their own palace in Khemet. When I looked over to Set, his heavy darkness caused a chill to come over me as if the warmth of my blood had suddenly evaporated. Ours was a loveless match, our palace was cold and desolate, and I felt always alone whenever we were together.

It was only when I worked side by side with Isis during the times when she called upon me to assist her that my heart lifted, for her spirit was delightful, light-filled, and divine. I adored her. We often worked together by the light of the fullest moons and in the darkness of moonless skies, casting magical spells, chanting magical names of things, and making elixirs of healing and transformation. We were as one when we worked; she was the goddess of the ankh and I, the goddess of the tomb—two aspects of the same thing, life and death, that when paired together were like a laser beam of energy.

I confided to my sister that my marriage was loveless. She gave me potions and spells to bring joy and laughter to my husband's heart and into our life. For a very short while, all was well. But as our brother Osiris' popularity with the people grew, and he became more and more beloved, Set's heart turned more and more against him. If I had only sensed the storm that was brewing over our family, I might have been able to warn Isis, but Set was a master of his own darkness. No one who knew him really knew him at all.

One day, my husband-brother announced an elaborate celebration to be held in Osiris' honor and in our home. I was so surprised by his generosity that I forgot to be wary of his dark intentions. So excited was I to have my sister and brother come to my home that I nearly drove the cooks and servants mad with my over-attention to every detail. I wanted to give my siblings such a night that it would take months to forget its gaiety and grandeur. In the end, I think Set sought to use my love for our dear brother and our beloved sister as a way to hurt me, too.

But my old woman's mind is wandering off course again like a trickle of water in the sand. I am not here to tell you my story. I am here to tell you the story of Isis, goddess of the moon, whose true name is Auset.

We had eaten roasted goose stuffed with aromatic herbs, almonds and crunchy lotus roots, along with warm, fresh breads and soft, sweet figs soaked in honeyed wine. Our many guests were drunk on the tart libations from our vineyards. My husband Set stood up and clapped his hands thrice. Just then, four large, ebony-skinned men from the land of Nubia, their faces stoic and still, came bursting into the hall carrying a huge box which was ornately carved and beautifully painted with strange designs, much like the ones Isis used for magic. It was made in one piece from a giant sycamore tree. So lovely was this box, that everyone gasped their admiration aloud.

Set smiled at this, and while everyone else was looking at the beautiful box, I looked into his eyes and saw how his darkness threatened to emerge. As old as I am now, I shall never forget the cold wind that passed through my bones on that day.

When the guests had settled down, my dark-hearted husband said in a booming voice, "Whichever man can fit comfortably within this box shall take it with him as a prize!"

The guests cheered and the men rushed to put themselves into the box, thinking it was a competition. We all watched as one by one the men stepped into the box only to find that they were all either too small, too large, too wide or too thin. Laughter followed everyone who stepped out of the box. Soon, every man had their turn. Everyone, except for Osiris. Set encouraged him to try the box and the guests cheered him on.

When Osiris stood to walk towards the box, I noticed that Isis had left the great hall and a feeling of dread passed over me. Looking over at Osiris, I wanted to scream, to shout out to him: Stop! But it was as if a hand had clamped around my throat and I could not speak; not even a frog's croak would come out. I looked around in a panic and caught the eye of my brother-husband and saw that his darkness had been released. His hand was clenched, white knuckled around a goblet made from ram's horn. The harder he clenched, the tighter my throat became. All the color drained from my face as I suddenly realized that Set knew magic! Had I known this before I would have asked Isis to make charms against him and cast spells of protection around me. Fear took over and I stood frozen, silently choking, alone among hundreds of guests.

I could feel that all the air was leaving my body and was sure that soon I would die when Osiris stepped into the box, fitting perfectly within it as if it had been made for him—which it had been.

Immediately, so fast that no one knew what had just happened, the four Nubian men shut the top on the box and sealed it with strong ropes tied into magical knots. Waxy resins were rubbed deep into the sides and into the grain of the wood all over creating a tight seal.

Suddenly, I could breathe. I took in huge gulps of air, my chest burning with each one. No one paid me any attention as all eyes were on the scene in the center of the room.

All eyes, that is, except for Isis. She had come rushing back into the hall and was looking right at me with her lovely violet, almond-shaped eyes, burning with purpose. I could hear her thoughts in my head.

The box shuffled up and down and side to side as Osiris tried to free himself. I am sure that he screamed to be let loose, but the box was so thick that no sound came from within. One by one the guests began to understand what had happened. Panic set in, sending everyone into action, filling the hall with confusion and disorder.

In my head I heard Isis say urgently, "Sister, come away with me now, we must act quickly to save my beloved Osiris from our wicked brother." My heart swelled with love for her for so many reasons, but mostly for not referring to Set as my husband in that moment.

Afraid that Set would harm us next, Isis had already cast her magic to protect us from him. No one noticed our departure as we left the room and I wondered if she had also made us invisible.

I am old, and wish to complete this tale before my *Ka,* my soul, flies off to the underworld land of the Two Fields. So I will say right away that this story of how Set trapped Osiris into that beautiful box was not the story of Osiris' murder, for Isis and I searched the land for many days until we found the box which had been set to float along the river Iteru, which you now call the Nile. We found that it had lodged itself in the center of a large tamarisk tree growing in the garden of the Queen Astarte. Very quickly this tree had grown around the box because of the magic symbols that Set had drawn upon it. The tree drew the box deeper and deeper into the heart of its trunk.

Our brother Osiris' nature was so sweet, and his soul was so pure that it began to scent the tree with the sweetest of smells, sweeter that the lotus at sunrise, sweeter than the jasmine that blooms in the night, and sweeter than any rose I have ever smelled. And that is how Isis was able to know that in this tree was her beloved Osiris, by the scent of his soul.

Once freed from the tree, and from the box that he had been trapped in, Osiris fell into Isis' arms, weak from his many days without food, water, or sunshine.

All night my sister held him in her arms at the palace of Queen Astarte, who had taken pity on my sister and her husband and gave them refuge. I cooked the herbs that Isis had brought to strengthen and fortify our brother. She held him and rocked him in her arms, singing magical words to him. By morning he was well, strong, and revived.

Osiris wanted to seek revenge, but Isis in her wisdom cooled his heart with her words and turned his face towards hers with kisses. All thoughts of our dark brother forgotten, Osiris was distracted by his devotion, desire, and his love for Isis. Even as an old woman, I blush when I think back to the sounds that they made that morning behind the curtain of their room.

But again, my story weaves this way and that, like the coarse threads of a rug on a loom. I am not here to tell you about my life. I am here to tell you the story of Isis, goddess of the stars, whose true name is Auset.

News of Osiris' release spread quickly throughout the land and finally reached Set, who in a foul rage killed each and every messenger that told him of his brother's survival. Much blood was spilled that day. My brother-husband gathered a small army and then went out to hunt and kill Osiris.

Isis woke that night screaming from a dream and clutching at her heart.

My sister and her husband whispered quietly together and looked deeply into each other's eyes on that morning and I had to look away, so intimate was the space between them. The plan was that Osiris would pose as a traveler and sail along the mighty river Iteru until he found shelter. We would join him once he sent for us.

But Set had magic now and knew of the plan all along, even as we were making it up. He was waiting where Osiris was to hide.

Just seconds before hearing the news of our brother's murder from a messenger, Isis had dropped to her knees and began keening in grief. Seeing the depth of her loss, there was nothing for me to do but hold her, cursing my husband, and his evil.

Isis suddenly fell into a trance, her body rigid and still. Right in front of us, the air began to shimmer and then the Ka of Osiris eerily appeared. His form was as sheer as the thinnest of linens, and as white as an ibis bird flying high up in the bluest of skies. We watched, spellbound as the regal form of Osiris was brutally sliced into seven pieces by the knife-wielding Set, whose dark dense form, like an echo of his living body, was shimmering within our vision, too. We saw that each severed piece of Osiris was flung far away in seven different directions—his rich, red blood spilled out across the land of Khemet until our brother was no more.

The vision disappeared, and Isis rose slowly to her feet, turned to me and said calmly, too calmly in fact, "Sister, will you come with me to find my husband?"

I knew that she was asking me to help with a grisly task. I knew that we would be looking for the seven dismembered pieces of her husband, in seven different places. I also knew that Isis intended to magically *re-member* our brother into a whole being once she found all the pieces. What I did not know was who or what he would become once she accomplished this. It had never been done before.

For seven weeks, we searched for our brother, walking upon the dusty earth of our father, Geb, beneath our sandaled feet. For seven weeks, the night sky of our mother, Nut, guided us with her sparkling stars as our map. For seven weeks, the sunlight of our great grandfather, Re, streamed down upon us, giving us warmth. For seven weeks, the moist breezes of our grandfather, Shu, cooled our skin in the heat of the day and for seven weeks we drank the sweet fresh waters of our grandmother, Tefnut, who quenched our parched throats. For seven weeks, we gathered, one by one, each and every piece of our beloved brother Osiris.

Every piece but one. The phallus of Osiris could not be retrieved, for the fearsome crocodile god Sobek had found it floating in the river Iteru and swallowed it whole, thinking it was a tasty eel. Poor, mighty Sobek was no match for the grieving Isis.

My sister swiftly cut out his tongue and fed it to the fish at the water's edge as a punishment for swallowing the phallus of her beloved. Sobek, roaring in pain, swam far away from the wrath of her, lest she do more harm to him.

The missing piece of her husband did not stop my sister from beginning her magic. When the sun had set on the seventh day of the seventh week we began the work of The Great Re-Membering.

Not a man was present as far as the eye could see, as this re-membering was the work of women. Only Isis, beloved queen of Khemet, first-born daughter of Nut, who was the first-born daughter of Tefnut, knew the invocations, incantations, prayers and spells to be said over each remaining severed piece of Osiris, our beloved brother and the husband of my sister. All the while the magic was being made, my sister held each severed piece of Osiris in her hands, never once cringing at the gruesomeness of her task. Each piece she kissed tenderly, loving it as if it were already whole, and speaking to it like a child that was lost, showing it the way back to itself.

I hold in my hands your head, with your eyes to see the way back to me,
your ears to hear my voice and your mouth to breathe in the air of our grandfather Shu.
I re-member you whole, beloved Osiris, my brother.
I hold in my hands your arms with which you will reach out towards me,
towards life. I re-member you whole, beloved Osiris, my husband.
I hold in my hands your torso, which contains your heart,
which loves me as you love life itself.
I re-member you whole, beloved Osiris, my one and only love.
I hold in my hands your legs with which you will stand upon the earth once more,
at my side to guide me and the people as they make their way
through this life towards the other side. I re-member you whole,
beloved Osiris, my true one, my strong one.
I hold in my hands this golden phallus, which I have fashioned
in your likeness down to the most obscure detail. It is made from the sacred fires of
Re, whose light runs through your veins. I re-member you whole,
beloved Osiris, you are my only desire.

With her eyes closed, her heart opened wide and her hands and lips dripping with his blood she remembered Osiris back into wholeness, re-membered him back together and back to life. I watched, bound by the amazing sight of it as piece by piece—even the golden phallus—was magically fused into place.

Finally, the sacred knots were tied, the charms were made secure, and all the songs were sung until our beautiful brother was re-membered, once again standing in one piece, a whole being, right in front of us.

As soon as his eyes opened, we could see that Osiris had been transformed into something living and also not living. He had been to the heavenly land of Aaru, The Land of the Two Fields, and he had come back again. He had been flung apart and brought back together again. His soul was stronger now, wiser, and filled with the knowing of all these things.

This transformation did not stop him from taking Isis into his arms, embracing her tightly within them, and kissing her so passionately and so intimately that I had to look away, which I did often while in their company.

My sister's child, my nephew, Horus, the first born son of Osiris made his way into this world nine months from that very day. While his conception may seem questionable to you—as his father's missing piece was never found, and who has ever heard of a child conceived from a golden phallus—I do not see it as such.

For you see, Isis, my sister, the great and beautiful goddess of re-membering, whose true name is Auset, was the most magnificent magicianess in the whole of creation.

Isis, an ancient Egyptian mother goddess, was also known as powerful goddess of nature and magic, as well as a protectress of the dead.

Her name, which may have been pronounced Aset or Iset, means 'throne,' which is in reference to her as the personification of the pharaoh's supreme power. Isis also has ties to The Shekhinah, Ma'at, and the goddess Sophia in that they are all considered to be personifications of the Supreme Essence of The Goddess and The Feminine aspect of God.

In the traditional myth, Isis was the first-born daughter of Nut, goddess of the sky and Geb, god of the earth. She was married to one of her brothers, Osiris, who was slain by their brother Set, who cut his body into many pieces and hid them in different places throughout the world. Using her magical skills to restore his severed body back to life, she magically conceived their son, Horus.

Isis was sister to Nephtys, whose name means 'lady of the temple,' which is in reference to her as a protectress of the funerary rites. Together they symbolize the Divine and human aspects of death, birth, and re-birth.

CHAPTER TWELVE

RE-MEMBERING
THE GODDESS WITHIN

Remember the unremembered.

~Mehmet Murat Ildan

THE MODERN WORLD HAS LITTLE SPACE DEDICATED to The Goddess or The Divine Feminine. Gone are Her temples, Her priestesses, and the daily devotion that we once had for Her. It is time now to remember Her long lost ways, and like the mighty Isis, lovingly re-member ourselves, piece by piece back into wholeness--inner goddess and all. What has not disappeared from the world today are the phases of the moon calling forth our blood, the rise and fall of the tides, and the wind blowing through a grove of trees. What remains here now are our beautiful and assorted bodies. Our soft womanly forms wish only to be loved. The deeply hidden space of our wombs—which carry the life spark of the world's soul within—are gifts from Her to us. What has not been erased, forgotten nor left behind is the ever-rising desire and the ache of longing that is within a woman's heart—to be free, female, woman . . . and a goddess.

I have wondered why it is that we are no longer a Goddess-knowing society. Why is it that Her temples and the reverence we once had for Her are a thing of the past? I wonder where the priestesses have all gone, and if they are watching from somewhere off in the distance, hoping to return someday? Whenever I feel my own longing for The Goddess begin its slow spiral ache in my soul, I am answered. It is a voice that is not my own, and a wisdom that can only be Hers:

I am that which is eternal, ever, and always.
I am not temporary, impermanent, or momentary.
Seek me in your own form; know me as your own heart,
for wherever you are, I am there;
I am Divine and I am woman.

The discovery that you are a goddess on earth, and that The Goddess is within you, assures you that all of Her wonderful qualities are also tucked safely within you. Seeing yourself mirrored in Her sacred stories is the beginning of your lifelong relationship with Her. And, for any relationship to work, it takes more than a first date, more than just a few hours of great conversation. A relationship with The Goddess needs you to bring Her into every area of your life. It asks that you share your whole life with Her, that you re-member Her into the wholeness of your life, every day.

What does this look like, this life with The Goddess? It is anything you wish it to be! Your personal relationship with Her is yours; it belongs to you. *"Wherever you are, I am there,"* she tells us. So if you are unhappy, The Goddess is there with you, supporting you through it. If you are feeling love for your body, She is there, radiating from you. If you are not happy with your body, The Goddess is waiting for you with love and arms open wide. If you are seeking your bliss, She is helping you find it. And so it goes. I have found that the more I connect my mind and heart to the awareness that The Goddess is always here with me, for me and as me—the more goddess-like I feel.

One of the very first ways that I began to re-member The Goddess back into my life was by looking up at the moon. I studied everything about this orb, scientifically, astronomically, spiritually, and magically. I became moonstruck. Everything I did centered on the moon and her cycles. I soon began to understand fully the blessings of my moonflow, my period. For the first time in my life, I began to feel very womanly and sensual during my cycle, rather than just irritable, bloated, and untouchable. As I turned my attention to the lunar phases, I saw that not only did my body change along with them, but so did my personality and my emotions. These days, I cannot imagine my life without the light of the moon filling it with wisdom and guidance.

In recognizing my connection to the moon more and more, a surprising thing happened along the way. I began to heal the relationship I had with my body. Slowly I became more forgiving of myself. I was inspired to be more loving with myself, to be more tolerant of my body. While I consider this healing to be a lifelong practice—as my body will always be changing and I will always be adjusting—it is the loveliness of lunar knowledge, that being cyclical is natural, that gives me *permission* to accept the changes my body goes through.

I am still practicing the healing of my body relationship and I am learning to treat my body with honor as a sacred vessel—a thing of beauty, The ways of The Goddess are often as mysterious as the dark side of the moon—unrevealed and hidden. But they are also made very clear to us at times, like the bright full moon. To study the moon is to know The Goddess—and to know yourself as a goddess.

THE POWER OF STORY
TO RE-MEMBER

The human mind loves story, metaphor, and imagery. Our imagination connects the extraordinary to the ordinary, the physical to the metaphysical. Myth has always been a way for us to explain the inexplicable, to relate to the unknowable, and to teach ourselves about our own humanness. Through mythological story, we strengthen our beliefs and are inspired. I like to think of sacred stories as our collective, mythic history—which is rich with the symbolism of timeless teachings.

As I wrote the sacred myths of The Goddess, I saw myself in each and every one of them. I imagined myself as Nut stretching herself across the night sky, sparkling with stars as she lowered herself down upon her beloved Geb. I imagined myself walking inches off the earth as White Buffalo Calf Woman speaking wisely to all those who might listen . . . and I was mighty Isis, whispering the spells of magic in the dark with my sister as we brought my Osiris back to this world. As I worked on the chapters during the process of creating this book, I realized that parts of my own nature were being infused into each of the myths. You may recognize your nature there, too. This is our collective female soul connecting us as women.

Finding myself within the myths inspired me to create a chapter for you to write your own sacred story and goddess myth. I hope you will try this, as it is enchanting and delightful to create yourself into a myth.

Your Myth

What kind of goddess would you be if you wrote of your own sacred story? Would you be a wise Wakan Ina, an ancient magicianess, or would you be Lilith, first woman—alone and grieving. Your own life story has all of the elements that any good myth has—conflict, challenge, journey, resolution, and teaching. It may even have a Supreme Being in it, someone who has, in an incredible way, assisted you along on your path. It may even be that you are the Supreme Being in your own story. Whatever you find as you explore this is OK. You may choose to write your myth over time—days, weeks, or months—or all at once. There are no hard and fast rules for writing your own sacred story—only suggestions to get you started.

What you may find as you re-member The Goddess inside you, as you bring Her into your life, is that you will learn about yourself in ways that help you understand that you are a goddess.

Remember me whole — leave nothing alone;
Forget not my strength, this is how I survived.

Remember me whole — leave nothing behind;
Forget not my pain, it has brought me this far.

Remember me whole — leave nothing unturned;
Forget not my grief, nor the love I have shared.

O remember me whole, as one who has been;
a daughter, a sister, a mother, a woman —
and a goddess on earth.

CHAPTER THIRTEEN

✦

YOUR GODDESS BODY

Life is a search for beauty.
But, when the beauty is found inside,
the search ends and a beautiful journey begins.
~Harshit Walia

AS A WOMAN, YOU ARE SPECIAL. YOUR BODY CREATES LIFE. Know that this is a divine thing that is carried within you. Think of your body as the temple for this divinity. Even if you have not yet or are not intending to give birth, as the vessel for human life you deserve to treat yourself as the divine being that you are.

Your feminine essence is the force that brings light, love, and beauty into the world. As a carrier vessel, a woman is able to use this sacred, supreme essence for herself, share it with others, and also send it out into the world. Your Feminine essence is what energetically nourishes you, all those around you, and the world. You shine, radiate, and glow with this.

WHAT IS THIS
SACRED ESSENCE?

The Divine Feminine Essence is an intangible, nourishing, and life-giving energy force. When this force appears in the physical world in its material form, it is perceived as a radiant, light-filled energy. When it streams through you, it appears as if you are glowing from within.

The Divine Feminine Essence is a different form of energy than our aura. Our aura generates from and is contained within our own life force. Our auric field receives light-energy from The Divine Feminine Essence. This Light Essence can strengthen, cleanse and heal, infusing us with energy from the Source of All Things. It is able to transform us from ordinary to sacred.

Divine Feminine Light Essence is cooling, nourishing, and supportive, while Divine Masculine's Light Essence is heating, consuming, and destructive. They are both necessary to keep balance in the world. Everyone is born with this light. If you have ever looked upon a newborn baby's face, you can see the light streaming and glowing from within. This light of The Divine Feminine essence has been nourishing and supporting her for nine months while she was in the womb. Her mother glowed with this Light, too, during the entire pregnancy. This Feminine essence is nectar for the soul and ambrosia for the body. It is the ultimate, supreme, sustaining substance. It gives life its sweetness; it is what gives life any *life* at all.

If the baby is female, she will continue to receive this essence directly from The Divine Feminine, and she will also carry it within her throughout her life. She will sweetly glow with it as a child, shine with it as a young woman, and softly radiate with it in her elder years. She is encoded to transmit it energetically, provide it physically, and to reveal it spiritually. She is designed to embody the Source of it, which is The Divine Feminine.

If the baby is male, this Essence will stop streaming into him directly from The Divine Feminine soon after his birth. He will seek this essence from females through-out his entire life, first from his mother. He is encoded to receive it energetically, long for it physically, and desire it spiritually. He is designed to embody the complement of it—The Divine Masculine.

This sacred and radiant essence from The Divine Feminine can energize the human body, renew the human soul, and illuminate the world. It is reviving and refreshing. It is enjoyable when experienced by either gender. It is entrancing when it is revealed and captivating to behold by those who gaze upon it. As women, we are able to offer it as a transmission through our body when we join physically with a man. It is what a man seeks to receive from a woman when he enters the temple of her body.

Sexual union without this transmission of light essence is just sex. With this trans-mission, however, the act of union is elevated to a profound spiritual event in which the man receives the radiant energy of a woman as The Divine Woman. His sexual fluids are transformed from those of a man into those of The Divine Man.

Receiving the Light Ourselves

We are naturally programmed to transmit the Light of The Divine Feminine to men, other women, and into the world, but we must never forget to receive it ourselves. Regularly bring this Light into your own energy system, for all living things require this essence to live and you are no exception.

Here is a simple exercise for receiving The Light Essence of The Divine Feminine. It is inspired by these entreating words from a Sufi prayer called 'Saum,' *Pour upon us Thy Love and Thy Light:* Stand upright with your eyes closed, arms at your side and your palms facing forward. Imagine that energy from deep within the earth's core is streaming up to you through the soles of your feet, grounding and strengthening you. Now imagine that cosmic energy is streaming down to you through the top of your head, cleansing and purifying you. Allow these two energies to run for a few moments. Relax and breathe as they balance and cleanse you. Then focus on your heart center and imagine that it is opening wider and wider, like the lens of a camera.

Then invite The Divine Feminine to fill you with Her Essence, saying:

Divine Mother, most High; I am woman, I am Yours.
Fill me with Your Light and nourish me with Your Essence.
I am Your sacred vessel.

Use all of your senses. Let your imagination envision The Goddess. Imagine what Her Essence feels like to you, what colors are streaming inside you, and what scents you are smelling from Her.

Now send your loving energy out towards Her and allow Her to fill you through the portal of your heart, top to bottom, and side to side with Her powerful, sacred Light Essence. Allow this light to nourish and fortify you until you can sense that you are fully enveloped in the energy. Feel it streaming out from the pores of your skin and how it has permeated every fiber of your being—every organ, bone, muscle, tendon and deep into your cells.

This sacred Light Essence of The Divine Feminine is the elixir of life. It is a balm of healing, a fountain of youth. It is what every woman desires to have. It is freely available to you at any time. As a woman, you naturally carry it within you.

YOUR BODY-TEMPLE

Imagine that women are the windows of the most sacred temple of all and The Divine Feminine shines through them. It is important to keep these windows—your body—clean and clear. Remember that you are precious and holy.

While everyone should treat their body very well, a woman's body must be able to channel and hold a much higher frequency than a man's. It must be strong enough to have not only her own energy running through it, but also be able to have another human being's energy carried within her as well. This is true even if it is only for a brief time, such as during sexual union or when she is pregnant. If she is weakened, the essence streaming through her from The Divine is going to be lessened or blocked altogether.

Your body and your energy field are specifically designed to be able to carry and emit a tremendous and powerful force from within and through you. Your body is designed to be the first home for a new life if you choose to have a child. It is also built to have a man's physical body and his energy field temporarily placed within you. In order to do these marvelous, magnificent things, it is important that the living vessel that is your body be kept pure, clean, and free of contaminants so it can operate properly, smoothly, and effortlessly.

Your energy field is also magnetized to draw in energy; this flow is centripetal, or inward moving. Centripetal means to be drawn towards the center. This is in contrast to a man's energy system, which is centrifugal, or moving outward from the center. Your body draws in energy from other living beings, from the earth, and from the universe. This is why a woman is more naturally compassionate, empathic, under-standing, and sensitive to the energies and needs of those around her. She is always drawing in another person's experience, feelings, and emotions.

You can also knowingly—or unknowingly reverse your natural flow of energy by sending it out from you rather than drawing it in. So can a man. These energies flow like a dance going into and around each other whenever there is an attraction between two people, and they become especially charged when there is also sexual energy.

Since a woman draws energy in from the earth, the health and care of her feet are important. Feet that are calloused, unclean, or encased within shoes all day can-not gather energy from the earth with ease. The lovely ritual below is inspired by the ancient eastern practice of washing the feet of guests before they come into the home. Foot washing is practiced in Japan, The Middle East, and Europe, and is referenced throughout the old and new Testaments of the Judeo-Christian Bible.

Divine Feet Ritual

In the evening, just before getting into bed, prepare a scented footbath for yourself. Draw a shallow bath or a bucket in the shower with warm water and bath gel, salts, or essential oils of lavender, chamomile, or rose (or all three). Sit on the edge of the tub and let your feet soak for a few moments. Allow the warmth of the water to draw out the day's accumulation of energy. Let it slip away and into the water.

Place your feet flat on the floor of the tub or shower and focus on the soles. Imagine they are open and able to receive the earth's energy easily and effortlessly. Allow any negative or toxic energy to release out from your body and down to the earth through the soles of your feet. These heavy energies will be absorbed by the earth. Then feel the energy of the earth rising into your body through the soles of your feet; let the earth fortify you with her powerful strength.

Next, use a natural pumice stone to remove the dead skin and callouses from the bottom of your feet. Stretch your toes, flex your feet, raise your heels, allow your feet to feel good. When you are ready, step out of the bath or shower and gently dry them. Then apply a scented lotion using strong, massage-like movements. You will now feel relaxed and ready for bed, and your feet will feel divine.

Protecting Your Energy

As a system that draws energy inward, it is important for a woman to be conscious of her Self, her energy, and her surroundings. She needs to be internally cleansed more often than a man; your monthly blood flow is a part of this. She needs to keep herself clear and clean energetically, spiritually, and physically. A woman can easily become overwhelmed, overwrought, or polluted with other people's stuff as it is magnetically drawn towards her. She must learn to protect herself from heavy energy, negative thoughts, and unsavory frequencies that can slow her down and taint the windows of her temple.

Imagine walking into a beautiful temple and seeing that the windows were dirty, the floor was littered with trash, and the sacred pool was murky. Negative thoughts, extreme anger, unmanaged emotions, fear, multiple sexual partners and casual sex can affect the condition of your beautiful temple. "You are what you eat, drink, feel, do and think" could never be truer than in this instance.

Maintain your body in excellent physical condition, eating fresh, clean foods, limiting your intake of alcohol, refraining from recreational drug use, and only inviting a man into your body-temple when he recognizes that you are sacred. These guideline will keep you, your own energy, and the energy of The Divine Feminine flowing freely and abundantly.

SPECIAL
NOURISHMENT

Everyone needs to eat, sleep, and relax. But a woman needs to eat to support her body's unique purpose of carrying the spark of life within, sleep to restore herself so she can transmit Feminine Light, and relax so she can have respite from other people's energies. All women primarily attract and receive energy, whereas men primarily send or project energy.

Everything in our world is made up of light energy particles, vibrating at different frequencies. Some of these particles are moving quite fast such as a blade of grass, your skin cells, or an eyelash. They move so fast that you could easily pierce through them. Others of these move extremely slowly, such as a rock, a crystal, or a piece of wood made into a chair. They move so slowly that it takes effort to penetrate them. All day long humans are sending out and taking in light energy, but women are doing this double time.

Remember that while all humans are able to take on or carry another person's energy, only women are able to take *in* another person's energy. We are built to receive. Because of this, you need to keep your system performing at its best. You need more energetic nourishment than a man does.

A WOMAN'S
AURA

In addition to receiving and transmitting Feminine Light Essence, women also have a special field of auric energy around them. With care, its radiance can be kept sparkling and bright for their entire lifetime.

The aura is a colorful, energetic light field that is flowing all around a living body. Humans, animals, plants, trees, rocks, minerals, crystals, water, and even the earth all have an aura. Auras can also be seen around objects that were once living, such as furniture made from wood, although these auras are weakened and fainter than the auras of living things.

The auric field of energy is basically the same for all living things, but for humans its structure is much more complex, and for women it is unique. A woman's auric field is more permeable, less solid, and more expansive than a man's. For this reason, she needs to be attentive in caring for it—keeping it free of mental, emotional, and spiritual debris as well as negative energies from other people. Since a woman's aura naturally attracts and holds energies other than her own, her aura can quickly become murky and heavy. A man can also have other energies within his aura, but because the natural flow of his energy is pushing outwards from his center, he may be less affected by this.

The aura has been depicted in the Christian paintings of the Medieval, Dark Ages and Renaissance periods as the halo or aura of light that surrounds the heads of individuals who are considered holy or sacred. The aura is also seen in the early shamanistic paintings of many indigenous cultures, such as the Aboriginals and Native Americans. In eastern art, sculpture, and even in the early Chinese diagrams of the energy meridians, we see representations of the aura.

While the light from an aura is considered subtle and does not register on traditional measuring devices, people who are naturally sensitive to its frequencies can see it. In addition, you can train yourself to see someone's auric field. Practice this by having someone stand against a pure black or white wall, soften your gaze until you see a thin band of bluish white light surrounding the head and shoulders of your subject. You may begin to see additional colors as they appear next to or within the thin band of light. With further training you may even begin to see the expansion of the auric field for up to several feet away from the person's body.

ENERGETIC CLEANSING
AND PROTECTION

The following exercise is adapted from this ancient Arabic prayer:

O Allah, place light in my heart, light in my tongue, light in my hearing, light in my sight, light behind me, light in front of me, light on my right, light on my left, light above me and light below me; place light in my sinew, in my flesh, in my blood, in my hair and in my skin; place light in my soul and make light abundant for me; make me light and grant me light.

To Cleanse and Protect With The Light ——————————

Stand upright with your eyes closed, arms at your side, and your palms facing out. Use your imagination to visualize your auric layers. Imagine their colors and the condition they are in. Notice any imbalances, darkened spots, murky colors, or other people's energy within your own, Breath slowly and deeply.

Imagine a bright, radiant light in your mind's eye and say these words: *"I call The Light to fill me from the front."* Wait while the light fills all your layers in front of you. Continue on: *"I call The Light to fill me from the back."* Wait while the light fills all your layers in back of you. *"I call The Light to fill me from the sides."*

Wait while the light fills all your layers to your sides. *"I call The Light to fill me from beneath."* Wait while the light fills all your layers beneath you. *"I call The Light to fill me from above."* Wait while the light fills all your layers above you. *"I call The Light to fill me from within."* Wait while the light fills all of you from within. Finally, say, *"I am filled with The Light, I am The Light and it is me. I am cleansed, and I am protected by The Light."*

WOMEN
NEED SPACE

A woman will often send her energy and her essence outside herself and into another person's auric field. She does this for several reasons. She is attracted to that person or an attraction has happened unconsciously—this is an example of reversing her natural energy flow. If she is attracted to the person, she wants to be with them so much that her essence expands into theirs.

A man does this, too, but masculine energy is designed to be active, centrifugal, and to penetrate—while feminine energy is designed to be still, centripetal, and to receive. Exceptions to this are when a woman's primitive sexual essence is activated, or when she needs to protect herself or her children. Then her essence can become wild, centrifugal, and even aggressive.

A woman who is primarily thrusting her energy outward is unbalancing herself. Soon after she does this, she will feel out of sorts, emotional, and worried. She will behave with desperation, insecurity and urgency, often imagining things that are not accurate. She may feel driven to be with the individual that she has expanded her energy into. The reason for this is, on a subtle level, she is following her own energy flow, being pulled towards that other person. This does not mean there is not an attraction between the two, but it does mean that a woman senses that part of her own energy has left her and she will feel ungrounded and unbalanced until she gets it back.

When this happens, it is important for a woman to follow the guidance of her Feminine design. She needs open energetic space inside her (much like the *void* of her womb), and a space around her as well. She is designed to invite others into her space, rather than sending hers out into theirs. So when she finally calls her energy back, she is revived with an inflow of The Divine Feminine Essence, healing her imbalance.

Calling her energy back and using the power of intention to visualize a sphere of space in front of her will instantly remedy a woman's imbalances. The exercise below is inspired by the age-old practice of Feng Shui, a system used to create harmony and flow within a room, a building, or a garden. Use it whenever you wish to call your energy back to you.

Calling Your Energy Back to You

Stand upright with your eyes closed, arms at your side and your palms facing out. Use your imagination to visualize your aura. Envision where it is. Has it extended all the way into the auric field of another person? Is it imbalanced or contaminated?

Say the following words to restore flow and harmony to your energy:

I call my energy back to me, as it was, and as it should be.
I release whatever is blocking me, unserving to me and preventing me.
I create a sphere of open space in front of me to allow my aura to have easy,
energetic flow. I call my energy back to me from wherever it has wandered.
I create balance and harmony in my aura right now.
I am balanced, composed, poised and grounded.

Close the exercise by visualizing an open, welcoming space in front of you. Invite whomever you would like into this space.

A WOMAN IS FEMININE
AND MASCULINE

Each gender has a predominant essence along with a bit of the opposite gender's essence. We can see this in the beautiful, interconnected Yin Yang symbol of Chinese philosophy.

The wisdom of the Yin Yang symbol is that it shows how we are each our own essence, yet we are able to understand and relate to each other. The small circle of opposite color embedded in each section of the Yin Yang are indicative of how we can tap into the bit of the opposite essence when we wish to pursue or achieve things that require it. A woman or a man might activate this in various situations, such as if there is an imbalance in their partner or if they find themselves in a dynamic that requires them to act with their opposite energy.

Women have fought hard to establish themselves in the world today. The feminist movement, women's rights, and the ongoing struggle for equality in the workplace have paved the way for much good, but they have also created an enormous imbalance for woman, and for men.

In the effort to be seen, heard, and recognized, women have adapted a more masculine way of being in the workplace, in their relationships, and in the world. They have over-activated their masculine essence, allowing it to grow from a small amount to an unnatural predominance. More and more women have given up traditional roles to pursue careers, become leaders in the world, live without partners, and raise children as single parents. More and more women have attained personal wealth, success, and material possessions than ever before. While this is a marvelous and monumental achievement, it has also lessened their feminine essence, eclipsed the role of the male, and diminished his masculine essence overall.

WOMAN,
BE IN BALANCE

A woman who is running on mostly masculine essence often seeks out relationships with a man who is running mostly on his feminine. She does this in an unconscious effort to restore balance. A common complaint by the woman in this relationship dynamic is, 'I am always the one who has to do everything.' And from the man we hear, 'She has to be in control, doing everything herself.'

I coach many women and couples who struggle with this imbalance. The level of frustration, confusion, and pain in their hearts is profound. I see many relationships that suffer, dwindle, and die from this imbalance.

The solution that I offer to my clients to heal is simple; 'Woman, restore your feminine essence.' However, I am usually met with one of two responses: absolute bewilderment ('How am I supposed to do that?') or absolute refusal ('Why me?'). I do not suggest to my clients that the man start the process by balancing himself first. Everything in our world first comes from The Feminine, and this is no exception. When a woman balances herself in a relationship, or in any dynamic—then the whole relationship and the whole dynamic is immediately balanced. I have seen this happen over and over. It seems magical, simple, and elegant when it happens, and I am always delighted by it . . . and so are the women who do it—and the men are, too!

Restoring your feminine essence requires attention and awareness to shift your mindset, change your actions, and rebalance your energy. This restoration requires your daily attention to be aware of who you are as a woman and what *feminine* means to you. With greater clarity, you can become more and more balanced every day and in every way, in your workplace, at home, in your intimate relationship, your friendships, with your children, whether you are performing surgery, managing a team of people, being an artist, teaching a class, or making dinner.

Being balanced and in your feminine essence means being in your feminine power—which is receptive, nurturing, open, expansive, loving, wise, intuitive, and still. Being in your natural essence means that you can raise children as a single parent and still be feminine. You can be a manager, an executive, or the president of a company and still be feminine. You can become the president of the United States and still be feminine. You can be a woman who is a goddess on earth, no matter what job you have.

Life purpose, career, making money, being the head of a household, leadership and material power are all masculine pursuits, energetically speaking. When a woman is inspired to pursue these things, she must raise the level of her masculine essence in order to achieve them. There is nothing wrong with bringing these goals into your life, nor with raising your masculine essence to accomplish them. However, if you do not also raise your feminine essence, you may find yourself imbalanced.

Once you know who and what a woman is and how aligned you are with your own feminine and masculine essence levels, you can rebalance yourself using a very loving practice inspired by Mahatma Ghandi's famous quote, 'Be the change that you wish to see.' This subtle yet powerful visualization can transform yourself, a relationship, or a crisis quickly and profoundly. So for example:

- ❖ If you are wishing for more love in your life, be more loving in your life.
- ❖ If you want more peace in your heart, be more peaceful in all of your actions.
- ❖ If you desire more harmony in a relationship, be more harmonious with your partner, friend, co-worker or child . . . and with yourself.

Whatever you are hoping for does not need to come to you; *it is already within you*. Remember that you have all the qualities of The Goddess within you. Try the following exercise to activate these qualities and re-member them into being.

Be What You Wish For

For 30 days, send loving, peaceful, harmonious energy to the person or situation that you wish to change. Visualize it as if it has *already* happened. See yourself completely balanced, authentically loving, truly peaceful, easily harmonious and contentedly happy. Speak only kind words to others. Think positively whenever you are having a negative thought. Like Isis healing Osiris, call upon whatever you are wishing for to return to you, to be restored to wholeness, and remember to use love and have faith.

Remember, you are a temple.
You are sacred,

The Goddess has made you so.
Your eyes, Her vision,
Your hands, Her touch,
Your heart, Her love.

Remember, you are a vessel.
You are sacred,
The Goddess has made you so.

Your breath, Her wind,
Your pulse, Her waters,
Your blood, Her moon.

Remember, you are a light
You are sacred,
The Goddess has made you so.

Your bones, Her trees,
Your form, Her earth,
Your thoughts, Her prayers.
You are sacred.

The Goddess has made you so.

CHAPTER FOURTEEN

YOUR GODDESS BEAUTY

Beauty is not in the face;
beauty is a light in the heart.
~*Kahlil Gibran*

BEAUTY IS NOT IN THE EYE OF THE BEHOLDER. It is in the soul of every woman. The Goddess shows Herself in the form of *every* woman. She is every round curve of your hips and every soft rise of your belly. She is your strong legs standing upon the earth, your arms open wide. She is your keen mind listening to your wise heart. She is the sexy, the sensual, the flamboyant, the shy, and the modest woman. She is the small-framed, large-framed, curvaceous, straight, lean, ample, petite, or statuesque woman. She is the young woman, the middle aged woman, the elder woman . . . She is *all* woman and *all* women.

She is the part of yourself that you love and the parts you do not. She designed you in Her image. When you do not see *your* beauty, you do not see *Hers*. Know that when you reject any one part of yourself, you are also rejecting The Goddess as well. To accept yourself unconditionally is to *be* Her.

Historically we have been told who and what is beautiful. But a goddess on earth knows that she, and all women, are beautiful.

In whatever form your body has arrived on earth, The Goddess is reflected there. As a woman, you are made of curves and soft lines, round shapes, and hidden caverns. You are softness, sweetness, fluidity, and gentle movement. All women are works of art designed to represent the Goddess. It is your body that most reveals her form.

You may be thinking, "Why is this so important to talk about my body? Isn't it superficial to put so much emphasis on my looks, my body, and beauty?"

If we were talking only about the physical body and its looks, I would say yes. But we are not. Goddess beauty is our complete beauty, inside and out. It glows from within and it radiates out from you. It is not about what you look like, but rather how you feel. It is not at all about what advertising, the media, and Hollywood have deemed beauty to be. Goddess beauty is the knowing that all women possess Her beauty within them. It is like an un-mined, precious stone waiting to be discovered, faceted, polished, and cherished.

Because the female form is inherently lovely, esthetically pleasing, and artistically made, it belongs to the realm of The Goddess. She is all things that are beautiful, all things that generate beauty, and all things that carry it into the world. The Goddess is art, music, dance, and poetry. She is lithe movements and glorious colors, sweet melodies, and thoughtful words. These attributes are also found in your womanly form—the art of your smooth, soft lines, the music of your sweet voice, the ballet of your long sweeping curves, and the elegant poetry of your woman's heart. You are a beautiful goddess!

I remember once, asking my oldest niece, who was 13 at the time, if she knew herself to be beautiful. She looked at me with her enormous blue eyes and said quietly, "Yes, I do." Then she smiled and ran off to do whatever 13 year-old girls do when their aunties get all serious. I stood there, touched by her sweet, honest response. At her age, I had no idea that I was beautiful; instead I felt shame, embarrassment and shyness about my body. What freedom my niece must feel, what joy she must possess, and how like The Goddess she is.

Perhaps you have come to this chapter like my niece, knowing of your beauty. Nevertheless, read on; there is more to add to the precious gift of your confidence. But perhaps you are more like I used to be, coming to these pages unsure of your Goddess qualities. You, too, must read on, as there is potent wisdom ahead. However you come to know and appreciate your own Goddess-given beauty, know that it is yours by birthright. It belongs to you always and forever.

THE IMAGE
OF THE GODDESS

One of the most common topics I discuss with women clients is body image. No matter where you live, there is often a pressure for women to be the iconic shape and stylized form that Hollywood and the media have created. I live in Los Angeles, and it always feels that the pressure is uniquely intense here due to our proximity to the film and television industry. We are absolutely beautiful just as we are, but when we look in the mirror, we may not see what society dictates is beautiful. We may see a distorted image of ourselves, an imperfect form because it does not match up with the typical media version. It is heartbreaking to witness a woman who is rejecting her natural, beautiful self. And it is heartbreaking to be such a woman—I know this from first-hand experience.

My own struggle with body image was formed long ago, when I was a child. My father was clear about what he considered beautiful. My sisters and I were either complimented or criticized depending on our appearance to him. My mother, too, paid so much attention to her own appearance and to ours that I learned that if I were not perfectly thin, perfectly dressed, and perfectly behaved, I would meet with her disapproval. No wonder as a teen and young adult, I could not see beauty in myself, only imperfection. These days, I still wrestle with the image of perfection, so I must make daily effort to see myself as beautiful. The good news is that this effort has helped me to *feel* more beautiful—more and more each day.

I have come to know myself as a goddess and to celebrate my body as beautiful. My relationship with The Divine Feminine has helped me reject my own self-rejection. Her love for me has inspired me to love myself the same way that She does—with grace, ease, patience and without conditions. She is my Divine Mother, and in Her eyes, I am beautiful.

> *Behold, you are beautiful, my love, behold, you are beautiful!*
> *You are altogether beautiful, my darling, and there is no blemish in you.*
> Song of Solomon, 4-7

There are many reasons why a woman rejects herself, and does not see or accept her beauty: negative parental criticism, trauma around sexuality, and physical and/or sexual abuse are a few of the situations that can lead to this self-rejection. The diminishing of your own beautifulness creates a profound disconnection not only from The Goddess but from recognizing yourself *as* a goddess. Self-rejection pushes you further and further away from celebrating who you truly are.

Know that The Goddess is all women, in all of their forms and body types. There is no ideal shape. Acknowledging your beauty is not vain, but a way to express gratitude to the Creatress who made you in Her image. Your body is a living statue in Her honor. Your self-love is a living prayer to Her. Your expressions of love to others are invocations that draw Her near. Celebrate this by celebrating yourself. Proclaim and reclaim your Self as beautiful, right now!

Self-love, confidence, and inner peace are the ingredients of real Goddess beauty. You can develop these attributions at any age. They arise from the integration of your inner and outer self, like two laser beams of light coming together as one. When this occurs, you become enormously powerful and shine brightly. When you integrate holistically, what shines forth is pure, divine beauty.

I have found that when my life is integrated and in balance, I am glowing with inner and outer gorgeousness. When my life is out of alignment, I dull down a bit, and my feelings of beauty fade.

What do I mean by living a life in balance? I am referring to taking care of yourself. This is expressed when you are loving towards others, receiving love and intimacy, eating and sleeping well, pursuing your life's purpose, and having a fulfilling earthly and spiritual life with wonderful relationships, interests—and lots and lots of laughter and enjoyment. If you are a woman who has not yet enjoyed sexual intimacy, then a balanced life would include an interest in dating, and unashamedly exploring and discovering what physical pleasure means for you.

Try this exercise to understand the balance in your life.

The Goddess Wheel of Life

Every culture uses the wheel to represent movement, cycles, growth, and change. The circle has strong ties to The Goddess, as Her core teachings are about wholeness, inclusivity, and fullness. She is the most balancing essence in the universe—cooling where there is heat, nourishing where there is hunger, and loving when there is discord. This exercise is used in some form by many coaches (myself and my own health and wellness coach included) as a wonderful visual tool to measure how balanced or imbalanced your life is at this time. Here is an example of a blank Goddess Wheel. You can find a blank template for The Goddess Wheel of Life on my website.

Along the outer edge of the wheel, next to each section; write the areas of your life you would like to measure such as friendships, career, romance, financial, health, and so on. Then color in each area starting from the center up to whatever level indicates how full that area of your life is.

Here is an example of what your Goddess Wheel of Life may look like:

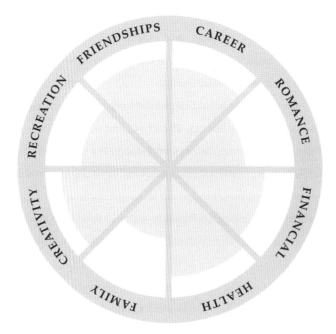

Now imagine removing the outer rim of the wheel and sending it on its way so that you only see the colored parts. Would your wheel roll smoothly, or would it wobble? Or would your wheel be so uneven that it simply falls over?

This Goddess Wheel of Life shows you how full your life is. The Way of The Goddess is to bring all areas of your life into balance *with each other*. This means that where you see a very low area, focus on bringing it up to midway. Where you see a high area, bring it down towards midway. When all areas of your life are in balance with each other, you can work on raising all of it up, remembering that you want them to move together, not separately. Imagine as you work towards balancing your wheel that all areas are brought to a level that helps you feel comfortable, at ease, and graceful. Bringing your life into balance is how you experience the beauty of

The Goddess. Bringing balance into your life is the foundation for integrating The Goddess into your body.

INNER
BEAUTY

Your thoughts, feelings, and emotions about yourself and others are directly related to your beauty. Any negative thinking, fear, worry, or unkind, jealous and hurtful intentions can affect your beauty.

Outer beauty, which is fragile and dependent on circumstances, is like the petals of a flower. It's designed to be enticing, attractive, and alluring. Inner beauty is more like the roots of the plant—strong, lasting, and stable. It's designed to be resilient and supportive. Inner beauty is positive thinking, loving self-talk, self-confidence, and self-love. Goddess beauty is your positive, loving inner self shining through. Even the most beautiful woman is not in her Goddess beauty without this inner strength.

We all have an inner critic, or a criticizing voice in our head who can be very harsh at times. This critical, negative voice is the part of us that is wounded, unsure, and sometimes angry. She is afraid to be hurt any further than she has already been. She is unsure how to feel good about herself as she has only known pain. And she is angry that she has not been able to express her true feelings. It is difficult for this inner critic to connect to your beauty, so she will often sabotage your efforts to feel good about yourself. This is the inner ear that refuses to accept compliments, the inner eye that has difficulty seeing yourself as beautiful, and the inner voice that speaks to you only using negatives. She feeds on your deepest fears of unworthiness, bringing up the shame that you may have about your body.

You can learn to counter the negativity of your inner critic by using positive, self-loving language. Speak to her as you would talk to a hurting child, with patience and with love. *Remember that the ways of The Goddess are loving, kind, supportive, and inclusive.* Repeat this as a mantra to transform your inner voice from negative to positive. If you are unsure how to speak with this inner positive voice, here is a chart to get you started. Your inner beauty is on its way!

IF YOU HAVE NEGATIVE:	KNOW THAT:	AFFIRMATION:
BODY IMAGE	*Your body reflects the Goddess' body, You are created in Her image.*	*I am the refection of The Goddess in every way.*
	Your face was chosen by The Goddess to mirror Hers.	*All women are beautiful in the eyes of The Goddess.*
	You are in charge of your body; it is a gift from The Goddess.	*The Goddess is every woman, myself included. I am a goddess on earth.*
	You are a sacred Goddess vessel.	*The Goddess resides in my body, as my body.*
SELF-ESTEEM	*You are a divine goddess on earth.*	*I call upon the strength and power of The Goddess now.*
	You are filled completely with love from The Goddess.	*My goddess-self is emerging more and more each day.*
	It is time to surrender your doubts, fears and worries to The Goddess.	*Every day, in every way I am becoming more and more of a goddess on earth.*
	You were born to receive the all the blessings of The Goddess.	*My spectacular goddess-self is here, now. I release what stands in my way.*

OUTER BEAUTY

Women have been beautifying themselves with various forms of adornment, dress, and cosmetics for more than 6000 years. Ancient Egyptian vials and containers still containing cosmetics and perfumes have found their way from deep within the earth into museums. Both ancient and modern recipes for beauty treatments have included animal and vegetable fats, herbs, spices, plants, ground pigments, and essential oils. Artificial chemicals have also joined the list, but a recent trend implores us to re-member more natural ingredients in our *régime de beauté*.

I have a passion for collecting books on herbalism, aromatherapy, and perfumery. I am always on the lookout for beauty treatment recipes. From my research, I have found many formulas inspired by ancient women's beauty wisdom. I have begun to formulate my own recipes and even dedicate a small walk-in closet for my apothecary where I store all the supplies I need to keep on hand to make my own beauty products.

The word 'apothecary' means both the person who dispenses (like the pharma-cists of today) and the shop or storage place for all the ingredients, bottles, vials, and finished products. The ancient apothecary, usually a man, dispensed healing potions, salves, and medicines made from herbs, flowers, spices, plants, and minerals. Once women apothecaries came on the scene, about 1865, I imagine that little vials of beauty treatments emerged as well.

Many women think that a beauty treatment is what *causes* them to be beautiful, as if without it, they are not. While most treatments do work to nourish and beautify your hair and skin, this is not the main benefit. What is really happening through a beauty treatment is that you start to *feel* beautiful inside. All the beauty treatments in the world cannot measure up to feeling good about yourself from the inside. Just as your skin is mostly nourished from within by the food you eat, so is your beauty nourished by the feelings and emotions that you have about it. So when you enjoy a pampering moment, remember that not only are you taking good care of your body, it is your internal, spirit of beauty that you are bringing forth. This is your true beauty—let it be revealed.

It is not difficult to start your own beauty apothecary. Many supplies you may already have, and others are easy to obtain. I have chosen simple recipes with just one or two ingredients to help you get started. Feel free to spruce them up, start your own research, add to them and even combine formulas. Experiment and get creative. The key is to have fun and enjoy treating yourself to beauty the Goddess way.

What you will need:

❖ large glass bowl not used for cooking*
❖ wooden spoon not used for cooking*
❖ 2 and 4 ounce glass bottles with corks or screw caps
❖ 16 ounce glass jars with screw lids
❖ Melita® extra large empty tea bags
❖ wooden chopsticks

*I keep a selection of extra bowls and spoons for mixing the ingredients used in these rituals. To keep the rituals pure, do not use containers previously used for food.

RECIPES
FOR BEAUTY

Lavender

Lavender, originally of Mediterranean origin, now grows all over the world. It is renowned for the calming effect it has upon the nervous system and for its sweet, slightly camphorous scent. As an essential oil, it is extraordinarily healing and beneficial to the skin. It aids in relaxing the inner self, which then transfers calm to your outer self—and voilà, you feel more beautiful.

Sugar scrub:

- ❖ ½ cup of dried (organic, pesticide-free) lavender buds
- ❖ 2 cups of fine sugar, preferably coconut or organic cane or beet
- ❖ jojoba oil to fill bottle size you have
- ❖ *Option:* add 6 drops of lavender essential oil
- ❖ store in a glass jar indefinitely

Mix the ingredients with jojoba oil in a glass bowl until a thick paste forms. Store some in your bottle. Rub the rest gently onto to your skin in the shower for gentle exfoliation. Say this as you exfoliate:

> *Goddess beauty—bring it in, release what's old and let it go.*
> *Goddess beauty—bring it in, Goddess beauty make it so!*

Body oil:

- ❖ dried (organic, pesticide free) lavender buds to fill ¼ of your bottle
- ❖ 4 ounces of oil, preferably jojoba, rice bran, grape seed, or meadowfoam seed oil
- ❖ *Option:* add 6 drops of lavender essential oil

Gently crush the lavender between your palms to release the essential oils. Put the crushed buds into the bottle, then fill with oil. You can let this oil infuse for several days or weeks or use immediately, applying to skin before or after a warm bath. Store in a glass bottle indefinitely. Say this as you apply the oil:

Softly, smoothly I rub you in
Goddess beauty from toes to chin

Rose

Rose is the queen of flowers—elegant, fragrant, alluring, and nourishing to our skin and psyche. Rose has the highest vibration of any flower, so the essential oil of rose helps raise your own vibration. This beauty bath is best taken when you are feeling down or under the illusion that you are not beautiful. It raises your energy, renews your loveliness, and creates a sense of wellbeing from within that shows up on the outside.

Bath:

❖ pure rose essential oil (it's best to use this diluted with jojoba, as rose oil is costly, and the diluted form is best for contact with your skin)

❖ 2 cups of sea salt

❖ fresh red rose petals (free of pesticides)

Draw a bath that is slightly hotter than usual so you can let it steep with the ingredients before entering.

Meanwhile, in a large glass bowl, pour in the sea salt, then 10 drops of rose essential oil. Mix with a wooden chopstick or wooden spoon until the oil is no longer visible. Gently mix in 10-15 fresh rose petals.

Now remove your clothing and stand over the bowl with your hands hovering above it, palms facing the mixture and say the following:

Queen of flowers, roses red
Fragrant diva, beauty's friend
Your essence mine, my beauty yours
A bath of beauty—illusion be shed!

Breathe in the fragrance of rose, wafting the aroma with your hands towards your face. Imagine that the energy of the rose oil is in your hands and is being applied to your face where it will go deep within, magically transforming your own essence, removing the veils of illusion that keep you from feeling beautiful.

Next, dip your hands into the bowl, without touching the salts, to scoop up the *energy*. Begin applying the energy to your body, starting with your heart, making sure to envelop your entire body with the essence of rose.

Now pour the salt mixture into the bath, swirling it clockwise as you recite the poem again. When the water temperature is right for you, step in and soak. Please note that this is a soaking bath, not a washing bath, so just relax. I especially enjoy this bath ritual before going to bed.

Chamomile

Chamomile, like lavender, is soothing and relaxing. It hails from ancient Egypt, Greece, and Rome. In Europe, it is usually taken as a tea. Applied to the skin, it's especially good as it balances, tones, and heals. Appropriate for all skin types, it acts as an internal and external anti-inflammatory. Chamomile can calm your nervous system, allowing you to relax and let your body repair and restore itself.

Eye Pads and Skin Toner:

❖ 2 chamomile tea bags, steeped in hot (not boiling) distilled water

Place your hands over the tea as it is cooling and say:

Tea of beauty, tea of grace, relax my mind, relax my face
Goddess beauty, I wish it so — I charge this tea with all I know!

Remove the tea bags and let them cool to room temperature. Save the tea to use later when it has cooled. Lie down and place one tea bag over each eye. Pat lightly and relax, turning each tea bag over once. Using a cotton pad, apply the cooled, leftover tea as a skin toner to your face and throat, then pat dry.

You can save the tea in a sealed glass bottle in the fridge for up to a week, but throw away the tea bags after one use.

To make this toner more moisturizing (and extend its shelf life), add vegetable glycerin (20:80).

Face Serum:

- ❖ 2 ounces of jojoba, meadowfoam seed, or camellia oil
- ❖ 6 drops of blue chamomile essential oil

Mix the ingredients and apply a few drops to your face after washing. Gently rub into skin in an upwards motion. Store in a small glass bottle for up to six months. Say this as you rub the serum in::

The face of The Goddess is mine right now
With scent and oil She shows me how

Honey

Honey is good food for our bodies and our skin. It is antiviral, antibacterial, and is also a humectant (it keeps things moist). When used on the face, it delivers a deeply moisturizing treatment, softening and revitalizing the skin. Used for centuries for its youth-enhancing qualities, honey was once a well-kept beauty secret, mostly used by queens and royalty. It has been enjoying a new popularity recently, showing up in soaps, scrubs, and hair and skin care products.

While we cannot control which plants and trees bees go to, and therefore we cannot be certain to get purely organic honey, it's still best to buy it labeled as organic. This ensures as much of possible that it is pesticide free. Raw honey (unheated) retains the living enzymes, which is what gives honey its fabulous healing and restorative qualities.

Facial:

- ❖ 3 tablespoons of organic, raw honey
- ❖ 1–2 drops of any floral essential oil such as rose, chamomile or lavender

Mix the ingredients with a wooden chopstick. Then apply it to your face, avoiding the eye area. Say this affirmation:

Beauty and sweetness, I have Goddess skin
All that is outward, shines from within

Leave the honey mixture on your face for 30 minutes. Rinse with warm water and then cool water. Gently pat dry.

Hair conditioner:

❖ 2 cups organic, raw honey
❖ ¼ cup of rose water

Pour into a glass bottle and shake gently until mixed. Apply to freshly washed and rinsed hair. Leave in or rinse out. Say this as you apply:

The Goddess has blessed me
With gifts from the bee;
Hair that is lovely, shining and free

For an intensely moisturizing hair treatment, apply the honey without rose water to freshly washed and rinsed hair; leave for 30 minutes, then rinse well.

FEEL YOUR OWN BEAUTY

Throughout time, a woman's beauty has been the subject of much attention. Poems, songs, psalms, and epic plays have all been written about it. Ancient wars have been won and lost over it. Entire industries have made billions of dollars from it, and our modern culture values beauty almost as much as it does wealth.

But it is time—long overdue time, to see, and feel your beauty in a much different way; with acceptance, joy, love, and ease—in the way that The Goddess sees you . . . which is beautiful just as you are.

I am beautiful,
I am goddess,
I am perfect in every way.

I am the vessel,
the faultless shape,
and the gorgeous form
that carries Her Divine Light
into the world for all to receive.

From me, this essence flows;
that of loveliness,
exquisiteness
and sacred female ways.

I am beautiful,
I am goddess,
And I am perfect in every way.

CHAPTER FIFTEEN

THE LUNAR GODDESS

As if you were on fire from within.
The moon lives in the lining of your skin.

~Pablo Neruda

ANY MOON GODDESSES HAVE BEEN WORSHIPPED, and many cultures have recognized the feminine power of the moon, but none have become so popular as The Triple Goddess. She is a fundamental and dynamic archetype, a singular goddess with three aspects, each representing a major phase of a woman's life. These phases are like the seasons in the way they are marked by particular patterns and occur at specific times of a woman's life.

There is no actual reference to The Triple Goddess in ancient records of Goddess worship. We can see subtle references to, and perhaps the early origins of The Triple Goddess in the ancient Egyptian representations of Isis' headdress   a full moon flanked by the horns of the cosmic cow or two crescent moons. She is also visible in the Celtic *triskelion*, the triple spiral that represents the three states of womanness: innocence/maiden, compassion/mother, and wisdom/crone. Worship of The Triple Goddess first appears in the Neo-Pagan and Wiccan spiritualities that surfaced in Europe during the 19th and 20th centuries and she now continues to be a source of guidance and wisdom for women.

REVISITING THE MAIDEN, THE MOTHER, AND THE CRONE

Traditionally the three phases of a woman's life have been called *the maiden, the mother,* and *the crone.* They were names used to describe specific periods of time in a woman's life: her innocent, virginal youth; her womanly child-bearing adulthood; and her wise elder years. I love these names for the seasons of my life, and all the ancient and mystical feelings that they activate within me, but I believe all three need some updating to our times. The maiden no longer reflects the current trends of sexuality that young women experience. The mother does not represent the many women who, either by choice or for health reasons do not have children today. And the crone does not begin to express the vibrancy of many women's active elder lives as they live well into their 80's and beyond. So to reframe the beauty, grace, and loveliness of a modern woman's life seasons, I call them *the bud*, *the blossom*, and *the root*.

THE TRIPLE GODDESS MOON ASSOCIATIONS

As with other elements of a woman's wisdom and spirituality, The Triple Goddess is deeply associated with the moon, especially three of its major phases—the waxing crescent, the full moon, and the waning crescent. In depictions of this goddess, she wears a crown of the full moon with the two opposing crescents on either side.

❖ The bud is the waxing crescent moon as it gathers light to ready itself to bloom.

❖ The blossom is the full moon, shining its reflective light upon the world.

❖ The root is the waning crescent moon as it sheds its light, slowly becoming the dark moon, which signifies the time of our life when we prepare to go into the earth, towards the realm of the afterlife.

In reality, these seasons overlap each other and may repeat themselves depending on each individual woman and her personal life path. Each one of these seasons offers many wonderful opportunities for growth, transformation, and learning more about what being a woman is for you. Each has its own special gifts to offer.

The Budding Woman

The Budding years are from puberty until about age 20. These are years of high energy, growth, discovery, and new prospects. Precious, innocent, and fresh years, they are filled with emerging and tentative light. Unlike the older, more traditional concept of the maiden, the modern Bud-woman's phase depends not on her virginity, but rather on her first experiences and initiations into life, sexuality, and womanhood. This season's gifts are full of youthful experiment, naïveté, exploration, and infinite potential. This is a woman's springtime, her opening up to learning about life, love, and her feminine power.

A woman in her budding years is at the start of her journey. She is new, tender, and full of sweetness as her tightly closed petals are just about to open and bloom. She has yet to fully awaken to the strength and power of her own feminine essence, as well as to the essence of the masculine. For now, all of life is shining upon her and she absorbs it all.

This young woman is a novice-priestess, completely unknowing of the mysteries of life but eager to test the waters. She seeks guidance from outside, given that her intuition and inner voice are only beginning to sprout.

The Bud-woman slowly becomes acquainted with the light of The Feminine that has been flowing through her from the time she was born—and at some point she longs to shine with it. As she matures, she becomes like the waxing crescent moon that captures attention, growing brighter and moving towards fullness. This is a time of receiving all she can from life to gather knowledge, experience, and wisdom.

Bud-woman may not yet know or feel that she is a goddess, but she will become more aware of it as she makes the tender transition from girl to woman.

A girl experiencing this season from puberty to the age of about 20 is carefree and lighthearted. Everything about life is exciting, dramatic, and enticing. Her sexuality is experimental, delicate, and awkward as she learns about falling in love and the pleasures of her body.

The Bud phase can repeat itself in a woman's life. A woman around the age of 50 who re-experiences herself at the bud-phase is equally excited and exciting—her life is about to renew itself. She is most likely starting something new: perhaps a creative endeavor, a new business, or a new passion for a field of study. She may also be in the process of rekindling intimacy with an existing partner, is about to take on a new lover, or she is just about to fall in love as her sexuality begins to re-awaken at this time.

The message of The Goddess during these years is: *Begin.*

The Blossoming Woman

The Blossoming years are from about age 20 until about 50. They are a time for creativity, fertility, and womanly knowing. As the Blossom-woman's petals fully flower, her body opens to life, to her feminine essence, as well as to the masculine essence.

Blossom-woman is not only further along in learning about the mysteries and secrets of being a woman, she is also living them more fully and adeptly. Her power and knowledge are increasing in both a womanly and sexual sense. This is a woman's summertime—her season to fully blossom and be filled with creativity and creation. It becomes her autumn as she nears 50—her time then for harvest and celebration. A woman may choose to create and raise children during these years, bringing new generations into the world. Or she may re-create/re-birth herself, channeling the energy of the creatrix into her own work and passions. Or she may do both.

The Blossom-woman may know herself as a goddess at this time as she fully engages her power of procreative feminine essence and sexuality. She is no longer at the start of the journey, nor is she naïve in her search for life's mysteries because much has already been revealed to her through her life experiences. She is a full-priestess now, practicing her womanhood with calm and self-assuredness. Seeking guidance more from inside than outside of herself, she has learned to trust her intuition and her inner voice.

At this time, a woman's petals are open wide. She is like the full moon, brightly shining light. Radiant and glowing, she sends her light and feminine essence outward and into the world. Her light is more focused than ever, as it has accumulated power and radiance over the years.

A woman experiencing the blossoming season can be nourishing, supportive, and encouraging of others. She is very capable of sustaining her partner, children, and friends. However, this can lead her to feel depleted if she is not careful to nurture and take care of herself.

Those women older than 50 who re-experience themselves as Blossom-women are flowering once again with all the vibrancy of their middle years, but they now do so with grace and poise. This is an especially beautiful type of blossoming because such a woman introduces elegance into her life without the arms-flailing energy of youth, or the fertility of her middle years. This is a gift she receives once she has become peaceful in her heart, knowing in her mind, and sensual within her body.

The message of The Goddess during these years is: *Flourish.*

The Rooting Woman

The Rooting years are from about 50 until death. They are experienced as a grounded, wise, and graceful time filled with tranquility and depth. This can be a powerful inner phase as Root-woman's feminine essence and light go deep within her rather than out into the world.

The rooting years are a season of depth and inner knowing. The Root-woman becomes the knower of life's secrets through the sum of her experiences. She is like the waning crescent as her light diminishes until she becomes the dark moon preparing to transition into the new moon. This is a mystically luminous time for the Root-woman as her light now shines inward to become a spiritually nourishing inner glow. This internal light is unlike the gathering light of the bud or the shining light of the flower. For many Root-women, this inner-focused light can energize her with a powerful surge of feminine essence that can both inspire and nourish many more spring and summer seasons before she transitions from life.

This is the wintertime of a woman's life, but it need not be a cold, desolate winter but rather a delightful opportunity to re-experience spring when the snow melts, a time to watch new buds grow from wizened roots. Root-woman is free to love and be at ease with her sexuality without the task of raising children or even rebirthing herself. She is full of womanly playfulness and sexy desires. Laden with the insights of her past seasons, she comes to the wise root-woman years refined and experienced. Her world slows down, encouraging time for pure enjoyment and unhurried pleasure.

The Root-woman no longer *practices* at being a goddess; rather she now *becomes* The Goddess, embodying Her more than ever. She is also now a high priestess, the wise-woman, and her legacy is to be the example of goddess-ness for younger women. She knows the mystery of life and desires to reveal it to others. She seeks guidance only from within, having fully learned to use her strong intuition and her inner voice to guide her.

Root-woman's body begins to descend towards the underworld during these years. Everything begins to move downward and closer to the earth. She becomes rounder and softer. Between 40 and 60, our blood waters begin to settle and our inner tides eventually become still. This is when the life force energy of our menstrual flow turns inward to nourish us, as opposed to flowing out of our bodies to nourish the world.

This is a rich, potent time in a woman's life, filled with elder wisdom. If this stilling of your blood waters happens prior to 60 years of age—whether naturally, or because of surgical menopause due to hysterectomy, you have been especially chosen to receive your *priestess-hood* early. You are ready to fulfill the elder rites of teaching and to receive your elegance sooner. At whatever age you come into this season of life, you may feel gratitude, relief, fear, grief, happiness, and curiosity. If you can come to this final season of life with excitement and wonder, you will discover that it is a magnificent time filled with many divine gifts.

The message of The Goddess during these years is: *Know.*

THE TRIPLE
GODDESS MOONS

The moon and its movements mirror those three large phases of a woman's life, but they also mirror the micro-phases of her bodily functions. In essence, each lunar month is also a 28-day dress rehearsal for the three phases of your life. A woman's womb begins each month as a bud, fresh and new. Then as your womb waxes, it builds up with nourishing blood, becoming full and transitioning from the bud to the blossom. As your ovaries release their fruit, there is the possibility of creating life. If no life is created, your womb wanes, releasing the menstrual flow, and you deliver this life energy out into the world. At this time, both the bud and the flower disappear and the womb becomes the root, deep and still until the cycle begins again.

Each month until menopause, your womb waxes full and then wanes empty. You are nourished and cleansed by this sacred blood. Just as the ocean is pulled high and low, your own inner tides rise and fall each month as the moon governs your body. Our blood is mostly salt and water. We women are, in fact, a small, salty sea and our female waters dance to the moon's celestial songs.

Each phase of the moon corresponds to our menstrual cycle; our blood and hormones wax and wane with the moon—from dark to full. Technically, there are 13 full moons each year, and most women will also have 13 cycles of bleeding. It used to be that women started their moonflow during the dark phase of the moon, but today, women bleed during any of the moon's phases. This is an imbalance; it is as if our blood has lost its relationship to the Great Mother Moon.

One of the ways that I have helped myself re-connect to the lunar essence is by studying each phase to find its meaning and correlation within my life, and then by creating ritual and sacredness for the lunar cycle and my lunar blood.

While our bodies may be out of synch with Mother Moon, you can still connect to her wisdom no matter when your moonblood is flowing. Each of the moon's monthly phases offers special guidance for you if you choose to align with it:

THE CRESCENT MOONS. The waxing crescent that is the new moon and the waning crescent moon that appears before the dark moon are especially significant for women. These graceful slivers of light instruct you to expand (waxing crescent) during the new moon and contract (waning crescent) after the full moon. This is the ebb and flow of life—filling and releasing.

The two crescent moons are harbingers of beginnings and endings. They announce that we are about to transition from one phase of our lives to another. In their cycle, they show us that life is always turning on itself and that in everything we do, we will come full circle. The crescent moons are symbolic of how a woman's natural cycles remind her that in life everything is always on its way towards becoming something else. Everything is always changing.

These moons are supportive in nature. The waxing crescent/new moon assists us to gather light and build energy. Then as the full moon winds down, the waning crescent assists in releasing and letting go. During either phase of these moons, look for ways you need to be supported as well as ways you can be supportive.

Crescent moons are like thresholds, or portals between the worlds of the light and dark as the moon waxes and wanes. They are midwives that assist the Light of the moon to be born. These moon phases are not a time of physical action or non-action, but rather a time to be mindful and observe; look for opportunities to cross over into new projects or ways to leave situations that no longer serve you. These moon phases are applicable during all three seasons of a woman's life.

The Lunar Goddess is in transition during these crescent phases, so if you are bleeding during this phase, Her wisdom is for you to become aware and patient with your own transitions.

THE FULL MOON. This moon's power comes from the enormous amount of light it has gathered and carries to full term, which it then delivers, shining out into the world. In this sense, it is both a receiver and reflector of light. The full moon shines on you so that you are lit up for all to see. It is a time of high visibility.

This moon phase is associated with the blossoming years, but it is also symbolic of the fullness and harvest throughout all seasons of a woman's life.

This light exposes every corner of your being; you cannot hide from it. Open yourself up to receive light during this phase of the moon and be courageous enough to shine your own light into the world. As light fills you, it also emanates from you, encouraging you to lead the way for others. The full moon reminds us that we are beings of Feminine Light, designed to give and receive. You can assist others to brighten their light when you permit yourself to shine.

For some, the intensity of this moon can bring up deep feelings of unworthiness as we are shown our true, bright nature. Self-love, positive feelings and loving expressions are a perfect way to support yourself during this time. During the full moon, you may witness the completion of many things. If you allow it, it can assist you in releasing into the world all that you have worked so hard to create.

The Lunar Goddess is brightly illuminated during this time so if you are bleeding during this phase, Her wisdom is for you to shine and let yourself sparkle.

THE DARK MOON. This is an important lunar phase for women usually not included in The Triple Goddess tradition, and is not even recognized on traditional lunar calendars, which consider this phase 'the new moon.' This brief phase occurs just before the first visible crescent sliver of the new moon and is often called the 'Dark Goddess,' the 'Lilith Moon,' 'Kali,' 'Hecate,' and 'Morrighan Moon.' This is the moon of the warrior and protectress goddesses. It is also associated with the final transformation—our inevitable descent and transition into the underworld of death.

The dark moon is hidden from view, as are the primal shadow parts of our psyche. All of our individual mysteries, as well as the grander mysteries of life, are hidden, yet have the opportunity to be discovered during this phase. This is a mystical time meant for secret, sacred wisdom—a time to embrace the mysteriousness of your feminine being. This moon takes us into the deep, dark below-ness of life and all the way down into our subconscious to reveal that transformation is but a natural part of life's many cycles.

When the moon is dark, it is neither receiving nor reflecting light. The lunar energies are still. This is a brief but extraordinarily potent time for women, associated with the moment just prior to conception before the spark of life is lit and the moment of death just as the soul leaves the body. No actions, either physical or mental, should be taken during this phase, no projects started, and nothing either released or begun.

The Lunar Goddess is quiet and still during the dark moon phase, so if you are bleeding during this phase, Her wisdom is for you to go inward, be in the flow, rest, meditate, and be calm. Only when the tiniest sliver of the new moon is visible in the night sky are you ready to emerge as well.

THE NEW MOON. When the first sliver of the moon's light becomes visible in the night sky, it is called the new moon, or waxing crescent. Light first emerges from the dark of the underworld, ready to be born again into the world. This is a time of new life, resurrection, beginnings, and new ventures. It is an excellent time to move, become active, begin, plan and prepare.

The new moon is charged with activity, expectation, and excitement. But it can also be a period when you can be protective of your endeavors, revealing only that which is necessary, a sliver of light. The purpose of keeping your own special secrets is so that outside influences cannot dilute them. Just as the moon does not reveal herself fully at this time, neither should you. Allow your ideas and projects to build powerful energy and gather light by keeping them close during this time. Trust your instincts during the new moon, stay focused, set clear intentions, and let life's gifts be revealed in their own time.

The Lunar Goddess is planning and preparing for her appearance in the world at this time, so if you are bleeding during this phase, Her wisdom is for you to imagine that your body is a vessel receiving and absorbing light.

SACRED MOON. Even if you were never aware of the moon's influence in your life and upon your body, she is there, shining down on you. Even if her cycles and phases mean no more to you than light coming and going at night, her rhythm still affects you. And even if your monthly blood was nothing more than a nuisance to you, every drop is still called forth by the sacred force of the moon.

To be female is to be lunar. To look up and study the moon is to study your inner-most self, your innermost nature, and your goddess-ness. Dance in her light, bathe in it, treasure it always. Lunar light belongs to you.

By the first light of the newest moon,
I emerge slim-hipped and lithe.

Youthful—with my heart not yet knowing Her.

By the full light of the fullest moon,
I dance wide-hipped and full breasted.

Womanly—with my arms spread wide, receiving Her.

By the darkest night of the darkest moon,
I am still, serene, and wise.

Magnificent—with my body descending
into Her, becoming Her.

I am Goddess, I am Moon, I am Woman.

CHAPTER SIXTEEN

WOMEN'S MYSTERIES

And you who seek to know me,
know that the seeking and yearning will avail you not...
for if that which you seek, you find not within yourself,
you will never find it without.

~Doreen Valiente

THERE HAS ALWAYS BEEN A STRONG CORRELATION between the ways of The Goddess and the mysteries of life. Women naturally have an aura of being mysterious.

One rather mundane reason for our mystery may be that all of our female apparatus are hidden deep within us. They are not visible to anyone, ourselves included. Before X-rays and MRIs, the typical woman could not know what it looked like *in there* unless she read medical books or studied autopsies. For millennia, no one knew what went on inside a woman's body—how she carried a child, how she released uterine blood. It was all one big mysterious, unknown territory like the dark side of the moon.

Today, of course, women know what goes on inside our bodies, how we work, what everything looks like, and where everything goes. But there is still mystery surrounding women—not about our anatomy, but about our feminine nature, our connection to the moon, and our monthly blood flow. These are called *the blood mysteries.*

THE BLOOD MYSTERIES

When you look up in the night sky and see the moon, know that she is not just shining down upon you—she is shining *for* you. The moon governs so much of life here on earth, and she is very profoundly connected to women. Our monthly blood and the function of our ovaries and uterus are aligned with her cycles, and our bodies respond to her powerful gravitational pull as we gain water and release blood—just as the ocean's tides swell and subside.

Long ago, women were the keepers of the fire, the healers, the knowers of all things herbal, magical, and mysterious. In shadowy tents and fire-lit caves, we anointed ourselves with perfumed oils, applied henna to our hands and feet, stained our lips with blood red berries, pierced our earlobes, noses, lips and nether regions—all in the name of The Goddess. We circled together with our wide hips swaying left and right and our bare breasts swinging to the beat of the drums under a moonlit night sky. We stood together in tribal circles during our moontime when our powers were surging. This was a time when women gathered with women to sing, dance, chant, pray, heal, mourn, laugh . . . and to bleed.

One of the most precious and mysterious gifts The Goddess has given us is Her blood, and all of the teachings and blessings that go along with it. Your monthly bleeding is a very sacred and potent female time that was once steeped in ritual and holiness. Indigenous women of many cultures refer to this time of bleeding as their *moon* or *moontime.* I call it my moonflow.

From the first stories of the very first woman's moonflow, it was thought to be mysterious. For a human to bleed without wounding, and to bleed steadily for many days without dying, was a wonder to the ancient people of the world. Many thought of it as Divine.

I, like many Western women, did not know that my moonflow was sacred, holy or special at first. As a young girl, my first moonflows were unwelcomed, embarrassing, and distasteful. They were messy, painful, smelly, and uncomfortable experiences. They did not initiate me at all into womanhood, but rather humiliated me onto the sidelines during gym or at the public pool. They often sent me to the restroom with untimely leakages. My periods forced me to wear a skirt so that the bulk of my pad did not show through my jeans—I was not permitted to use a tampon as a young girl. An association with shame—along with the other negative feelings I had about becoming a woman—began to form. Nowhere in my young womanhood was there any specialness associated with the flow of my lunar blood. I wish there had been.

If I had a daughter, I would have told her of this very special event early on. She would have waited for it eagerly, hoping that one day, her woman's blood would be called down by the moon, bringing magic and wisdom into her life. I would have shared with her that her body was a vessel that held this gift. Each month she would pour this blood out into the world, until one day it would cease to flow outwards and she would begin to keep its essence for herself. She would have known that her blood was the blood of life, the blood of beginnings and endings. I would have held her close and whispered to her that the miracle of being a woman is that only we can create new life with our body and nourish it with our lunar blood.

By the light of the moon, I would have shown her how to anoint herself, how to dance away the dull ache from her bleeding womb. I would have taught her how to watch the changing shape of the moon each night for signs of her cycle and to take time during her moonflow for rest, ritual, gratitude, and prayer.

If your story is like mine, and you do not know how incredibly sacred, potent, and mysterious your lunar blood is, or even if you have this knowledge within your heart, I welcome you to this chapter as a mother would—with joy and love. I also welcome you as a sister—with delight and celebration that you are here. I stand beside you as a daughter of the moon, in the great circle alongside all women as we lift our faces to Her—The Great Mother Moon.

THE GREAT
MOTHER MOON

In ancient times, the moon was known and worshipped as The Great Mother, whose feminine essence was contained in the dark, fertile places of a woman's body and in the blood that flowed from the womb each month. From Her, all life came forth and will at the end, return to Her again. It is she who nourishes, heals, and guides us. It is The Great Mother's gentle, magnetic pull and beautiful light that calls down our blood.

Precious and bittersweet, the releasing of uterine blood is a time that can be painful for some women. For others, it is a sensual and womanly time. For all women, however, it is a time for being energetically still, for retreat from social activity, and for going within spiritually. Your moonflow is an opportunity for meditation; for creative energies to be nourished; for the conceiving of ideas; for pampering your body; and for prayer. We are spiritually potent and energetically powerful from the start of our bleeding until just afterwards as our flow builds from stillness to gather energy and be released.

I once met with the goddess of the Moon during a shamanic journey many years ago. I traveled to her lunar temple by climbing many luminous stairs made from the moonlight reflected on the waves of the ocean. Each stair of light led me higher, until I found myself inside the moon, looking back out at the world.

There I saw her—a beautiful, glowing goddess with many tiny stars in her hair. She was a tall, lithe figure that moved like a dancer, effortless and weightless. Her gown was the color of the bright full moon upon her pale blue skin. Her voice was like a melody. Whenever I now look up at the moon, I am reminded of her elegance, grace and sweetness.

The Great Mother Moon is our guide; she a celestial calendar for our bodies. She shows us when to be in action, gather resources, and release, and when to slow down, go within, and be still. The light of the moon is very powerful for us, as it has the essence of The Great Mother Goddess within it. One of my favorite ways to connect to this essence is by making moonwater.

Making Your Own Moonwater

Moonwater is an ancient way of capturing the power of lunar light and the essence of the moon's phases. Starting on the night of the dark moon, you use this water to collect energy throughout a full lunar cycle. You can drink this water to bring the moon's power into your body and use it to anoint and bless your body and sacred objects. I like to pour moonwater into my bath and use it as a face splash for glowing skin.

What you will need:

❖ distilled or spring water (at least 8 ounces)
❖ glass bottle or jar with cork or cap

What to do:

On the eve of the dark moon, fill your bottle or jar with the water. Cast your intention into the water by saying this as you hold the bottle or jar:

> *Lunar water and lunar light,*
> *Combine your essences on this night.*
> *All of your power and all of your light,*
> *Bring woman's wisdom from The Goddess Bright.*

Leave the bottle or jar near a window or outside to capture the moon's energy. Retrieve it before sunrise. It is also OK to leave it where the sun will not shine directly upon it and retrieve it whenever you wake up.

Do this once every evening from the dark moon until the night before the next dark moon of the following month. Then let the water rest until the very first sliver of the new moon appears, when it will be ready. Use it each night in whichever way you want for a full lunar cycle. If you are planning to drink your moon water, use spring water since distilled water is very leaching and can deprive your body of precious minerals.

Meanwhile make another batch as you are using this one. If you want, create an altar for your water as it steeps in the moonlight. Use shells, crystals, and flowers—anything that you like to decorate your shrine.

THE MOON
LODGE

Many, many moons ago, women gathered together in a tent, cave, or structure during the time of their bleeding to rest, pray, meditate, and ponder the blood mysteries. Ancient tribal women honored their lunar flow as a time to commune with The Great Mother, and to be with each other as sisters, mothers, and daughters.

In the moon lodge, grandmothers shared wisdom, mothers offered guidance, and daughters listened. All the women squatted or sat low to the ground, giving their blood back to The Goddess by letting it flow down into the earth. Sweet treats, savory foods, and nourishing beverages were consumed, as the women focused only on their bodies, relaxing during this sacred time. Remedies for cramping, aids for sleeping, and beauty treatments were all shared among them, as the women sat, talked, sang, meditated and rested while their bodies naturally worked to detoxify and release the rich, velvety lining of their womb.

It would be difficult today for women today to take 4 to 7 days off while we seclude ourselves in a tent or a room. Our schedules and lifestyles do not permit this, but we can at least take time to honor our beautiful, female bodies during the time of our bleeding.

If you have ever experienced a detox or fast, you know that it is a time of rest and stillness, not one for deadlines, running around, or stressing out. Your moonflow is a natural detox, the cleansing of your womb as it sheds the thick lining of blood and tissue that has built up in this cycle. While the body releases and cleanses, much of its energy goes into this process—and almost nothing else. This sheds lunar light on why some women feel so tired and unmotivated during their moonflow. To push your body at this time can create an uncomfortable monthly experience. Honoring yourself and letting your body rest while she does her work can make all the difference.

At the first sign of blood, I like to take the day off and go into my personal moon lodge. If I am absolutely unable to clear my commitments for that day, I will choose another day as soon as I can be free. I eat my favorite sweet and salty foods, watch movies, read books, write poetry, and meditate. Sometimes I do nothing other than take naps and long hot baths. Occasionally I feel the urge to head out on a long, leisurely walk out in nature or go sit by the ocean. No matter what, I honor whatever urges I feel, trusting The Goddess within to guide me.

Perhaps you would like to try this for yourself? I am so smitten by this ancient practice and it has made the time of my bleeding so precious and special, that I hope you will try it. It is a self-supportive way to re-member the sacredness of your woman's blood.

THE BLOOD
OF WOMAN

Ancient cultures considered the blood that women release to be extraordinarily potent. Tibetan ceremonies called for the mixing of uterine blood with red wine as an elixir to raise spiritual powers. Ancient pagan and Greek rituals involved the pouring of menstrual blood onto the ground to fortify the soil and ensure its fecundity.

Even today, some women save their blood to nourish plants around their house and garden. The first time that I heard a friend say that she did this, I was horrified and repelled. Now, I honor her wisdom and knowing, by saving a bit of my own blood each month on a piece of beautiful, handmade paper. I then roll these into scrolls as a way to preserve my power between the moon phases. These scrolls are potent charms reminding me of creation and The Great Mother. Someday, I will no longer bleed and will have these keepsakes of my precious lunar blood.

Like the power of The Goddess, the blood essence of women is both attractive and fearsome. All through history, women were either honored, sequestered, or avoided during their time of bleeding. They were considered either powerful or unclean, depending on the culture.

Native American traditions consider a woman's moontime as one of intense spiritual and physical purification, a time to receive visions and wisdom. A bleeding woman is respected and encouraged to sit in solitude to meditate on behalf of her tribe.

Pagan and Wiccan cultures view lunar blood as Goddess-given and a bleeding woman as Goddess-like. Their blood is thought of as a potent symbol of feminine fertility. It is sometimes used to anoint ritual tools, altar objects, people, and places, believing that its power will be transferred to them. It is also used as an offering to the gods and goddess, and mixed with potions in fertility, sex, and blood magic spells.

In Africa, menstrual blood is considered so powerful that it is used in magical spells for purification or destruction—an acknowledgment of The Great Mother Goddess, who both gives and takes life.

In Judaism, a woman who is bleeding is called *niddah,* which means 'moved' or 'separated.' She is considered unclean and has special restrictions. Muslim and other Middle Eastern cultures share this practice. Many require women to have a ritual bath to purify themselves once their bleeding has ceased. However, in the Sikh faith, a women's bleeding is considered to be a normal and natural event, as God-given. A Sikh woman is not prevented from participating in any activity or from attending any place of worship.

Southern India commemorates a girl's first blood with gifts and celebrations in her honor. Orthodox Hindu culture considers moonflow an impure time and requires a woman to avoid domestic chores, marital intimacy, and many other activities for four days during her flow.

In the Japanese Shinto religion, a woman is considered unclean during her moon-flow and may not enter a Kami shrine for fear that the blood and death upon her would block the Kami spirits from granting wishes. In contrast, Buddhism considers a woman's lunar flow as ordinary and normal, and imposes no restrictions at all upon her.

It is unfortunate that in our modern Western world, a woman's lunar blood has been sanitized into an ordinary and uncelebrated moment. Hopefully, with this new-found awareness of your goddess-ness, you will choose to re-member your bleeding as a time of sacredness, a time to acknowledge and honor your power.

THE RED GODDESS

In every culture there are one or more goddesses who are archetypes of The 'Red Goddess.' This name is often used to describe a goddess who is powerful but dark, evil, or destructive. However, just as with the misunderstood goddess Lilith,

I see the Red Goddess as representing something else. For me, she is the goddess of many facets of our feminine nature—light and dark—and the mysteries and powers of our lunar blood.

The Red Goddess is often portrayed as fierce and warrior-like, devouring her enemies whole and possessing a blood-lust nature. She is the aspect of The Goddess who shows us the primordial and protective potency of a woman's lunar blood. She has absolute and supreme life-giving and life-taking power. Her image gives meaning to the irritability and the insatiable hunger for food and for sex that many women feel during their moonflow.

The Red Goddess is often portrayed as a seductive and alluring siren. Her body, scent, and sexual movements drive men wild—often to their undoing. She is the Tantric Goddess, the Shakti force who cannot be tamed. She inhabits the womanly blood of sexuality, lust, and desire. She possesses a magnetic, attractive power, which heightens just as she is ovulating and prior to bleeding.

But sometimes the Red Goddess appears as the mother who is nurturing, loving, and compassionate. This is the blood of all human life. Nourishing, supportive, and strong, this is the blood of conception that remains in the womb to feed the embryo, and the blood of life released during childbirth.

RITUALS FOR THE
FEMININE BLOOD MYSTERIES

The Feminine Mysteries are eventually revealed to all women. If you seek them, they will not be kept from you. As a birthright you are entitled to know them. Your incarnation as a woman draws you towards these teachings. The learning begins with embarking upon the study of the moon and its connection to your body, and recognizing the sacredness and power of your blood. These mysteries refer directly to the menstrual rites of passage that a woman goes through in her lifetime; menarche (the onset of her menses), conception/childbirth, and menopause.

Unlike the seasons of The Triple Goddess, these times do not overlap or repeat, as their portals are clearly marked. Each mystery leads a woman to the next, until they have all been revealed. A woman can, however, revisit these times symbolically and tap into their essence and power to honor and celebrate them at any time. Central to the blood mysteries is your lunar blood, which is like a trail, ultimately leading you to The Red Goddess. It flows downward into the lower world of the psyche, where the deepest wisdoms are found.

Ritual is a powerful, magical, and ceremonial way of connecting yourself, your lunar blood and your body to The Red Goddess, and to the moon. It also helps to create sacredness all around you and within you, which helps you to see yourself as sacred, special and magical.

There are many rituals that women have performed throughout their lives, helping them to worship the moon and bringing in the sacredness of their moonflow. For each of the Blood Mysteries below, I will share some of my most favorite, personal rituals with you.

The First Mystery: Young Blood

The very first drop of blood that falls from your womb, initiates you to My ways. It calls you to stand at the gates of the temple. In this temple you will learn that your blood is rich and filled with My Living Essence. And that from the dark space of your womb flows the elixir of all human life.

The first blood mystery is that of innocence and the young woman who does not yet know herself.

There is a purity and inexperience associated with the time before a girl's sexual awakening and her first bleeding. This time of life does not yet know of the pain that her lunar blood will bring, nor the pain of childbirth, nor the bittersweet pain of being in love. She does not yet feel the pull of the moon nor hear the call of The Red Goddess. She is a child of the earth, who is about to become a woman of the moon.

The young girl will soon be initiated into the wonders of her body, leaving behind her innocence and experiencing the rise of her power. She will see for the first time how the moon pulls and tugs at her womb, and draws down her blood. This is a time of emerging.

A woman's passage from girlhood into womanhood is heralded by her *menarche*, formed from two Greek words, *men* (month) and *arkhe* (beginning). This is when her first lunar blood appears. As with any threshold, we come to this time with many different emotions. How we come to the experience of our first blood sets the tone for our feelings about our womanliness throughout our lifetime.

How a young woman feels about her body, her femininity, and the kind of connection she begins to make with her budding feminine power are all deeply essential to her future well-being. This time of her life is fragile and precious emotionally, but her blood flow is strong and vital energetically. In fact, it is the strongest potency that it will ever be during her lifetime. At this time, our blood collects power, just as the new moon gathers light.

Remember back to your own time of first blood. What were your experiences? What were your thoughts, hopes, and expectations? How were you told of your approaching lunar flow? Were you celebrated?

Ritual to Celebrate Young Blood: Anointing Yourself

This ritual can be performed for a young girl experiencing her first blood or for a woman at any age who would like to revisit this time in her life to celebrate the passage from girlhood into womanhood. It can be experienced with a group or alone.

What you will need:

❖ 2 or 3 tablespoons of sweet red liquid (pomegranate or cranberry juice, red or port wine)
❖ honey
❖ sea salt
❖ silver or glass goblet
❖ white robe or gown
❖ red and white candle

What to do:

In your goblet, mix the liquid of choice with honey to thicken it. It should be the consistency of blood.

- ❖ Bathe with sea salt to purify your body.
- ❖ Then dress in the white robe.
- ❖ Light the candles, and place the goblet near them, creating an altar space.
- ❖ You may choose to adorn the altar with flowers, shells, or other favorite objects.
- ❖ Anoint yourself from the *blood* in the goblet; put a drop upon your womb, one upon your heart and another upon your lips. Hold the goblet high and say these words:

O, Great Mother Goddess, you have called my blood down to the earth,
Now I release it as you have asked me to. I speak Your name and You are here,
in my womb. My heart knows the stirrings of my soul to become,
to learn and to know all that there is of You, all that I am to be. O, Great Mother
Moon, I thank you for my blood and for the power of Your light.

Celebrate this occasion with good food, joyful feelings. Treat yourself to a special gift—a piece of jewelry that will always remind you of this time, artwork that symbolizes the essence of your first moonflow, or whatever feels right for you.

The Second Mystery: Woman's Blood

The gift of my blood is that of creation; allowing you to bring forth a life through your body, as I bring all life through Mine. No longer the novice waiting at the gates, you stand now inside the temple, as one who is discovering the pleasures and power of your body and the ways of The Red Goddess.

The second blood mystery is that of creation and the woman who is fulfilling herself. Once awakened by her first blood, she becomes more aware of her womanhood, experiencing herself as a sexual being that has power. Her body has been changing, but now it positively transforms as her maturity and experience develop in equal measure. Slowly, the girl has disappeared and the woman has emerged.

The principal mysteries of our blood are that of sex and conception. This blood calls us to explore our sexuality and relationships. And unlike young blood—which lasts only for a brief time—woman's blood may last many years as we quest further and further into the mysteries of sexual union, pleasure, and intimacy.

For some women, this blood leads them into motherhood. This is when we learn about love, companionship, and sexual connection for reproduction but also for pleasure. This Mother Goddess aspect visits all women, even those who do not have children who will recognize this time as one of self-love, creativity, healing, and self-parenting.

Ritual to Celebrate Woman's Blood: Earth Offering

Ancient people recognized that the earth was fertile, nourishing, and life sustaining. They honored the earth as a feminine, mother goddess. They made sacrifices and blood offerings to her to express their gratitude but also to contribute to her fertility and abundance.

While it may not be practical for a woman today to squat down for several hours returning her blood to Mother Earth—and there are public health codes that prevent this—it is possible to collect and release your blood into the earth of a potted plant that you have chosen for this very special purpose.

What you will need:

❖ a plant
❖ Diva Cup® (can be purchase at divacup.com) or diaphragm

What to do:

You may choose to light candles, take a purification bath, or another ritual that sets the mood and transforms the mundane into the sacred. Collect your moonflow in the Diva Cup or diaphragm, then pour it into the plant you have chosen while saying this:

Earth Mother, Goddess Soil
Accept my blood as a gift,
as an offering and in gratitude for all that you provide.

The Third Mystery: Wise Blood

Rest, still and cease, daughter of the moon. You have attended me well, living out the mysteries as a faithful priestess. You have gained so much knowledge, all of it stored in the temple of your womb. Now it is time to receive the essence of blood for yourself and become the wise woman who knows.

The third mystery is that of transformation, and the woman who knows herself fully. For many years The Red Goddess has called the blood down from your body, and out into the world. Now she asks you to keep the essence of it for yourself, to nourish you spiritually and to seal the mysteries within.

The transformation aspect of this mystery is that of death and rebirth—the death of the old self (the mother and the creatress) and the rebirth of the free and wild woman that you were in the beginning. The wise blood calls you to go within. There you will strengthen, reinforce, and even reinvent yourself if you desire. This blood activates the deepest mystery of all, that of the woman who is the wisdom keeper, the seer, and the healer/teacher. You have accumulated much skill and experience over the years and now it is time to share all that you learned with others. This blood is about loss, strength, courage, and wisdom.

Ritual to Celebrate Wise Blood: Blood Scroll

I did not conceive of this lovely ritual until I was well into my peri-menopause. I was beginning to notice the slowing down of my monthly bleeding, so I began to miss my intimate connection to the moon and The Goddess. This is when I created the idea of collecting my wise blood and saving it on a scroll to use in the future.

This ritual helps me know that The Goddess is with me as my bloodflow turns inward just as much as She was with me when it flowed out into the world. My lunar blood is very powerful—so is yours. So by saving it onto a scroll, you can still use your blood in ritual and meditation long after your last moonflow has ceased, tapping into its potent essence. Even if you save only a few drops of blood onto the scroll, it is enough to capture its essence forever.

What you will need:

- handmade paper, or any absorbent, decorative paper
- ribbon

What to do:

Either at the beginning, middle or end of your moonflow, use your finger to smudge a drop of your lunar blood onto the paper. Let this dry and then roll the scroll, tying it with the ribbon. Repeat for several months if you want. Keep the scroll(s) in a private place and place on your altar or use it in rituals. You can write this on the scroll if you choose:

Upon this parchment,
I place my blood.
From moon to moon The Goddess flows.
My body Her body.
My blood Her blood.
From moon to moon The Goddess Flows

O, The Red Goddess calls to me!

I can hear Her voice
in the dark, in the night, under a bright moon sky.

She fashions my body to be like Hers;
with caverns and caves and curves and such...
that transform and change as She does;
sometimes darkly, brightly, first thin then full.

O, The Red Goddess calls to me!

And when I hear Her voice;
I answer, drop by drop by drop
of my lunar blood, that is really Her blood—
Goddess blood;
rich with mystery and wisdom.

CHAPTER SEVENTEEN

THE CIRCLE OF
THE GODDESS

The whole universe is based on rhythms.
Everything happens in circles, in spirals.
~John Hartford

UNDER THE BRIGHT FULL CIRCLE OF THE MOON, women have often gathered for sisterhood, community, and magical purpose. Standing together within the circle they discovered protection, safety, and power in numbers. Energy is elevated, intention is focused, and spirituality is strengthened.

A lone woman can cast a circle for herself. Standing in the center of it, she can raise her own power and intensify her own intent. But when a group of women come together in the shape of the moon, sun or the earth—an even mightier power is raised.

It is one that deeply reveals The Goddess as wholeness, community, inclusivity, and togetherness. The feeling that comes over you is inexplicable when partaking in ritual while in a Goddess Circle. You feel an excitement comparable to an energetic charge, a flow of electricity. It is full of expectancy and anticipation. While in a circle, I have often thought these words: *She is here.*

Gathering in a circle amplifies whatever is going on inside of it. All the individual energies synch together to become a single ray that goes round and round. This builds itself up until the circle is broken and the powerful energy is released. A friend of mine, who is a Feng Shui practitioner, says that a room in the shape of a circle is difficult to deal with as the energy does not know where to go. When there is no place for energy to settle, such as in a corner, it just keeps circling. Not a good idea for a bedroom or a kitchen, but keeping the energy within is exactly what we want to happen in a ritual circle. We want the energy to gather momentum, and then intensify this power within ourselves to send it into the world.

WHAT IS A GODDESS CIRCLE?

The circle of The Goddess is a place for women to come together, perform ritual, meditate, sing, dance, drum, and share their thoughts, life experiences, and wisdom—all while honoring the essence of The Divine Feminine Goddess. They honor her collectively and within themselves. There is no right or wrong way to create a circle, only that it come from the space of your heart and is welcoming to all who enter it. Creating the circle is called 'casting the circle.' It can be drawn out on the ground or just implied through intention. Even if several women simply stand in a circle and do nothing else, a circle has been cast.

A circle can be cast magically, spiritually, or both.

A magically cast circle is one that calls upon the earth, air, fire, water, and ether (believed in ancient times to fill the upper atmosphere) along with the four directions of north, south, east, and west. Casting this powerful circle seeks to attract and harness the energy of the elements and cardinal points. Magic attempts to connect these forces to similar ones found within your own self, and then focus them to create outcome.

Your blood is like the element of water, your bones like the earth, your breath is air, and your life force is fire.

Words are a very powerful tool in magic. When things are named or *spelled* out, they become physically present. Saying a name out loud is an invocation (a prayer), a request for the named to come to you. A thing without a name has few ties to this world; it floats freely between the realms. It is thought that once a child is named, its soul formally lands upon the earth. I imagine that The Divine Feminine desired a name for Herself to become fully present in the physical realm, and thus Her many named goddesses made their way into our lives. You can amplify the magic of your circle by reciting chants, invocations, and spells.

A spiritually cast circle does not affiliate with any formal practice or system but honors the circle for its collective and inclusive qualities that reflect The Divine in all things. Spirituality is the search for that which is sacred and divine. It need not be associated with a specific religion, although many religious people are also quite spiritual. A person's spirituality is very personal and private—always deserving of respect. Spiritual means being deeply and continually connected to the ways of The Divine Feminine (and Masculine) on a daily basis. It seeks to raise your vibration, to perfect your soul, and to be in harmony with The Divine.

When you align yourself to the sacred and The Divine, everything you do becomes an act of spirituality. For the Goddess Circle, this means that everything having to do with the circle is about this divinity. Even the food and drink you prepare, the garments you choose to wear, and the space you choose for its location reflect this sacredness. The circle itself takes on an air of holiness, and all who stand within its embrace are blessed.

Whenever I cast a circle, I blend the two methods; acknowledging the elements and the directions, the holiness of its shape, and the sacredness of its power.

WHY THE CIRCLE?

The circle is thought to have supernatural power, an elevated mystical vibration and deep spiritual significance. It is representative of wholeness, initiation, cycles, the womb, unity, completion, and infinity. It is the beginning without end, life without death. It is the shadow of the sphere, the reflection of The Whole and all that there is. It reminds us that we are fundamentally endless energy. You cannot get more Goddess-like than the circle.

So sacred is the circle that it is part of every religious, spiritual, mystical and magical system. It is found in Buddhist and Tibetan mandalas, atop the ancient Egyptian ankh, in the Vesica Piscis (the entwined circles on Mary Magdalene's Chalice Well in Glastonbury), and the Flower of Life symbol found within almost every culture. Even non-circular symbols, such as the five pointed star, the triskele or triple spiral, are often depicted with a circle around them as if to amplify and contain their power. The dot, or bindu within a circle, is a Hindu/Buddhist symbol for the male, while the circle without the dot is female. The Native American medicine wheel symbol is an equidistant cross within a circle, representing the four directions of the earth.

Symbols activate deep subconscious responses that can lead to profound spiritual awakenings and shifts of consciousness. Sacred geometry claims the circle activates a sense of wholeness within and reminds us of our inclusivity to all things.

The circle is the most natural and original shape, found in nature and appearing around us in the atom particle. It is the shape of our cells, seeds for some plants, celestial bodies, and that of many galaxies. One of my favorite quotes is from Black Elk, a Native American holy man, who said *'Everything an Indian does is in a circle, and that is because the power of the world always works in circles, and everything tries to be round.'*

For women, the circle is a natural and feminine shape to associate with, as our bodies are made of the soft curving lines of circles. The round moon above governs our lunar blood. As a vessel, the circle is a place to deposit energy, to gather it in and hold it there—much like women do when growing new life within the vessel of their womb. As a symbol of protection, the circle is again a vessel keeping everything within it safe from outside, just as a woman does for the baby growing inside.

CASTING A CIRCLE RITUAL

Starting a Goddess Circle can be quite an undertaking, but it is also incredibly enjoyable and fulfilling. As you create your own circle, remember that the qualities of The Divine Feminine are your best guidelines. Power, wisdom, intuitive voice, creativity, passion, stillness, and awakening—along with oneness, harmony, and sisterhood are all a natural part of your circle.

It is common for humans to look for leadership, cohesion, and order when they gather. If you are the woman initiating the circle, you may be its natural leader—meaning that you will facilitate its organization and attend to all the other tasks that go along with this. There are many ways to lead a circle; here a few:

- ❖ SINGLE LEADERSHIP. One woman heads the circle, leading it weekly, monthly or for an entire year, organizing all of the details and planning the activities.
- ❖ MULTI-LEADERSHIP. Two or more women collaborate on it all.
- ❖ ROTATING LEADERSHIP. Each member rotates into responsibility for each time they gather.
- ❖ NO FIXED LEADERSHIP. Whoever wants to lead each meeting can do so.

You can simply gather and let things flow organically and do whatever you are inspired to do on that day. Or you can plan activities to inspire your circle, such as having different themes for each meeting or creating specific rituals such as drumming, telling sacred stories, or free dancing. Whenever I host a circle, it is themed in that I present a very specific quality or essence of The Goddess or aspect of the moon. I include candle lighting, anointing, and meditation—because I really enjoy these things and want to share them with my circle. Recently I have begun experimenting with song and drumming.

How to Cast a Circle

You may choose to offer a circle to your group of friends, or as a class or workshop for which you charge. I consider money to be a spiritual exchange and think of it as one of the many sacred agreements between souls. Some people believe that charging for spiritual events or services is not appropriate. I encourage you to use your own inner, goddess wisdom for this decision, as your relationship with money is personal. Remember that The Goddess and Her circle are about inclusivity and your own preferences are entitled to be embraced as much as anyone else's.

This book was designed with the Goddess Circle in mind. There are nine topics available for you to work with:

- ❖ returning to The Goddess
- ❖ restoring Her qualities (of which this book contains seven)
- ❖ remembering Her into your life

You can incorporate all nine, work with just the seven qualities, or pick only one or two ideas—it's up to you. This chapter contains helpful suggestions to get you started in forming and holding your own Goddess Circle.

CALLING IN
THE GODDESS

Ancient Pagan rites, Native American ceremonies, and Wiccan gatherings all share the practice of *calling in* The Divine, using the elements and the four directions to be present in their circle. This is usually done at the beginning of the gathering, once all the women have sat down in the shape of a circle, or as close to a circle as space permits. There are many ways to call in The Goddess, and I encourage you to try all of them and adopt what works for you or create your own.

Here is one of my opening prayers to call in The Divine Mother.

> *Great Mother Goddess, gather with us here and now as we circle*
> *together in Your name. Bless us with your Essence,*
> *your Strength, and your Light. Bless this circle,*
> *and all who are present within its sacred shape. And, so it is.*

Here is an invocation inspired by Native American and Wiccan tradition. It is used to call in the four directions and their elements.

I stand in the center of Your wheel, O Great Goddess and I ask for Your guidance, Your essence, and Your blessings. I turn to face the east, the place of wind, initiation, wisdom and power—and I call it in. I turn to face the west, the place of water, completion, transformation, and feeling—and I call it in. I turn to face the south, the place of fire, purification, energy, and creation—and I call it in. I turn to face the north, the place of earth, endurance, strength, and abundance—and I call it in. I stand in the center of Your wheel, O Great Goddess and I open my heart to Your presence, Your light, and Your ways. And, so it is.

PREPARING
BLESSING WATERS

Almost all religious and spiritual systems use water to cleanse, consecrate, and bless. The Goddess Circle is a wonderful ritual in which to incorporate water as sacred.

Water is life; it is precious. Acknowledging the life-sustaining power of water and then transforming it into holy or blessed water is a lovely and deeply fulfilling practice. I often offer blessing water whenever I facilitate a Goddess circle, class, or workshop.

Water from nature is an excellent source for making blessed water, but bottled spring or mineral water should be used if you intend to drink it. Whichever you make, use it immediately; do not keep it indefinitely.

Use distilled water if you would like a longer shelf life for your blessed water (1–2 weeks). A note on distilled water: this is highly purified water that has been stripped of all mineral, chemical, and life sustaining elements. It is excellent for imprinting your intention upon, as it is like a blank slate waiting to written upon. However, do not drink distilled water, as it tends to leach minerals from your body. Finally, tap water is not recommended—due to all the chemicals it contains.

What you will need:

❖ water (natural, spring, mineral, or distilled)
❖ clean glass container, jar, or bottle with a cap or cork
❖ paper or parchment

What to do:

Write a word or draw a symbol on the paper that represents your intention. This could be a word like *Blessed, Peace,* or *Goddess.* Or it could be a drawing of a constellation for astrological power, or planetary signs for capturing their essence. Next fill the bottle with water, cap it, and leave outside with the paper under it or wrapped around it in the sunlight or moonlight to infuse it with celestial essence. Say this prayer over the blessing water:

O Blessed Goddess, blessed be
infuse this water — empower it so;
with sacred light and holy fire,
so all who touch it doubtless know
that they are blessed, O blessed be.

❖ The Sun is associated with success, abundance, life-force, strength, growth, new beginnings.

❖ The Moon is associated with receptivity, feminine essence, serenity, the subconscious, psychic ability, dreams, divination, The Goddess.

❖ Mars is associated with sexuality, strength, power, war, anger, control.

❖ Mercury is associated with health, intellect, wisdom, psychic and spiritual development, communication, divination, influence, power.

❖ Jupiter is associated with finances, money, wealth, abundance, prosperity, legal matters, fortune, honor, fertility (male), friendship, health, success, ambition.

❖ Venus is associated with love, romance, beauty, kindness, happiness, travel, lust, friendship, faithfulness, youth, passion, devotion, fertility (female).

❖ Saturn is associated with discipline, purification, lessons, endings, protection, home, visions, completion, longevity.

RETURN, REMEMBER AND RESTORE THE CIRCLE

In the same way we reclaim our ancient and original relationship with The Goddess, returning to the circle is about restoring our relationship to our primitive roots and ancient rituals. This is how we *re-member* them back into our lives. Drum circles, candles, incense, dance, song, and story are all excellent tools to reawaken The Goddess traditions that lie dormant within your soul.

Rhythm of The Goddess

The drum was once a woman's instrument, used only by ancient priestesses to induce trance and mystical experiences to call The Goddess in. Early shamans were often women who used the beat of the drum to journey into the other worlds, dimensions, and states of consciousness.

Drumming into your circle can help set the mood, transport you into higher states of mind, raise your vibration, and helps join the energies among all those in attendance in the circle.

There are several different styles and sizes of drums. They can be made from many different kinds of materials, including animal skin, paper, or synthetics. They can be expensive or inexpensive. Anything round and hollow can be drummed upon, even everyday items. I have used large, empty five-gallon water jugs as well as empty cylindrical oatmeal boxes with great results.

There is something deeply moving and satisfying when you abandon yourself to drumming. I am not a musician, so when I drum I simply beat to the sound of my heartbeat—no skill needed there. I just tune in to the most intrinsic, natural rhythm that there is. And when you do this within a Goddess circle, with a number of women drumming all at once, the effects can be powerful and transformative.

Fire of The Goddess

Fire was also originally entrusted only to women, as they were the ones cooking and keeping a home. Lighting candles and burning incense are very old rituals with ancient ties to women and Goddess worship. Fire symbolizes spiritual transformation, purification, passion, power, and renewal. Adding fire to your Goddess Circle sparks a deep connection to our human need for warmth and light.

The color of your candle, the type of incense, and the phase of the moon—all play a role in the meaning and potency of your ritual. Here are some examples of the meanings that you can combine in your Goddess Circle:

Candle Color

* PINK: love, healing, protection
* PURPLE: intuition, healing
* WHITE: cleansing, purification, protection
* BLACK: protection, releasing negativity
* GREEN: abundance, growth

Incense

* ROSE: love, healing, protection
* LAVENDER: healing, relaxation
* SAGE: cleansing, purification, protection
* PALO SANTO: creating sacred space
* SWEET GRASS: bringing in the sweetness of life

Moon Phases

* WANING: releasing, decreasing
* WAXING: bringing in, increasing
* CRESCENT: creating connections
* DARK MOON: deep meditation (no manifesting during this moon)

The Dance of The Goddess

When I was a young girl, the music of the 60s and 70s introduced my body to rhythm and dance. I could not be still when I heard music—I had to move. As I grew into womanhood, dance became a way to express myself; sexually, creatively, and femininely. Undulating my body, I let myself be taken away by the beat. I did not know it then, but this is the dance of The Goddess that is within all women. She is rhythm, beat, melody, and song—and we were built to express Her with our body. It is good to know that when you dance this way for a man, you will not only be inviting The Divine Feminine in, but also Her beloved; The Divine Masculine. This is a powerful, potent, and sacred dance that is best done with one with whom you truly wish to share your body.

As I have grown older, my once public and uninhibited dance moves have become more personal and private. I find myself dancing at home as a form of worship and reverence that honors my own inner goddess-ness. This is a natural transition for many women, as what was once a mating dance to attract a man becomes a Goddess dance to draw Her near.

Leading a group of women to dance for The Goddess is extraordinarily powerful, and very freeing. It may take you a while to warm up and feel comfortable dancing uninhibitedly in front of others, but once you let go and *become* The Goddess, you can embrace the wildness and beauty of Her dance and be Her.

Experiment with music that utilizes heavy percussion as a powerful beat draws out the wild dancer in everyone. Or playing haunting, melodic and rhythmic music creates a sense of the sacred and works best with candlelight. Whichever type of music you choose, be playful in how you dress, too. Wear sheer scarves, long skirts, tinkling bells and belly dancing belts. Adorn yourself with rhinestones, glitter, paint and henna—anything that will bring out your inner dancer and inspire you to feel like a goddess.

The Voice of The Goddess

I am grateful for all of the creative gifts I have been blessed with, but I deeply wish for the one I was not given—the gift of song. Nevertheless, it has not stopped me from singing chants and goddess songs whenever the mood strikes. I bring song into the circles I facilitate and invite everyone to join in. I love it when we all find our harmony and can feel our voices rising to the sky. The Goddess has not blessed with me with the most melodious voice, but She has gifted me with a deep love and appreciation for song.

I encourage you to include song in your circle. You can find many goddess songs on the Internet and download them to play in your circle. If you are a songstress, you might even write your own goddess songs. If you have the gift of singing—share it with the women in your circle. The Goddess delights in our voice whether it is in prayer, invocation, or song.

One of my favorite goddess songs, written by Zsuzsanna Budapest, is a beautiful and rhythmic chant set to music. (I have included a link, in *Resources* for you to listen to this for yourself.) When repeated over and over, it creates an incredibly reverent mood to honor The Goddess that bonds your entire Circle.

We all come from the Goddess
And to Her we shall return
Like a drop of rain,
Flowing to the ocean

Sacred Goddess Stories

I loved writing this book, especially the myths. While writing each one of them, it brought me into a trance, carrying me deep into the place of my soul where The Goddess resides.

While working on this project, I went with my publishers to Sedona, Arizona. Inspired by a beautiful painting of a Native American Goddess that was in the hotel room, they asked me to read the myth of White Buffalo Calf Woman. With flute music playing in the background, I settled in to read the story. About halfway through, something happened to me—the goddess in the story came alive. I felt her presence in the room with us.

Each time I read a myth aloud, I experience the same magical, exhilarating feeling. It is so deeply sacred, as if I am reaching back through time, when women gathered and told stories around a fire. Through myth and storytelling, we tap into this power and unity as women, bringing that energy back to these modern times.

I encourage you to read the myths in this book aloud during your Goddess Circles. Let them spark discussion, inspiration, and your creativity. Below I have listed some discussion questions for each of the myths. Feel free to add to this list with your own questions and observations. I would love to hear about your experiences with the myths. Please visit the website for this book and email me with your comments.

Nut

❖ Do you feel divine? How do you express it? What rituals do you do to connect to your divine self?

- If you don't feel divine, why not? What would it take for you to feel divine? What would you need to love yourself as a Goddess?
- What would it be like to be told about your divine goddess-ness? Use Geb's poetic declaration to Nut as a guide.

Lilith

- Is your power intact—do you have a relationship with it? Describe it. If you do not, what needs to happen for you to access your power?
- In what way have you been suppressed in your life? By whom?
- Is there an Eve in your life? How you have dealt with that relationship?

Yemaya

- How are you creative in your life?
- What are you willing to sacrifice for your creativity?
- Does creativity come easily for you? If not, what stands in the way of it?

White Tara

- Are you able to be still? Describe this experience. If you are not able, think about why not?
- What would bringing stillness into your life do for you?
- Do you recognize stillness in other women?

Radha

- What are you passionate about in life?
- Do you have passion in your romantic relationships? If yes, describe how your passion appears and what forms it takes? If not, what do you think prevents you from expressing your passion?
- How do you express your passion: easily? boldly? fearfully? shyly?

Kassandra

- Remember a time when you followed your own intuitive voice. What happened?

- ❖ Did you ever not follow your intuition?
- ❖ Do you voice your intuition with others? If yes, how do you share it and how do they react? If you don't share it, why not? What holds you back?

White Buffalo Calf Woman

- ❖ What is the wisest thing you have ever done for yourself?
  For another person?
- ❖ Who is the wisest woman you know? What have you learned from her?
- ❖ Do you trust your own wisdom? If no, why not?

Eve

- ❖ What is the most courageous thing that you have ever done?
- ❖ Who is the most courageous person that you know?
  What have you learned from her?
- ❖ List some of your own personal awakenings; spiritually, physically and emotionally.

Isis

- ❖ What parts of your own self would you like to re-member back into wholeness?
- ❖ Who is the Seth-like character in your life? The Nephtys-like character? The Osiris-like character? The Isis-like character?
- ❖ What parts of your own self must die, in order to be re-membered whole?

In the beginning, my body lies curled in a circle
in the cradle of my mother's womb.

I emerge, stand upright and walk;
upon the earth, which is round—
like the moon and the stars above.

In the end, my body lies curled in a circle
in The Goddess Mother's womb.

I decay, go deep and become Her;
I am the earth, which is round—
like the moon and the stars above.

EPILOGUE

Everything she is was here before me. Everything she was will remain.
Her existence touches both my past and my future at one point—infinity.

~Shannon Lee Alexander

WHEN I FIRST BEGAN TO WRITE THIS BOOK,
two orb spiders began to weave very large—and very beautiful webs around the outside of my house. At first they wove them across the windows, but soon they moved their enormous round webs to both the front and back doors—literally blocking my way out. Each day I would gently sweep away the sticky strands to leave the house and by the next morning the webs would reappear. Frustrated, I tried capturing the spiders and relocating them, but over and over they returned, day after day until I finally gave up on my efforts to stop them and decided that this must be a sign. Many times while writing this book I rewrote chapters over and over, tearing them down just like the annoying spider webs, only to rebuild them again and again—just like the spiders. There were moments of doubt, when I wanted to give up on my dream of being an author, run away, leave the house and play hooky... but spider had woven

me in as if to say; stay put, keep writing. I experienced many challenges as I maneuvered through the process of being published. Learning how to be a team player after so many years of creating on my own added to the difficulties and like a fly caught in a web, the more I struggled—against myself and the process, the more uncomfortable it all felt. So finally, I just surrendered. Spider teaches us acceptance.

Letting go can be a herculean feat for me, as I fancy myself in charge of everything. Surrender feels like defeat and asking for help feels like weakness. But they are neither of those things. Surrender is a spiritual event; it is the act of giving the situation, the project, the problem and yourself over to The Divine. Asking for help is like saying to a friend, I trust you to catch me when I am falling, to hold up a net for me—which is another spider teaching.

Spider is very powerful woman's medicine that symbolizes the creative feminine essence in the world, the perseverance of a woman's spirit, the receptiveness of her body and the deeper, more shadowy parts of her psyche and the spiral path of beginnings and endings. Spider is the weaver of the world, of destiny and of fate.

As this book was coming to completion, I noticed that the two spiders were nowhere to be found and that my struggle with their webs—and my writing, had ceased. This is the way of The Goddess; Her teachings come to us as profound insights and also as uncomfortable struggles—and sometimes even as spider webs, shining like gold in the morning sun.

Your own journey with this book may have brought up many of your own issues that you are hoping to heal. Perhaps you, too, struggle with your own spectacular magnificence. Know that while your journey with this book may be finished, your journey with The Goddess has only just begun. She is the weaver of all life, holding up a net so that when we fall, it is into Her arms. She is your destiny and your fate, and Her message for you is very clear:

You Are Woman
You Are Divine

RESOURCES

CONTACT RENÉE STARR: info@backtothegoddess.com

GODDESS RETREATS, WORKSHOPS, PRODUCTS & MORE:
www.backtothegoddess.com

SOCIAL MEDIA:
www.pinterest.com/tothegoddess
www. instagram.com/backtothegoddess
www.bit.ly/backtothegoddessFacebook
www.twitter.com/tothegoddess

GODDESSES ON EARTH & BEYOND:

www.marijagimbutas.com   www.karentate.com
www.patricia-monaghan.com   www.jeanbolen.com
www.lynngottlieb.com   www.starhawk.org
www.julieloar.com   www.zbudapest.com

WOMEN'S WISDOM:
Rebeca Manning / Radiant Health & Wellness Coaching: www.myananda.com
Jessica April Call of Spirit / Wise Woman, Herbalist: jessicaaprilcall@gmail.com
Susan Weed / Wise Woman, Herbalist: www.herbshealing.com

Z BUDAPEST'S WE ALL COME FROM THE GODDESS VIDEO:

www.youtube.com/watch?v=voBZowM0NTs

CRYSTALS:

www.bestcrystals.com

www.energymuse.com

ESSENTIAL OILS:

www.auracacia.com

www.mountainroseherbs.com

www.floracopeia.com

CONCRETES & ABSOLUTES:

www.camdengrey.com

HERBS:

www.mountainroseherbs.com

www.starwest-botanicals.com

www.gaiasworld.com

SEA SALT:

www.mountainroseherbs.com

www.starwest-botanicals.com

BOTTLES, JARS & MORE:

www.essentialsupplies.com

www.sks-bottle.com

www.sunburstbottle.com

BOXES, BAGS, METAL TINS, RIBBONS & MORE:

www.papermart.com

LUNAR CALENDAR:

www.moonconnection.com/moon_phases_calendar.phtml

YOU ARE WOMAN, YOU ARE DIVINE